Bad Medicine

Bad Medicine

SETTLER COLONIALISM AND
THE INSTITUTIONALIZATION
OF AMERICAN INDIANS

SARAH A. WHITT

DUKE UNIVERSITY PRESS : *DURHAM AND LONDON* : 2025

Project Editor: Bird Williams
Designed by David Rainey
Typeset in Arno Pro and TheSans C4s by
Westchester Publishing Services

Library of Congress Cataloging-in-Publication Data
Names: Whitt, Sarah A., [date] author.
Title: Bad medicine : settler colonialism and the institutionalization
of American Indians / Sarah A. Whitt.
Description: Durham : Duke University Press, 2025. | Includes
bibliographical references and index.
Identifiers: LCCN 2024022129 (print)
LCCN 2024022130 (ebook)
ISBN 9781478031260 (paperback)
ISBN 9781478028048 (hardcover)
ISBN 9781478060253 (ebook)
Subjects: LCSH: United States Indian School (Carlisle, Pa.)—
History. | Canton Asylum for Insane Indians—History. | Ford
Motor Company—History. | House of the Good Shepherd—
History. | Indians, Treatment of—United States—History. |
Indians of North America—Crimes against—United States. |
Inmates of institutions—Abuse of—United States. | Settler
colonialism—United States. | BISAC: HISTORY / United States /
20th Century | SOCIAL SCIENCE / Ethnic Studies / American /
Native American Studies
Classification: LCC E93 . W59 2025 (print) LCC E93 (ebook)
DCC 305.897/0730904—dc23/eng/20241216
LC record available at https://lccn.loc.gov/2024022129

Cover art: The piece featured on the front of this book
is entitled *Jerry (after Horace Poolaw)*, created by artist
Thomas Poolaw (Kiowa/Delaware), who holds a BFA in
painting from the University of Oklahoma. Jerry, who is
Horace Poolaw's son, served in the Navy and had returned
home in 1942 when the original photograph was taken
by Horace. I extend my sincere gratitude to Mr. Thomas
Poolaw and the Poolaw family for allowing this piece to be
featured on the cover of *Bad Medicine*. Yakoke.

FOR ALL INDIGENOUS PEOPLE IMPACTED BY INSTITUTIONALIZATION

table of contents

acknowledgments

Bad Medicine is a collective work; many people sustained the writing process and this book could not have been completed without their support. I think of my mother, Donna Akers; my grandmother, Mary Ellen Leftwich; and my great-grandmother, Ruth Dodd, each time I sit down to write—so I must first acknowledge that I would not be who or where I am today were it not for them. To my son, Asa Leflore, who grew inside me, was born, and grew before my eyes during the completion of this project: I have you to thank for so much. You served as a reminder—in more ways than I can count—to soften and smooth out the rough edges.

This book was with me through many challenging times, following me around like a comforting, familiar old friend. I am grateful to Shari Huhndorf, Tsianina Lomawaima, Juana María Rodríguez, and Raúl Coronado for the incisive feedback they gave on early iterations of the writing and framing of this research and the stories that emerged from it. The COVID-19 pandemic forced me to return to this work, revising it into the book it would eventually become. I am grateful to Cliff Trafzer for his support during that period of reflection, quietude, and revision, and for the many conversations we had about life, academia, and the perils and power of writing history during a time when the whole world was shut down. Thank you, Cliff, for your intellectual companionship and shared excitement over community-based histories and new lines of inquiry. Juliet Larkin-Gilmore's laughter buoyed me throughout the revision process, and Olivia Chilcote's priceless friendship and sense of humor saw me through the finish line (for reasons that I won't put down in print).

I met new colleagues, strengthened old bonds, and forged many friendships as I wrote and refined the book's central argument, which helped me to find the meaning at the heart of the colonial archive. To Fantasia Painter, Tiara Na'puti, Amy Lonetree, Ari Kelman, Brianna Theobald, Adria Imada, Susan Burch, Traci Voyles, Sharon Block, Vibhuti Ramachandran, my amazing editor Courtney Berger, and many others: our conversations stretched and expanded the conceptualization of this work and the insights derived from it. To the incredible archivists who assisted me with this research, I thank you all sincerely. Stephen Spence offered invaluable expertise on the National Archive's holdings at Kansas City, and I am so thankful to have had the good fortune of getting to work with him on my many cherished trips to the archive. I am similarly grateful to Jim Gerencser at Dickinson College's Carlisle Indian School Digital Resource Center and to Richard Tritt of the Cumberland County Historical Society, both of whom offered valuable assistance. Thank you also to Paul Conrad, Martin Summers, Katherine O'Donnell, and Susan Burch, whose shared historical interests and generosity with archival and other materials helped to enhance this research and point to new threads to follow. Susan—thank you for your constant support, feedback, and incredible generosity of spirit, which has surely made me a better scholar and thinker. I am grateful, as well, for the generous support of the UC President's Postdoctoral Fellowship Program and the American Council of Learned Societies, which enabled me to revise and finish this book.

Finally, I owe a debt of gratitude to the many community members, descendants, coconspirators, Native-led organizations, and Tribal Historic Preservation Officers who have contributed to this research and offered invaluable perspectives, experiences, expertise, feedback, and knowledge. In particular I would like to thank Anne Gregory, Thomas Biron, Megan Baker, Deidre Whiteman, Ian Thompson, Pemina Yellow Bird, Brad Angerman, Bed Rhodd, David Grignon, Tom Parker, Steven Curley, Rose Miron, the National Native American Boarding School Healing Coalition, the Native Justice Coalition, and the Choctaw Nation of Oklahoma's Tribal Historic Preservation Office and School of Choctaw Language. May our collective work help strengthen Indigenous futures.

On December 17, 1916, a twenty-one-year-old Mescalero Apache man named Pablo H. wrote to the superintendent of the Carlisle Indian Industrial School, Oscar Lipps, to report some recent difficulties. Pablo was a former enrollee of Carlisle—the first federally funded off-reservation institution intended solely for American Indian people in the United States—and he had traveled from Pennsylvania where the school was located to the Greenville Indian School in Northern California, where he was employed as disciplinarian at the time of this letter's writing. As Pablo explained to Superintendent Lipps, "No doubt you will be rather surprised to hear that I intend to resign as Disciplinarian of this school. . . . I know you will think that I have been a failer [sic] as Disciplinarian but after you hear what I have to say you will think different."[1] He continued,

> The Superintendent [of Greenville] and I have been having some trouble of which no doubt he has already told you. This trouble started over the Assistant Matron, [who reported] me to the Superintendent, saying that she had seen me talking to certain girls out on the front porch. . . . Well this matron is always finding fault with every thing. . . . I have tried in every way to please her but have failed, she is always going to [the Superintendent] with things that do not amount to nothing.
>
> I have been treated very unjustly here. . . . I have done all in my power to put up with all that was said about me but cannot any longer. . . . I wrote to Washington for a transfer, but they wrote and said that there was no vacant places at present, so I wrote that if I could not get another place that I would resign.[2]

Pablo closed, "I think that after I quit here I am going to work up at the mines. . . . If I do not get another place [in the Indian Service] then I want to go to Haskell [Indian School] and take a Commercial Course. . . . I am only twenty one years old and feel that I need lots of schooling yet because it is very hard to get along when a fellow does not know very much."[3]

I quote Pablo's words at length because I think they capture something powerful about Indigenous people's experiences at Carlisle, and in the United States more generally, at the turn of the twentieth century. For one, Pablo's letter registers the paternalism and influence that Carlisle officials like Superintendent Lipps continued to assert over former enrollees who lived and labored thousands of miles away from Pennsylvania. But Pablo's letter also illustrates how, although he was employed at an Indian school and thus ostensibly free of the kind of surveillance he experienced as a Carlisle enrollee, his behavior was still constantly under scrutiny by his white colleagues—a fact that showcases the pervasiveness of white supremacy and the malleability of settler institutions in maintaining power over Native people. As Pablo's experiences illustrate in stark relief, even though he was the person responsible for *administering* discipline to the students of Greenville, to his white colleagues, Pablo would *always* be a disciplinary subject.

"It is very hard to get along when a fellow does not know very much."

I often wonder why Pablo felt he didn't "know very much." If we take stock of the details contained in Pablo's letters—of all the things he *did* know—the apparent misalignment between his experiences and his sense that he didn't "know very much" becomes even more pronounced: Pablo knew, for example, that his colleagues at Greenville discriminated against him, perhaps on the basis of Indigeneity; he could also identify the source of his trouble—the boys' matron—who gossiped about him to his supervisor, and thereby wielded a subtle form of disciplinary power—a phenomenon discussed in greater detail in chapter 1. According to archival documents contained in his Carlisle file, Pablo was also a relatively educated man: he had attended Carlisle for six years before securing a coveted position with the Indian Service. When he made the decision to resign from Greenville, he had also devised several contingency plans, which illustrates his competence in negotiating available employment opportunities: he would work in the mines, earning three dollars and sixty-two cents a day, and try to get another position at an Indian school. If all else failed, he would attend business classes at the Haskell Institute in Lawrence, Kansas—another large, off-reservation boarding school for American Indian people that existed alongside Carlisle in the early years of the twentieth century.

Given all of these details—all of the things Pablo *did* know—it seems surprising, then, that he expressed the sense that he didn't know very much. But in the context of an era in which Indigenous men like Pablo were often presumed by US officials to be always already in need of white oversight and management, his words register something more subtle: they speak to a broader awareness of the structures of supremacy—white hegemony, labor discrimination, criminalization, and racialized punishment—he negotiated as a Mescalero man, as well as to his determination to direct the outcome of his life.

:

Bad Medicine places the experiences of Indian people like Pablo centrally within broader struggles over race, Indigeneity, power, and settler colonialism at the turn of the twentieth century. In so doing, the book reveals interconnected histories of Indigenous punishment, pathologization, and labor exploitation in Progressive Era facilities that claimed to educate, contain, reform, or punish Indian people in the United States at the turn of the twentieth century. The institutions examined in the following pages are seemingly discrete: they are public, private, federal, state, and religious facilities that professed to educate, employ, reform, "cure," or care for Indian people and, in some instances, other members of the general population, during a period of immense upheaval and reform. The Carlisle Indian Industrial School (1879–1918) in Carlisle, Pennsylvania, is the subject of the first chapter. Indigenous experiences in the private labor sector at the Ford Motor Company in Detroit and at a nurse training program at the General Hospital in Lancaster, Pennsylvania, form the basis of chapter 2. The Good Shepherd Home in Reading, Pennsylvania—a Catholic "reform" institution—is the subject of chapter 3. Chapter 4 turns to experiences of forced institutionalization at the Canton Asylum for Insane Indians in Canton, South Dakota, which was the United States' first and only federal facility intended solely for the "care" of Indian people declared incompetent or "insane." This book also analyzes the significance of other brick-and-mortar sites—such as local jails—through which Indian people moved, and *to* which they were often confined or disappeared.

At first glance, then, the institutions discussed in this work appear to be autonomous; yet as *Bad Medicine* argues, each played an important role in furthering colonial objectives, maintaining white hegemony, and fortifying settler-citizens' power over Indigenous people and their tribal nations. As philosopher Gilles Deleuze (thinking with Michel Foucault) has observed about the ways in which disciplinary power traverses institutions, "Discipline cannot be identified with any one institution or apparatus precisely because it is a type of power, a technology, that traverses every kind of apparatus . . . linking them, prolonging them, and making them converge and function in a new way."[4] Viewed in this way—from the vantage point of the institutions' effects on Indigenous people and the way they facilitated settler empowerment—the discrete facilities discussed in the following pages are revealed to be interlocking and, in many ways, interchangeable in their objectives. Together, they comprised a formidable structure that functioned—sometimes exclusively—in the service of the settler society. Similarly, this book illustrates the mutually reinforcing relationship between institutions that maintained white citizens at the top of the racial hierarchy in the United States, in part, by enlisting them to participate in the punitive practices of the settler state.

In examining punitive connections between distinct spaces of American Indian education, labor, reform, and medicine, *Bad Medicine* demonstrates the interrelated nature of settler institutions and argues that the practice of confining Indian people helped concretize, maintain, and expand networks of white racial power. As illustrated by the dynamic between Superintendent Lipps and Pablo, this research reveals how diverse institutions deputized white American citizens as the disciplinary agents of Indian people and how Indian people uniquely experienced institutionalization as a tool of US settler colonialism. Building on extant scholarship in Native American history and settler-colonial studies, *Bad Medicine* argues that the intake or commitment of Indigenous people to settler facilities was inherent—rather than coincidental—to the broader work of US settler colonialism at the turn of the twentieth century.

Indigenous boarding school experiences continue to be an important subject of analysis in Native American and Indigenous studies scholarship, as well as for the tribal nations who continue to feel the effects of the "boarding school era" and its legacy. While previous boarding school scholarship has focused on the experiences of Indian children, however, my research finds that adult Indian women and men eighteen years of age and older were a significant proportion—and from 1912 to 1918, the majority—of Carlisle's institutional demographic.[5] In centering the experiences of this overlooked cohort of adult Carlisle enrollees, and the noneducational experiences of adult Indian people more broadly, the book argues that attempts to control, subordinate, and punish Indian women and men occurred across institutions that coexisted in the so-called Allotment and Assimilation Era of federal Indian policy—generally understood as the period stretching from 1879, when Carlisle was founded, until 1934, when Commissioner of Indian Affairs John Collier formally repealed much of the era's policies with the passage of the Indian Reorganization Act.

The punitive phenomena examined in this book occurred against a complex backdrop of political volatility, class struggle, philanthropy, and social reform.

I.1 Society of the American Indian, 1911. Ohio State University, Inaugural Conference, Columbus, Ohio, 1911. Thompson Library Rare Books Stacks, Thompson Library Special Collections, Ohio State University Libraries.

. . . .

Heterogeneous groups comprised of Indigenous people and white Americans, such as the Women's National Indian Association, the Society of the American Indian, the Indian Rights Association, and even the "Friends of the Indian," mobilized public sentiment to further the "Indian cause" (fig. I.1). Assuredly, there was good that came of these efforts; in other cases, however, organizational objectives were misguided and paternalistic, rooted in the belief that Indian people needed rescue, civilizing instruction, and oversight from those who knew what was best for them. The structures of discipline and power analyzed herein are anything but monolithic, just as the aims of the historical actors who participated in the institutional and social networks examined in this book were complex and varied. Indeed, Indian women and men, such as Wallace Denny (Oneida) and his wife, Nellie Denny (Sisseton; née Robertson), participated in Carlisle's institutional regime and the social milieus of other networks, and the fact of their presence and the presence of other Native employees in overwhelmingly non-Native spaces surely made a difference to the Native women, men, and children who navigated these complicated sociopolitical environments.

Yet as *Bad Medicine* argues, Indian people navigated a generally antagonistic stance in the so-called Assimilation Era—attitudes and ideologies that buttressed and naturalized the institutionalized patterns of discipline, punishment, infantilization, and exploitation that seized on Indian people and their sovereign nations in complex ways. The presence of Indian Service employees who were also Indigenous—Wallace and Nellie Denny, Gertrude Bonnin (Dakota), and Charles Dagenett (Peoria), for example—within this broader settler and institutional regime thus would have had a limited impact on the inequitable power dynamics inherent to settler spaces like Carlisle or the Indian Office, which (unevenly) furthered the objectives of capital accumulation, land acquisition, and Indigenous cultural eradication. The punitive phenomena analyzed in the following chapters reflect the ways in which the institutions of the state enticed and enabled everyday citizens to participate in policing Indian people as a form of racial power, to obtain cheap labor through the Outing system, and to collaborate in an expansive network of Indigenous surveillance that reinforced white Americans' own national belonging. Yet, as illustrated by the many historical actors discussed in this work, one did not have to be a white American citizen to participate in and contribute to settler structures of empowerment, just as one did not have to be an Indian person to resist them. Still, in many ways, participation in the diverse institutions that claimed to improve the lives of Indian people furthered the interests of the settler state in subtle and not-so-subtle ways. In finite detail, *Bad Medicine* explores how settler power worked, and how settler institutions worked together.

Carlisle is often remembered as the flagship boarding institution for American Indian people in the United States. Many elements of its institutional regimen provided a model for the dozens of facilities that would be established in the decades following Carlisle's founding: enrollees received a rudimentary elementary education in English, reading, and writing; students were segregated by gender; and at the height of its operation, enrollment figures could top one thousand individuals in any given year. Carlisle is also often remembered as self-sustaining: enrollees lived at the institution across all years of its operation and were rarely permitted to leave or visit home; the labor they performed sustained the operations of the facility, helping keep overhead costs down; former enrollees and graduates returned to Carlisle as Indian Service employees; and siblings and children of former attendees also enrolled at the institution year after year, keeping alive the very real feelings of pride and sentimentality that many families felt toward their alma mater.

Inasmuch as Carlisle seemingly comprised its own self-contained universe, however, the school also maintained significant ties to other institutional spaces—

many of which were not under the oversight of the Office of Indian Affairs (OIA). These connections were sustained by white as well as Indigenous employees— Richard Henry Pratt, Oscar Lipps, Moses Friedman, John Francis Jr., Angel DeCora (Ho-Chunk), "Pop" Warner, and Dakota activist Gertrude Bonnin (Zitkala Ša), to name a few—who helped create and maintain lines of affinity between Carlisle, Indian reservations and communities, and other sites of contested settler power and oversight (fig. I.2). Additionally, because Carlisle enrollees hailed from disparate parts of the country as well as from other boarding schools, they too created and maintained connections between and among their diverse home communities and the institutions they traversed in this era. Examining the effects of these complicated networks of power, punishment, labor, and mobility, *Bad Medicine*'s attention to the noneducational experiences of adult Indian people in diverse spaces of Indigenous education, labor, "uplift," and reform exposes sites of Indian-white conflict that were as integral to the maintenance of settler power as were the theft and indoctrination of Indian children in boarding institutions. In analyzing the heterogeneous experiences of Indian people across a network of settler facilities—rather than in boarding schools alone—the book similarly reveals the central role of the institution as a colonial tool of Indigenous confinement, territorial dispossession, and white American empowerment.

Carlisle looms large in boarding school historiography. It was the first residential facility intended solely for the indoctrination of American Indian children during the Assimilation Era of federal Indian policy, and, as Akwesasne Mohawk historian Louellyn White has pointed out, the institution holds "dizzying" historical significance for the thousands of enrollees who traversed its grounds—as well as for families, tribes, and descendants of enrollees who continue to grapple with the impact of the school on their communities.[6] Carlisle's founding is infamous: Captain Richard Henry Pratt, an experienced military man, established the school in 1879 as a way to "civilize" Indigenous youth by divesting them of their lifeways. The institution's stated objective, as Pratt famously remarked, was to "Kill the Indian in him, and save the man." From 1879 to 1918, when Carlisle was repossessed by the US War Department, Native nations resisted this aim with varying degrees of success.[7]

Yet, while existing studies about Carlisle and other Indian residential schools have extensively documented the experiences of Indigenous children and youth and the impact of forced child removal on tribal nations, *Bad Medicine* focuses on a demographic that has received less sustained scholarly attention—Indigenous

I.2 Hinook-Mahiwi-Kalinaka, or Angel DeCora (Ho-Chunk), ca. 1900. DeCora was a painter and employed as art instructor at the Carlisle Indian School from 1906 to 1915. Nebraska State Historical Society Photograph Collections.

I.3 Quarterly Report, December 12, 1912. National Archives and Records Administration, RG 75, series 745, Carlisle Quarterly School Reports. Image courtesy of the Carlisle Indian School Digital Resource Center, Dickinson College, Carlisle, Pennsylvania.

women and men eighteen years of age and older—who enrolled at Carlisle in the early twentieth century, and who also often spent time in other institutions that were dedicated, ostensibly, to the "uplift" of Indian people in this era. Adult Indian women and men attended Carlisle in large numbers; as I discuss in greater detail in chapter 1, after 1900, adults who were eighteen years of age and older—all the way up to forty-five years old, in one instance—made up an increasingly large proportion of the institution's population. From 1912 to 1918, enrollment ledgers reflect that adults were the demographic majority (fig. I.3).

Some Indian women and men were sent to Carlisle as a form of punishment, as was the case with Justin R. H. (Apache), whose experience of parole under Carlisle's jurisdiction opens chapter 1. Others enrolled voluntarily, by making their own application. Many older enrollees sought entrance to Carlisle in order to learn a trade so they could better their circumstances in life (the subject of chapter 2), and they were often dismayed by the poor treatment they received upon passing through Carlisle's gates. Other Indian people, like Pablo, believed that a Carlisle education would increase their opportunities in life and left the institution believing they had secured meaningful work—only to be greeted by intense forms of class discrimination and racism that jeopardized their employment status or their physical, mental, or spiritual well-being.

In oral testimonies recorded for posterity, some enrollees recount their former days at Carlisle fondly, while others articulate dissatisfaction with the institution's bland food, military-style daily regimen, and routinized subordination to white authority. Still others reveal complex feelings about their time at school, using humor as a vehicle for healing. In 1982, for example, James Garvie (Santee) was interviewed about his time at Carlisle, where he enrolled in 1912 at the age of nineteen.[8] In this interview, Garvie recounted a humorous story about Jim Thorpe, the famous Sac and Fox athlete and Olympic gold medalist whose accomplishments are often highlighted in connection with Carlisle's history. As Garvie explained,

> We would sing [hymns], you know. We stood up, and I stood with my hands folded behind my back and all of a sudden, I felt something in my hand. I thought someone had stuck their finger right there, so I said "I'll catch him," and I grabbed him. Here it was Jim Thorpe. He had put a prune in there, and when I squeezed it, the juice came out all over. . . . I didn't know who he was, so I asked [my friend], "Who is that guy?" "Why," he said, "that's an honor. That's Jim Thorpe who played that trick on you." And he said "That won't be the last one either." He was a prankster. Nothing that would hurt anybody's feelings, you know. He just liked to get into harmless mischief.[9]

I love this story because it illustrates how Native people found commonplace, clever, and subtle ways to cultivate connection in these austere settler institutions—the subject of much important literature on Indigenous boarding school experiences. For other boarding school enrollees, however, heartache, sickness, disconnection, and longing overshadow the archival record as well as their remembrances of their time at school. As I examine in chapter 1, the varied experiences reflected in archival records suggest that for many adults, Carlisle was not a school at all—it was a place where labor was performed continuously and where punishment was routine.

What do we gain from focusing on the punitive experiences of adults who spent time at Carlisle in the early twentieth century? Why does it matter that older enrollees increasingly populated Carlisle after 1900? At the turn of the twentieth century, new metrics were emerging by which to measure adult maturation, defined in opposition to childhood and adolescence. By 1920, Progressive Era reformers in many states had succeeded in increasing the age at which an individual could consent to sexual relations from ten or twelve to between sixteen and eighteen, the time at which puberty had been completed and childhood ostensibly concluded.[10] With these rulings, citizens debated the changing meanings of childhood against a backdrop of concern over the protection and control of young women's sexuality.[11] The early years of the twentieth century also ushered in child labor laws that mandated schooling until the age of sixteen, at which point Americans could enter the workforce.[12] According to psychologist Jaana Juvonen and colleagues, only one-third of American pupils transitioned from eighth to ninth grade between 1907 and 1911, a fact they attribute in part to the "irrelevance of the curriculum to the lives of everyday youths."[13] This meant that most of the American population left school in late adolescence, before society considered them to be fully mature adults. Emerging views about normative psychological development were embedded in these societal shifts, as reformers, citizens, and politicians debated the point at which an individual could adequately assume the activities associated with adulthood and generally agreed that sixteen marked the threshold of "adult" maturity.[14]

Many of the public debates about the duration, characteristics, and sanctity of childhood did not apply to Native nations, however. As historian Marylin Lake has observed of this chimerical era, "Progressive reforms could have profoundly undemocratic outcomes. . . . Indigenous societies were supplanted by settler communities, who resolved to bring into being new kinds of race-based polities that were not simply 'facsimiles' of the old but self-consciously innovative pioneering democracies."[15] Land was thus at the heart of emergent (and past) federal Indian policies; following on the heels of the passage of the General Allotment Act (or Dawes Act) of 1887, surveyors enumerated each male head-of-household and assigned Native families approximately 160 acres to live on and cultivate. "Surplus" land was thrown open to white settlement. In this way, over ninety million acres of Indigenous landholdings were lost.[16] Alongside the allotment of tribal lands in severalty, in 1891, Congress passed a mandatory school attendance law that compelled Indian parents to relinquish their children (whom the OIA defined as youth between the ages of six and eighteen) to boarding facilities like Carlisle, where they would perform manual labor for half of the day or more and be indoctrinated into a rudimentary English-only education.[17] Together, allotment and assimilation-via-indoctrination in boarding schools comprised the twin engines of an ostensibly "benevolent" era of OIA policy that stretched from the mid-1800s to 1934, when Allotment Era policies were repealed and the Indian "New Deal," as Reorganization was also colloquially known, was passed under Commissioner Collier.[18] US politicians believed that if subsequent generations of Indian people were to achieve "civilization," they would need to learn the value of hard work by performing manual labor—an inversion of reformers' hard-won fight for more stringent child labor laws for the general American public. In later years, however, curricular changes led to transformations in boarding school objectives and institutional demographics. After 1900, the OIA became increasingly skeptical of the efficacy of the boarding school system and encouraged the education of Indian children and youth in day-schools and American public schools closer to home.[19] Older enrollees, including adults eighteen years of age and older, thus increasingly filled Carlisle's enrollment ledgers. Despite this demographic shift, however, Carlisle officials retained the educational regimen and rules intended for school-aged children, and the institution's stated objectives remained largely the same.

US officials' promotion of a substandard curriculum for Native women and men who sought enrollment at Carlisle often meant that adults had fewer opportunities for economic or social advancement than did their white counterparts. In Carlisle's early years, founder Richard Henry Pratt was adamant that Indian people could compete with white Americans, and he stressed the importance of immersing them within Euro-American environments so that they might be better equipped to do so.[20] But with a change in OIA personnel that brought Estelle Reel's appointment as Superintendent of the Indian School Service in 1898, a new course of study for Indian schools gained traction. Reel's revised curriculum promoted expanded instruction in all manner of industrial work, domestic service, and menial labor, and this curriculum, circulated to all federal Indian schools after 1901, served as a template for Carlisle's course of study as well. Because Reel's views on Indian education were informed by a racial philosophy that asserted the inherent inferiority of Indian people, the training available to Carlisle enrollees was intentionally substandard to that which white Americans could expect to receive, thus offering little hope for Indian people—already adults upon "graduation" from Carlisle, in many cases—who aspired to obtain work outside of the routine management of the allotment farm and household.[21] In many ways, the limited nature of educational opportunities for Indian people was strategic; as Commissioner of Indian Affairs Francis E. Leupp remarked in 1905,

Of the 30,000 or 40,000 Indian children of school age in the United States, probably at least three-fourths will settle down in that part of the West which we still style the frontier. Most . . . will try to draw a living out of the soil; a less—though, let us hope, an ever increasing—part will enter the general labor market as lumbermen, ditchers, miners, railroad hands, or what not. Now, if anyone can show me what advantage will come to this large body of manual workers from being able to reel off the names of the mountains in Asia, or extract the cube root of 123456789, I shall be deeply grateful.[22]

US Census records reflect the efficacy of this limited plan of education; in 1920, for example, decades after the federal Indian policy of allotment had been established, 35.79 percent of the Indigenous population ten years of age and older was enumerated as being gainfully employed. Of the 63,326 Indian people engaged in labor for that year, 43,584, or 68.82 percent, were in the Agriculture, Forestry, and Animal Husbandry sector, which included general farming of the kind encouraged by policymakers. By comparison, 31.14 percent of the "native white" population was similarly engaged, thus illustrating the overrepresentation of Indian people among the agricultural and farming sector as well as the relative lack of heterogeneity in the occupations of Indian people in this era.[23] As these statistics reflect, while Indian people were fast-tracked into menial labor and farming, they were simultaneously being dispossessed of the land base necessary to assume this work successfully—to say nothing of the quality of the land and soil they were allotted, which was often inarable. The following chapters further examine how settler institutions limited educational and occupational opportunities for Indian people and, in some instances, eased the transfer of Indigenous land to white ownership—patterns and processes that illustrate the tensions, contradictions, and shadow projects inherent to the policies and institutions of the settler state.

For Indian women and men who had already attained self-sufficiency upon *enrollment* at Carlisle (and who, in some cases, had already married), Carlisle's curriculum and subjection to rules intended for children may have been rather disappointing. As disciplinary records reflect, the seeming misalignment between adult Indian enrollees' expectations and hopes and those of Carlisle employees created widespread problems at the institution. Indian women and men often refused compliance with the school's disciplinary regime, and records of conflict at the institution similarly show that Carlisle officials attempted to maintain control over adults by denying them, paradoxically, the rights and responsibilities associated with American citizenship and individual autonomy—both of which were held out as a reward for successfully graduating from Carlisle.[24]

In critiquing entwined processes of white American deputization and attempted Indigenous subordination, a process I refer to as *making children out of women and men*, this book stresses the importance of acknowledging that many of the "boys and girls" to whom Carlisle superintendents and US officials referred in correspondence were legal adults. In some ways, the issue is one of nomenclature: for many Carlisle women and men, designation as "adults" would have aligned with their own understandings of the roles they assumed within their communities or with their identities back home as wage earners, caretakers, cultural stewards, husbands, wives, siblings, knowledge bearers, and protectors.

Yet, the issue is also a political one, for the concept of Indigenous adulthood has historically held potentially threatening legal and social implications for the state. As K. Tsianina Lomawaima (Mvskoke) and Teresa McCarty have argued, Indigenous nations comprised of "self-determining adults exercising dual or multiple citizenships have been perceived as much more threatening than groups defined as wards, marked by the mental, moral, and legal deficiencies linked to the status of children."[25] To grant Indian people status as "self-governing adults" would challenge Chief Justice John Marshall's landmark 1832 ruling in *Cherokee Nation v. Georgia* that tribes were domestic dependent nations comprised of federal wards. Similarly, granting Carlisle enrollees adult status equal to their white counterparts would challenge the US government's assumption of federal guardianship over all Indian boarding school enrollees, regardless of age, and paternalistic authority over tribal nations and their children.[26] Indigenous cosmologies reckon with the responsibilities required of tribal members at various stages of physical, intellectual, and spiritual development in ways specific to each worldview.[27] Yet, at Carlisle, school authorities and Indian Office officials alike presumed that all enrollees were incapable of acting as their own agents—a view that actively undermined tribal sovereignty, as well as adult enrollees' self-determination, by disallowing them from transacting their own affairs, denying them autonomy over their allotments or annuities, and preventing them from tending to their responsibilities back home.

This hierarchical structure of settler power threatened the security of Indigenous resources as well. Archival records reflect that multiple Carlisle enrollees owned their allotments outright and made decisions about their resources while at the institution; other enrollees leased out their allotments for mining or other extractive purposes and garnered royalties from these activities. In many cases, archival records reflect Carlisle superintendents' and reservation officials' intimate involvement in the affairs of Indian enrollees: officials regularly conducted land transactions and facilitated annuity payments on behalf of Indian women and men enrolled at the institution.

In one example of the ways in which this structure of guardianship produced fraught circumstances for adult enrollees who were also landowners, in 1913, the field clerk at the Union Agency at Muskogee (later referred to as the Five Civilized Tribes Agency), George McDaniel, wrote Carlisle superintendent Oscar Lipps in regard to Walter A. (not to be confused with Walter S., discussed in chapter 1), a twenty-one-year-old Creek (Mvskoke) enrollee who held an allotment plus surplus land on the reservation. According to this letter, McDaniel and Walter's mother together had determined that it would be best for Walter to sign over the deed to his land to his mother, to prevent the allotment from being lost to grafters. As McDaniel explained to Lipps, "If Walter should once leave the school on account of his past habits and his tendency for drink, he would be an easy prey for any designing persons, and could be induced to sign a deed to all of his land for the proverbial 'mess of pottage.' It was, therefore, deemed advisable, as a matter of protection to Walter, that his lands be conveyed to his mother as a check against the contingency as above contemplated."[28] Evidently, this was done. As I document in chapter 4, similar kinds of conflicted interests and state intervention into Indigenous homelife complicated familial dynamics, and sometimes directly resulted in forced confinement. At Carlisle as well, US officials' interference into the affairs of adult enrollees underscored the power of the state to alter the lives of Indian women and men away "at school." These land transactions add another dimension to our understanding of Carlisle's legacy.

Seminal studies by K. Tsianina Lomawaima (1993), Brenda Child (1998), David Wallace Adams (1995), and Clifford Trafzer (2006) have focused on multiple aspects of student experience across a federal system that was comprised of dozens of large, off-reservation boarding institutions, including Chilocco in Oklahoma, Sherman Institute in Southern California, Haskell Institute in Lawrence, Kansas, and Flandreau Indian School in South Dakota, as well as smaller reservation day schools where Indian children and youth increasingly received an elementary education closer to home, especially after 1900. Newer work in this subfield, such as that by Kevin Whalen (2016), Myriam Vuckovič (2008), Mikäela Adams (2020), Sarah Klotz (2021), Natalee Bauer (2022), Maile Arvin (2019),

Caitlin Keliiaa (2024), and others, continues to nuance scholarly and public understandings of Indigenous boarding school experiences by addressing topics that range from the Office of Indian Affairs' power to shape the rhythm of enrollees' daily lives to the quotidian and extraordinary forms of physical, intellectual, and even linguistic resistance that Indigenous enrollees wielded with varying degrees of efficacy.[29]

While existing literature often examines the legacy of this system by analyzing boarding schools in isolation or comparative relief, *Bad Medicine* focuses on the ways in which white hegemony and supremacist notions seized on Indigenous people *across* the diverse institutions of the settler state. Indian people who attended off-reservation boarding schools are often regarded as being "away from home"—located in a place far away from their kin and communities.[30] But enrollees also recall experiences of moving from place to place and institution to institution—a phenomenon that disability studies scholars refer to as *transinstitutionalization*, or the movement from one institution to another, oftentimes forcibly. In addition to examining Indigenous punishment across institutions that existed contemporaneously in the boarding school era, a secondary goal of this book is thus also to demonstrate the significance of this particular pattern of transinstitutionalization for Indigenous people within the context of US settler colonialism. As the following chapters reveal, entrance into one settler institution was often entrance into a rhizomatic network of settler institutions. *Bad Medicine* extends boarding school scholarship by focusing on an underexamined cohort of older Carlisle enrollees and on elements of Indigenous experience that have received less attention in existing literature: transinstitutionalization, incarceration, punishment, sexuality, labor, mobility, and the ways in which white supremacy came to bear on the daily lives of those who lived and labored in and across settler institutions in the Progressive Era. While these and similar experiences are often acknowledged in Native communities as being part of our shared historical past, they have not been the subject of much sustained scholarly discourse. *Bad Medicine* thus seeks to denude the unspoken dynamics of white supremacy in this era while documenting and affirming what many Indigenous community members already recognize as being the commonly experienced legacies of state intervention into Indigenous lives, communities, and sovereignties.

The settler-colonial objectives of Indigenous elimination and territorial dispossession also figure centrally in the stories that unfold in the following pages. Building upon the work of scholars such as Lorenzo Veracini, Marylin Lake, and

Patrick Wolfe, *Bad Medicine* reframes interconnected histories of Indigenous punishment, pathologization, and racialization as experiences that reveal the inherently rhizomatic nature of settler institutions and the agents that oversaw them. In particular, this research draws on three of Wolfe's foundational insights: (1) settler colonialism is a structure and not an event; (2) settler colonialism has negative dimensions—elimination, for one—as well as positive outcomes, which include "erecting a new colonial society on the expropriated land base"; and (3) "race" is not a given, but is "made in the targeting."[31] Building on these key tenets, *Bad Medicine* reads across the grain of the colonial archive—in addition to reading against it—in order to deconstruct its "organizing grammar of race" and to examine the material realities and affinities of the settler institutions that impacted the lives of Indian people in this era.

Walter Benjamin, Lisa Lowe, Estelle Freedman, and others have described the methodology of reading "against the grain." In his famous essay, Benjamin observed that "empathy with the victor invariably benefits the rulers" and implored historians to "brush history against the grain."[32] Lowe notes that to her, the practice suggests reading "things in their contexts differently . . . to reconstellate a world that neither assumes the history of global capitalism to be even and inevitable, nor conceives of empire as a monolithic project."[33] I am inspired by these calls to action while recognizing that reading uncritically with the grain or skeptically against it does not always capture the productive capacity of the colonial archive and the attitudes and ideologies contained therein. In what follows, I thus often read across the grain of archival materials to expose the spoken and unspoken hopes, desires, assumptions, beliefs, and practices of the historical actors—many of whom were white American citizens—who authored them. In so doing, new patterns emerge from engaging with challenging institutional records about Indigenous people not as "true," but as truthful; a cross-grain analysis permits the historian to read seemingly familiar stories and events anew for what they might say about those who participated in the act of their creation.

This book's theoretical orientation has also been particularly inspired by Kelly Lytle Hernández's *City of Inmates* (2017), which reframes the history of human caging in Los Angeles and incarceration more broadly as a settler-colonial project of mass elimination. Similarly, I draw from the insights of Margaret Jacobs's influential *White Mother to a Dark Race* (2009), which examines the reach and scope of settler objectives through the lens of Indigenous child removal in the United States and Australia and, in so doing, crafts a historical narrative that traverses national identities, settler objectives, and continental boundaries. This book engages these works and other paradigm-shifting scholarship to contribute a view of Indigenous institutionalization as another "pillar" of US settler colonialism, as Hernández has described the centrality of incarceration to the creation of the state. *Bad Medicine* applies a settler-colonial framework to quotidian conflicts between white Americans and Indigenous people and goes further, to showcase how American citizens seized everyday opportunities to exercise punitive power on behalf of the settler state.

Recent scholarship in American studies similarly reframes master historical narratives of Progressive Era reform by placing the experiences of marginalized populations (women, people with disabilities, or nonwhite communities) centrally in analyses of familiar topics in US history—labor relations, the history of psychiatry—some of which are also examined in this work. Discussions about race and processes of racialization have increasingly dominated this kind of scholarship, as in Elizabeth Esch's *The Color Line and the Assembly Line* (2018), which revisits the history of the Ford Motor Company as one of race-making. Indigenous Brazilians are discussed in Esch's study, but the experiences of American Indian men who worked at the Ford factory in Detroit are omitted from her analysis and from other studies that focus on nonwhite populations at Ford, an oversight that *Bad Medicine* seeks to address. Similarly, Martin Summers's *Madness in the City of Magnificent Intentions* (2019) examines the history of St. Elizabeths, the United States' first federal psychiatric institution, from the perspective of Black Americans forcibly confined there. Like *Madness* in the context of African American history, *Bad Medicine* produces a counternarrative—one that focuses on the coarticulation of settler colonialism and ableism (or *settler ableism*, as discussed in chapter 4) in the administration of Indian Affairs to reveal the white-supremacist overtones of the history of Indigenous institutionalization in the United States.[34] Chapter 1 of this book also draws on Jacqueline Fear-Segal's insights in *White Man's Club* (2007), which investigates US boarding schools such as Carlisle (for Indian people) and the Hampton Institute in Virginia (for Freedmen and Indian people) as sites of white racial power, analyzing two schools in relation to one another but largely in isolation from other institutions. Building on this important scholarship, *Bad Medicine* highlights the transfer of white Americans' punitive power *between* and *among* the labor, medicine, and educational settings that Indian people traversed at the turn of the twentieth century. Indigeneity is distinct from "race," yet Indigenous people have been racialized alongside other nonwhite peoples in the United States; their histories are entwined. *Bad Medicine* thus argues for a broader view of divergent and intersecting forms of racialization, as well as the critical role of white supremacy—and specifically a phenomenon I refer to as *status-whiteness*—in the history of Indigenous institutionalization in the United States.

Although many of the settler institutions examined in this work promoted white supremacy, or the belief in the superiority of the white race, this does not entirely account for the "positional superiority," to borrow from Māori scholar Linda Tuhiwai Smith, that many white historical actors experienced over nonwhite people in this era. As such, I employ the concept of *status-whiteness* to demarcate a social role that many of the white Americans (and occasionally nonwhite people) discussed in this book adopted, were granted, or occupied—sometimes unwittingly. Not all white Americans held racial power in the same way, nor did they apply it evenly. But the many archival records examined in *Bad Medicine* illustrate how "whiteness" was a status that could be assumed and relied on in instances of interracial, gendered, and even class conflict. *Bad Medicine* contributes a new paradigm to Native American history and expands settler-colonial frameworks by demonstrating how white Americans assumed punitive functions over Indian people as a natural right—a pattern of deputization that heightened the efficacy of settler institutions, but one that has not been thoroughly explored in extant literature.

Chapter 1, "'An Ordinary Case of Discipline': Surveillance and Punishment at the Carlisle Indian Industrial School, 1879–1918," analyzes the deputization of white Americans as the disciplinary agents of older Indigenous enrollees who were punished at the Carlisle Indian Industrial School in Carlisle, Pennsylvania, before the institution's 1918 closure. In so doing, this chapter departs from existing boarding school literature to argue that patterns of white American deputization are most visible when we acknowledge the behavioral, physical, intellectual, and sexual distinctions between childhood and adulthood—as well as the messiness of these categories—that created racial conflict between historical actors in this institutional setting. After 1900, adult Indian women and men increasingly enrolled at Carlisle of their own accord and, once there, continued to exert autonomy and agency over their lives. They moved around, as they did back home, to greater or lesser degrees; they wanted to be able to come and go from Carlisle as dictated by the needs of their families and communities; and they often sought out romantic relationships with one another and with others in the

Carlisle vicinity.[35] As I explore in greater detail in this chapter, however, freedom of mobility often broke along racial lines of affinity—real or perceived—in the Carlisle region. This fact made the institution's immediate vicinity a dangerous place for Indian people, who devised creative ways of negotiating the class, race, and power dynamics they encountered in that time and place.

Drawing upon records held in Dickinson College's Carlisle Indian School Digital Resource Center (CISDRC), "An Ordinary Case of Discipline" reveals how Indigenous punishment figured centrally as an "ordinary" fact of everyday life at the institution. This chapter closely analyzes disciplinary files that document quotidian, punitive interactions between Indian women and men and white American citizens—interactions that range from explicit experiences of arrest and incarceration in the local jail, in the case of many Indian men, to Indian women's experiences of surveillance, gossip, and domestic discipline in Carlisle's "Outing" program, an exploitative system that placed Indian "students" in the homes of white Americans to perform menial labor. In addition to discussing instances of Indigenous punishment and resistance, however, this chapter also reveals the purpose Carlisle served for the settler society: it demonstrates how US officials deputized American civilians as the disciplinary agents of Indian enrollees and enlisted them to surveil and apprehend Indian people in the Carlisle vicinity—actions that curtailed Indigenous mobility throughout the Carlisle region and benefited the settler society by increasing its reach over tribal nations. These dynamics illustrate how, for many adults, Carlisle was not a "school" at all; it was a place where labor was performed continuously and where punishment was routine. Taken together, these experiences demonstrate how diverse historical actors worked together as part of the same system of white empowerment that spanned an entire region. These experiences also showcase the powerful methods of resistance that Indigenous people employed to resist this regime at Carlisle, and beyond.

A parable entitled "Hoe Handle Medicine," published in Carlisle's official student newspaper, provides the opening to the eponymous second chapter. This story introduces the concept of *medicinal labor*, which I use as an ideological lens through which to analyze the gendered experiences of Indian workers in the private labor sector. This chapter reads across the grain of archival records held in Dickinson College's CISDRC and, in so doing, centers the experiences of Indian men and women who trained to become automotive mechanics and nurses at the Ford Motor Company in Detroit and the General Hospital in Lancaster, Pennsylvania, two vocational "partnerships" facilitated by the Carlisle Indian School. At the turn of the twentieth century, US officials were confronted with addressing increasingly dire health crises on Indian reservations and in boarding schools, and often prescribed labor and remedial action—before medicine—as the cure for Indigenous ailments. This prescription dovetailed with dominant discourses that construed Indianness as pathological and underscored the Office of Indian Affairs' efforts to encourage Indian people to take up farm work and other menial occupations—objectives that were reflected at Carlisle and in white-dominated spaces of Indigenous employment as well.

Viewed through the prism of medicinal labor, "Hoe Handle Medicine: Medicinal Labor at the Ford Motor Company and Lancaster General Hospital" demonstrates how ostensibly new avenues of employment held out to Indian people in the private labor sector had profound medical, moral, and punitive connotations. The first section of the chapter begins with an overview of entwined histories of health crises and shifting labor opportunities in Indian communities and on Indian reservations—the paradoxical outcomes of an era of Indigenous "uplift." This discussion then shifts to close readings of disciplinary materials about Indian men at Ford and Indian women at the General Hospital, which reveal the prevalence of the ideology of medicinal labor—as well as profound instances of Indigenous resistance to the pathologization of their bodies, nations, and lifeways. In considering these contested experiences of employment training, pathologization, and punishment, this chapter argues that *hoe handle medicine* is an apt metaphor for diffuse settler labor that "cured" by attempting to exploit adult Indian women and men in the homes, factories, and fields of white America.

Chapter 3, "Sisters Magdalene: Entwined Histories of 'Reform' at Good Shepherd Homes," turns to another site of Indigenous punishment and forced institutionalization: the House of the Good Shepherd in Reading, Pennsylvania—a facility described in Carlisle correspondence as a convent or reform school administered by the Catholic order of the Sisters of the Good Shepherd. In 1914, at least three young Indian women were sent from Carlisle to the Reading home as punishment for various perceived behavioral infractions. Their experiences bear marked similarities to, and important distinctions from, the experiences of Irish women confined in Good Shepherd Magdalene laundries thousands of miles away across the world. The history of Magdalene laundries in Ireland and their impact on Irish women who were forcibly confined to these facilities between the eighteenth and twentieth centuries are well-documented; Magdalene laundries also existed contemporaneously in the United States, but their existence is less widely known. Placing these histories of forced confinement into conversation with one another, this chapter makes the case for expanding our understanding of the way the federal Indian boarding school system worked in tandem with other noneducational facilities in the Unites States to encompass and accommodate institutions that do not neatly fit the definition of a "school."

"Sisters Magdalene" begins with an overview of the purposes that Magdalene laundries served in Ireland and details important similarities and distinctions between Irish and US facilities. Drawing on oral testimonies of Irish survivors housed in the Digital Repository of Ireland, this section argues that the Good Shepherd home in Reading and other contemporaneous American "reform" institutions played an important role in the apparatus of the US settler state, akin to the role of Magdalene laundries in what historian James Smith refers to as Ireland's "architecture of containment."[36] Building on this discussion, I shift to an examination of archival records relating to the young Native women confined in the Reading facility, which illustrate how US officials used the Good Shepherd home as an alternative to the prison. The third and final section examines gendered distinctions in the punishment of Indian women and men, which further illustrates the use of carceral auxiliary institutions, such as "reform schools," as tools of US settler colonialism. As this chapter demonstrates, Indian women's experiences of confinement at the Good Shepherd home intersect with multiple histories of confinement, reform, and institutionalization; they also offer critical insight into the global impact of Magdalene laundries, while highlighting the ways in which the young Indian women sent to Reading uniquely experienced confinement as a tool of US settler colonialism. In light of the US Interior Department's federal investigation into the legacy of the boarding school system, it is critical that all institutions that intervened into tribal sovereignty be identified and come under scrutiny.

Following the policies of this era of bad medicine to their logical conclusion, chapter 4, "Care and Maintenance: Settler Ableism and Land Dispossession at the Canton Asylum for Insane Indians, 1902–1934," travels to Canton, South Dakota, to the Canton Asylum for Insane Indians—the first and only institution designed solely for the confinement of American Indian people on psychiatric grounds. Reading across and against the grain of medical association proceedings, boarding school publications, photographs, and Canton "inmate" case files held at the National Archives and Records Administration, this chapter shows how the medical confinement of landholding Indian people at Canton led to territorial dispossession on a small-scale, case-by-case basis. Records reflect that over four hundred Indian people were forcibly confined to Canton—often as a result of disagreements with boarding school superintendents, reservation agents, and other white citizens—and show that some Indian people were dispossessed of their landholdings while incarcerated there. Despite these facts, Canton is the subject of few academic publications and historical works. To date, *Bad Medicine* is the first monograph-length text written from a Native perspective (Choctaw) about Canton, although Susan Burch's excellent study, *Committed*, draws upon extensive community work with descendants of those institutionalized at the facility. Similarly, existing literature has not examined the motivations among white authorities that led to the long-term confinement of Indigenous people at Canton or the role that the institution played in piecemeal US territorial acquisition.[37]

"Care and Maintenance" thus broadens current understandings of the institution's legacy by examining extralegal processes that led to the forced confinement of Indian people at Canton, often until death. It begins by tracing anti-Indian sentiment in law, medicine, and popular culture that contributed to dominant Western pseudoscientific beliefs about Indian people and the prevalence, or lack thereof, of "insanity" in Indian communities. These discourses helped shape the racial common sense and conditions of possibility necessary for the incarceration of Indian people on the basis of "insanity," while further fortifying expressions of settler ableism in the United States. Building on this discussion, the remainder of the chapter shifts to close readings of case materials and utilizes biographical sketches and vignettes throughout to center Indigenous voices and perspectives. Together, these records reveal how reservation agents, boarding school superintendents, legal guardians, and sometimes disgruntled spouses or family members leveraged extralegal processes of commitment to disappear Indian people to the facility. "Care and Maintenance" shows how Canton was "run like a boarding school" and situates processes of Indigenous institutionalization deep within the settler state on a historical continuum of US policies aimed at the eradication of Indigenous peoples. Although forced confinement at Canton was characterized by radical power disparities, Indigenous women and men held at the facility vehemently protested and resisted their institutionalization, as did their kin and communities. "Care and Maintenance" documents these intimate struggles in finite detail.

⋮

A word on methodology is in order. *Bad Medicine* draws on records that are housed at the National Archives and Records Administration; the Library of Congress; the Carlisle Indian School Digital Resource Center at Dickinson College; the Cumberland County Historical Society in Carlisle, Pennsylvania; and other nontribal organizations. In so doing, this work joins that of Linda Tuhiwai Smith, Eve Tuck, Lisa Lowe, Saidiya Hartman, Michel-Rolph Trouillot, and many others who have critiqued the colonial archive as always already imbalanced and who have devised radical ways of listening and responding to an archival record that reflects troubling disparities of power. My way of listening to the colonial archive is specific to my positionality as a Choctaw woman, mother, daughter, community member, and scholar who hails from a long line of educators and troublemakers, whose research has been facilitated by graduate-level training and access to institutional spaces often unavailable to those outside of academia. I owe a debt of gratitude to the Indigenous community members, activists, and leaders whose perspectives are reflected in the book, and which supplement the inherently limited and limiting nature of the archival records engaged in this work. Many of the materials examined in *Bad Medicine* offer distinctively non-Indigenous viewpoints on Indian Affairs in the late nineteenth and early twentieth centuries; the stories of Indigenous struggle uncovered in the colonial archive suggest that US officials believed their institutions were "successful" not because they benefited Indigenous people but because they produced structures of power that fortified the settler society. Yet, Indian people were not passive bystanders in histories of forced or coerced institutionalization. In fact, as the following chapters reveal, the very opposite is true: they actively resisted subordination, infantilization, punishment, and white hegemony, along with the many other, myriad forms of bad medicine they encountered within institutions designed to further the interests of the settler state. *Bad Medicine* thus also illustrates how the Indigenous people who lived at the turn of the twentieth century and who were ensnared in the institutional apparatus of the settler state worked assiduously to maintain autonomy over their lives, relationships, and daily affairs; they used all of the resources at their disposal to achieve their goals or to seek out connection in these hostile institutional environments, and often, their very ingenuity was punished. Sometimes, they were able to successfully resist total subordination to white authority, as well as the most detrimental effects of these institutional regimes. In other cases, however, they could not. *Bad Medicine* finds that these behaviors, these resistance efforts, were historically significant because they reveal punitive patterns that might otherwise go unnoticed—patterns that continue to play out in the America of today.

To further intervene in the colonial archive's propensity to exclude Indigenous viewpoints, I place Indigenous perspectives centrally within the following analyses, whenever possible. Narrative cohesion and the production of history requires the selective incorporation and arrangement of facts, a process that Trouillot has famously problematized; in an effort to challenge settler hegemony and tell these stories of Indigenous struggle in a good way, I have also included an appendix of fully reproduced letters of correspondence authored by some of the Indigenous historical actors engaged in this book. Moreover, I make the stylistic decision to redact the surnames of the Indigenous people mentioned in *Bad Medicine* unless their names appear in previously published work or repositories, and I do so out of respect for their descendants and communities who retain the right to narrate their histories in a way that aligns with their own community protocols. To that end, tribal or community affiliations are used first to identify the Indigenous people referred to in this work, and I make the decision to retain tribal affiliations the way they were originally described in archival materials, in the hopes that this continuity might assist descendants and tribes conducting independent research in locating their kin. I use the terms *American Indian* (and Indian), *Native American* (and Native), and *Indigenous* throughout the book to refer collectively to the First Peoples, or original inhabitants, of Turtle Island.

The stories of Indigenous struggle contained in the colonial archive are often difficult to encounter. But they also document the fortitude of the Indigenous women and men who lived in this era, and who fought assiduously and unrelentingly on behalf of themselves and their loved ones—and in so doing, on behalf of future generations of Indigenous people. As illustrated by the accomplishments of our tribes, collectives, and communities in the interceding years, the policies and practices of this era of bad medicine were not ultimately successful. Today, as in the past, we forge our own paths forward. Our nations have always been strong; together, we carry on.

"AN ORDINARY CASE OF DISCIPLINE"

SURVEILLANCE AND PUNISHMENT AT THE CARLISLE

INDIAN INDUSTRIAL SCHOOL, 1879–1918

In 1912 a forty-five-year-old Apache man named Justin R. H. was paroled out under the jurisdiction of the Carlisle Indian Industrial School in Carlisle, Pennsylvania, the first federally funded off-reservation residential institution intended solely for American Indian people in the United States.[1] According to a proclamation signed by the governor of Arizona, Justin was charged in 1906 with the crime of murder in the second degree in Yavapai territory and had been serving his term of life imprisonment in the territorial prison. In 1912, however, Governor Richard E. Sloan commuted Justin's life sentence to a term of thirty years, and with time off for good behavior and the benefit of time served, Justin was released on parole to "his friend and advisor" Carlisle superintendent Moses Friedman. According to his "student" file, Justin was a former pupil; he was enrolled at Carlisle in 1884 at the age of seventeen but was returned home to the San Carlos Agency in Arizona four years later on account of ill health. Nearly a quarter of a century later, however, he would return to Carlisle not as a student but as a parolee—a fact that demonstrates the interchangeable nature of settler institutions and the malleability of their objectives in maintaining power over Indian people.[2]

The Carlisle Indian Industrial School (1879–1918) has received increased worldwide attention following US Secretary of the Interior Deb Haaland's June 2021 announcement of a federal investigation into the intergenerational impact of Native American boarding schools.[3] In public forums and other national discourse, Carlisle is often described as the first residential school intended for American Indian children during the so-called Allotment and Assimilation Era (1879–1934) of US federal Indian policy. Yet, American Indian women and men eighteen years of age and older composed a substantial proportion of Carlisle's population and were the demographic majority from 1912 to 1918, when the barracks were repossessed by the War Department.[4] As illustrated by the dynamic between Friedman and Justin, Carlisle served noneducational purposes as an institution that deputized white Americans as agents of the settler-colonial order and facilitated the punishment, incarceration, and proletarianization of adult Indian people—a dynamic that broadens our understanding of the institution's legacy and the ways in which its existence directly benefited the settler society.

As boarding school historians have amply demonstrated, policymakers of this era believed that the theft and indoctrination of Indian children was key to the successful assimilation of Indian communities. Their youth made them malleable— "measurably plastic," according to Commissioner of Indian Affairs Francis E. Leupp—and once removed from the protection of their communities, Indian children could be compelled to regard their ancestral lifeways with shame and accept "civilization" as the only alternative.[5] By contrast, reformers regarded adult Indian people as too "old school" to be educated in the American way and too committed to their worldviews to be completely assimilated. As historian David Wallace Adams recounts, a reservation agent to the Lakota believed that it was "a mere waste of time to attempt to teach the average adult Indian the ways of the white man. He can be tamed, and that is about all."[6] But if adult Indian people were inassimilable, as many US officials believed, why were so many adults enrolled at Carlisle? Why were so many adults punished, and what does this reveal about the shadow project of the institution in this era?

This chapter analyzes the deputization of white Americans as the disciplinary agents of Indian women and men who traversed Carlisle's grounds in the early twentieth century. In so doing, it renews attention to the adult Indian people who attended off-reservation boarding institutions in this era, and it places their punitive experiences within broader struggles over race, power, and settler colonialism. Carlisle officials kept extensive records about adult enrollees, and disciplinary documents made available through Dickinson College's Carlisle Indian School Digital Resource Center (CISDRC) provide a rich source for examining conflicts between adult Carlisle enrollees and US authority figures in key areas of adult experience, including labor, sexuality, and freedom of mobility.[7] In addition to revealing how punishment figured centrally as an ordinary fact of everyday life at the institution, these records show how white American civilians were enlisted to surveil and apprehend Indian people in the Carlisle vicinity—actions that curtailed adults' mobility throughout the Carlisle region and benefited the settler society by increasing the reach of its power over tribal nations. As historian Kelly Lytle Hernández points out, "Even as many settler societies depend on racialized workforces, settler cultures, institutions, and politics simultaneously trend toward excluding racialized workers from full inclusion in the body politic . . . and . . .

criminalizing them or otherwise revoking the right of racialized outsiders to be within the invaded territory."[8]

Disciplinary records about Carlisle enrollees were overwhelmingly authored by US officials, Carlisle employees, Office of Indian Affairs (OIA) agents, and other American citizens. As such, their attitudes about Indian people frame this chapter. These documents expose the ways in which Indigenous punishment dovetailed with the pursuit of white hegemony and highlight the interlocking and often interchangeable nature between Carlisle and other settler institutions, such as local jails. As revealed by the stories white officials and citizens told one another about Indian people, the practice of Indigenous institutionalization—the intake or commitment of an Indigenous person to an institution—enabled settler agents to profit from their involvement in the punitive structure of the settler state.[9] The interconnected relationship between settler institutions and the agents who oversaw them suggests that Indigenous institutionalization was inherent, rather than coincidental, to US settler colonialism in this era.

In examining Carlisle's complex institutional regime, this chapter also makes the case that institutionalization itself should be included as a positive dimension of the settler-colonial structure that historian Patrick Wolfe has famously described. Wolfe writes, "In [settler colonialism's] positive aspect, elimination is an organizing principal [sic] of settler-colonial society rather than a one-off . . . occurrence. The positive outcomes of the logic of elimination can include officially encouraged miscegenation, the breaking-down of native title into alienable individual freeholds, native citizenship, child abduction, religious conversion, resocialization in total institutions such as missions or boarding schools, and a whole range of cognate biocultural assimilations." Building on these insights, I argue that institutionalization in settler facilities that were interconnected often by design is a phenomenon that is distinct from the "resocialization in total institutions" that Wolfe has described and should be added to this list. Indian people were sent to settler institutions on the basis of Indigeneity and, once institutionalized, subjected to treatment that reinforced their racialized status as "Indian." This process furthered settler aims of Indigenous elimination—but did not always result in the loss of identity that defines total institutions. In some cases, as this book argues, institutionalization enhanced and underscored Indigenous people's identities and status as "Indian," even while divesting them of material rights.[10]

In analyzing the deputization of white Americans as the disciplinary agents of Indian women and men at Carlisle and beyond, this chapter forefronts a policy transformation that facilitated the increased enrollment of adults in an institution intended, at least initially, for children: Carlisle Superintendent Moses Friedman's official stance of accepting only "mature" Indian pupils after 1908 and the subsequent enrollment of adults in a "school" that shifted its focus away from book-learning and toward vocational training.[11] After this policy change, Friedman aimed to admit to Carlisle only those who desired to learn an industrial trade, and enrollment ledgers reflect that this policy change resulted in an older institutional demographic. Increasingly, Indian women and men eighteen years of age and older made their own application to Carlisle, and many stated a desire to enroll or reenroll at the institution to learn a trade or to take specialized courses in the hopes of securing work upon leaving Carlisle. The transformation in enrollment demographics that accompanied this policy change gave rise to a panoply of struggles between adult Indian enrollees and institutional authority figures—contests over power, labor, sexuality, and freedom that often distinguish the experiences of older Carlisle enrollees from those of younger children. Disciplinary documents enable us to examine the outcomes of these struggles for adult Indian women and men who were punished and the white Americans who frequently assumed this punitive function as their natural right. Although the focus of this chapter is on Indigenous punishment, Indigenous resistance and agency are both implicit and explicit in the stories that unfold.

After a brief overview of Carlisle's founding, the first section discusses the stakes of acknowledging older Carlisle enrollees' status as adults in order to critique entwined processes of American Indian racialization and infantilization.[12] As was the case with women, immigrants, nonwhite people, and people with disabilities in the Progressive Era, US politicians and social reformers regarded Indigenous people as political outsiders and perpetual dependents of the US government—conditions they asserted could be mitigated by oversight in institutions created, ostensibly, for their "uplift." For Indian people, however, institutionalization presented a specific set of challenges to tribal self-determination. The initial section of this chapter situates punitive patterns at Carlisle within a broader history of social reform and forced confinement at the turn of the twentieth century.

Building on this analysis, the next section centers records about two Indian men enrolled at Carlisle—George F. (Passamaquoddy, described as Penobscot in Carlisle records) and Justin R. H. (Apache)—which document quotidian punitive interactions with white citizens. These records show how white Americans assumed disciplinary functions over the Indian men as an inherent right and reveal how the policing activities of white citizens entrenched, rather than reconfigured, racial hierarchies endemic to the settler-colonial order. That Indian employees also participated in this institutionalized regime of Indigenous discipline and punishment underscores the structural nature of settler colonialism; one did not need to be a white American to participate in, or benefit from, this system. In a similar vein, Indian women at Carlisle were often less mobile than men due to the nature of their labor at the institution, which kept them indoors and under observation; I have thus elected to focus this discussion on Indian men for what these dynamics demonstrate about the very public nature of anti-Indian racism at Carlisle and in the surrounding area.[13]

The following section demonstrates how settler institutions and diverse historical actors worked together as part of the same system of white racial empowerment. Disciplinary documents reveal a seeming paradox: adult Indian women and men were punished for enacting the very characteristics—independence, autonomy, and self-sufficiency—that Carlisle claimed to be teaching them. Simultaneously, white citizens seized opportunities to participate in Carlisle's punitive network of Indigenous surveillance and containment, as revealed by coordinated efforts to apprehend and detain so-called runaway Indian men. Archival records also reveal that some Carlisle enrollees were landholders and reflect Carlisle superintendents' involvement in land transactions. These efforts highlight the potential utility of the institution in furthering settler objectives of resource management and territorial acquisition.

Finally, through an analysis of discursive forms of "domestic discipline," the last section analyzes how the white American women gossiped about Indian women domestic servants and, in so doing, expanded their spheres of influence outside of the private domain of the twentieth-century American home—actions that supplemented Carlisle's broader punitive regime. Disciplinary documents reveal that for many adult Indian "students," Carlisle was not a school at all; it was a place where labor was performed continuously, and where punishment at the hands of white Americans was routine. Together, these punitive phenomena expand current understandings of the way that white racial power worked in the United States and demonstrate the integral role that institutionalization played in furthering settler-colonial objectives of Indigenous elimination, land acquisition, and labor control. Simultaneously, the experiences explored in this chapter illustrate the subtle, profound, and intimate ways that Indian enrollees resisted Carlisle's punitive regime and retained some dimension of autonomy over their lives.

In October 1879, when Captain Richard Henry Pratt flung open Carlisle's gates, Indian men, rather than children, crossed over the institution's iron threshold. Carlisle's original disciplinary regime was inspired—indeed, was inextricable from—Pratt's experiences as military man and the time he spent as jailor to Indigenous warriors taken prisoner during the so-called Red River War. The "educational experiment" at Carlisle, as it would come to be known, thus had a military forerunner: a social experiment conducted in St. Augustine, Florida, that earned Pratt the confidence of the Interior Department and the support of the Secretary of the Interior Carl Schurz. In 1875, at the conclusion of the Red River War, President Ulysses S. Grant tasked Pratt with the oversight of seventy-two warriors of the Comanche, Kiowa, Arapaho, Cheyenne, and Caddo nations; it was Pratt who would lead the prisoners of war in chains from Fort Sill, Indian Territory, to Fort Marion. Before long, the warriors captured the attention of the American public, as visitors traveled from all over the United States to view them in their fortress. While there, the warriors' hair was shorn, Pratt taught them English, and provided them with paper and pencils—which many would use to depict their forced trek from Fort Sill to the old Spanish fort at St. Augustine.[14] In this way, as historian Jacqueline Fear-Segal has observed, Pratt turned "prisoners into pupils"—a phrase that powerfully illustrates the punitive and transformative capacities of Pratt's earliest "classroom."[15]

Following on the heels of his sensationalized time at Fort Marion, Pratt wanted to prove that if given a chance at a formal American education, an Indian could become an American like any other man. Pursuing this notion, Pratt thus arranged the transfer of twenty-two of the Indian prisoners of war to the Hampton Institute in Virginia, a school founded in 1868 by General Samuel Chapman Armstrong and intended for the education of African American Freedwomen and men. As Fear-Segal has also detailed, Pratt and Armstrong were influenced by competing notions of racial capacity, and soon found themselves at loggerheads with one another.[16] Shortly after his arrival at Hampton, in 1878, Pratt sought congressional support for a facility in which he could mold Indian people according to his own assimilationist racial philosophy, and he quickly secured approval to open an Indian-only school in the disused military barracks located in Carlisle, Pennsylvania.[17] With Carlisle's founding in November 1879, Pratt set to work implementing a militarized educational regimen modeled on the Fort Marion experiment and enrolled the first cohort of eighty-two "pupils," including fifteen of the Fort Marion prisoners. Thus, out of the dust of a facility used to train Confederate soldiers, the United States' flagship Indian boarding institution was born.

Scholars of Native American history have remarked on the severity of Pratt's institutional regimen as well as the trauma inflicted on Indian youth and their communities via forced enrollment at boarding school.[18] Ostensibly, Carlisle's founding marked the conclusion of a violent period of overt federal warfare, but as historians have demonstrated, the federal boarding school system—one that would by the early years of the twentieth century include over twenty-five off-reservation institutions—enacted its own pernicious form of cultural genocide. At its heart, the system was designed to eliminate Indigenous people and replace them with Americanized facsimiles. The effects of this era on tribal nations have been well-documented in a robust body of scholarship, but fewer works have analyzed how Carlisle served important functions in promoting white supremacy and furthering the settler-colonial aim of physically removing Indigenous people from white Americans' claimed territory via institutionalization, the focus of this chapter.

In 1905, just a year after Francis E. Leupp assumed his position as Commissioner of Indian Affairs, he declared in his annual report that the nonreservation school system had outlived its usefulness. Unlike Pratt, Leupp believed that academic instruction for Indian people was inapplicable to the lives they were bound to lead and that boarding school environments fostered "unwholesome" conditions. During his tenure, Leupp would work to implement a different kind of agenda in the Indian Office: "The foundation of everything must be the development of character. Learning is a secondary consideration."[19] "To my notion," he explained in his annual report, "the ordinary Indian boy is better equipped for his life struggle on a frontier ranch . . . his time could be put to its best use . . . [by learning] how to do the hundred other bits of handy tinkering which are so necessary to the farmer who lives 30 miles from a town."[20]

With Pratt's removal from his post in 1904, subsequent Carlisle superintendents found themselves tasked with maintaining an institution that had fallen into disrepute—as well as negotiating the changing objectives of the Indian Office. By 1905, Commissioner Leupp was adamant that Indian people could not, after all, compete with white Americans. He felt instead that government appropriations were better spent on day schools and American public schools, where Indian children could be educated closer to home, commingle with their white counterparts, and be induced to find contentment as "ditchers, miners, railroad hands, or what not."[21] These shifts occurred alongside broader changes in the US public sphere, as social reformers lobbied for the eight-hour workday, fought to keep children out of the work force, and petitioned for increased rights for white women predominantly. But these advancements were not intended for all; as historian Marylin Lake puts it, "Progressive reforms could have profoundly undemocratic outcomes."[22] The same impulses that bolstered reformist attempts to heighten workers' protections and improve the quality of citizens' lives did not extend to others—immigrants, people of nonwhite races, women of color, criminals, and people with disabilities—who were viewed as being threatening to or permanently outside of the national polity.

For many of those deemed antithetical to the "health" of the nation, segregation in racialized enclaves and facilities created for the "relief and care of the dependent and delinquent" was an everyday reality.[23] A turn-of-the-century US Census Bureau report on "benevolent institutions" illustrates the extent to which institutionalization was an everyday feature of modern life: in 1904, 4,207 facilities, including private orphanages, hospitals, and sanitariums, housed a total population of 2,040,372 "inmates," or 329 persons per 100,000.[24] By 1910, that number had leapt to 3,360,184, or 5,872 persons per million (587.1 per 100,000), while the number of private facilities had increased the same year by 1,201, to 5,408.[25] Institutionalization, in other words, had become society's answer for those "in need"—a status of immense stigma viewed by many as a condition of inadequate personhood.

Concurrent with the widespread warehousing of society's "unfit," tribal nations were dispossessed of vast tracts of land and corralled onto reservations.[26] With the passage of the General Allotment Act (or Dawes Act) of 1887, surveyors enumerated Indigenous heads-of-household, recorded their names and "degree of Indian blood" on allotment rolls, and assigned them approximately 160 acres of land for their families to live on and cultivate.[27] "Surplus" land was thrown open to white settlement.[28] The General Allotment Act stipulated that the US government would hold allotted lands in trust for a period of twenty-five years, after which time the allotted individual would be awarded a fee-simple patent, enabling them to sell or lease their plots.[29] According to historian Katherine Ellinghaus, from 1887 until 1934, the year commissioner of Indian Affairs John Collier formally repealed allotment policies through the Indian Reorganization Act, over ninety million acres of Indigenous lands had been lost to white ownership.[30] Additionally, as Luiseño scholar Olivia Chilcote has shown, many of California's tribes which are today non-federally recognized were forcefully evicted from their territories as Indigenous land fell under private white ownership.[31] Settler institutions facilitated these processes of land dispossession, as Indigenous people were declared incompetent or insane in a court of law, assigned legal guardians, and forcibly confined—often by reservation or school superintendents—to facilities such as the Canton Asylum for Insane Indians in Canton, South Dakota. As I discuss in chapter 4, landholding Indian women and men confined at Canton had their allotments leased, stolen, or sold right out from underneath them in a case-by-case process of small-scale land expropriation that demonstrates the myriad ways in which Indian people uniquely experienced confinement as a tool of settler colonialism.[32]

Alongside allotment, the OIA compelled tribal nations to relinquish their children to residential institutions where they would be indoctrinated into Western mores and provided a substandard education based on dominant beliefs about Indian peoples' inferior capacities. Just as employers emphasized vocational training for immigrants and nonwhite citizens while promoting "Americanization" and what labor historian Elizabeth Esch refers to as "white managerialism," Indian people were often fast-tracked into undesirable jobs that required little education or were encouraged to take up farming and agricultural work.[33]

Similarly, Commissioner Leupp's decision to de-emphasize academic instruction for Indian people appeared to signal that the heyday of boarding institutions was coming to an end. This created a new problem for Carlisle superintendent Moses Friedman, who assumed his position in 1908, the very year Leupp declared his intention of allowing the boarding school system to slowly deteriorate. As Leupp directed in June 1908, Friedman was to "Get rid of the little children and of all the academic students," and Friedman set about creating a "new order of things" in which instruction in "practical" trades would receive emphasis like never before.[34] The diminishing enrollment of Indigenous youth thus threatened Carlisle's demise and created an enrollment vacuum that Friedman would need to fill if his school were to remain in existence.[35] In response to Leupp's directive, Friedman wrote acting commissioner of Indian Affairs C. F. Larrabee that although enrollment numbers were down, he would act quickly to recruit "mature young men and women"—a solution that produced unanticipated consequences.[36]

Disciplinary documents tell a story of destabilized power relations at Carlisle that resulted from an influx of adults who fought to maintain autonomy over their daily affairs. These records also show that Indian women and men who enrolled at Carlisle did not view themselves as children or in need of permanent oversight. Similarly, Carlisle officials recognized that the school's population was becoming older, but they continued to describe enrollees as "boys and girls"—a fact that reveals how adult infantilization, *making children out of women and men*, was central to the logic of their settler grammar.[37] "Children belong in school," K. Tsianina Lomawaima (Mvskoke) and Teresa McCarty explain, "and the premise of school as the paramount Americanizing institution depends on the perception of 'different' peoples as immature."[38]

Carlisle officials may have regarded all enrollees as childlike regardless of age, but it was Indian women and men who would populate the institution in increasing numbers after the turn of the twentieth century. Unlike Indian youth of earlier generations, adults typically enrolled at Carlisle of their own volition; the OIA did not consider individuals older than eighteen to be particularly or appropriately "school-aged," and thus they could not be compelled to attend. There were wide-ranging reasons for adult enrollment: adults came to play football and other sports or to work—often to the exclusion of academic instruction—in training "partnerships" established in the years before Carlisle's closure, like the one at the Ford Motor Company in Detroit (discussed in chapter 2).[39] Some enrolled simply because they believed that a Carlisle education would provide them a greater advantage in the world, as was the case with my maternal relative Sarah Fowler (Choctaw), who went on to become an employee of Wheelock Academy after leaving Carlisle.[40] Reasons for punishment were similarly vast, and they were distinct from the reasons children were punished: adults attempted to come and go from Carlisle in order to tend to responsibilities back home; they sought out and engaged in romantic and sexual relationships; and they fought back physically against punishment at the hands of Carlisle officials.[41] Friedman's shifting enrollment policy thus resulted in a different kind of "student" body—an older demographic of enrollees who entered the institution hoping to better their circumstances in life, and who were met instead with a formidable regime of criminalization and infantilization.

STATUS-WHITENESS AND THE PUNISHMENT OF INDIAN MEN: JUSTIN AND GEORGE

Documents relating to Justin R. H. (Apache) and George F. (Passamaquoddy, described as Penobscot in his "student" file), two Indian men enrolled at Carlisle and punished under dramatically divergent circumstances, demonstrate the many ways in which white citizens seized opportunities to surveil, apprehend, and punish Indian people as their inherent right and civic duty. In addition to demonstrating how US officials deputized Carlisle authorities and white citizens as the disciplinary agents of Indian people, these records reveal how punitive interactions between white Americans and Indian people often entrenched, rather than reconfigured, racial hierarchies that structured relationships between settlers, Indigenous peoples, and racialized "Others."[42] As Wolfe has argued, "Different racial regimes encode and reproduce unequal relationships" in settler societies.[43] Similarly, as Hernández has observed, colonial conquest coheres around an oppositional guiding logic between criminal and citizen.[44] Despite Carlisle officials' stated aims of preparing Indian people to be independent and self-sufficient, disciplinary records show that white Americans viewed Indian men as potentially dangerous colonial subjects whose actions needed to be policed. Justin and George resisted punishment in different ways, but the surveillance networks in which they were ensnared reveal broader conflicts over Indigenous agency, labor, miscegenation, and freedom. Through these public acts of punishment, white civilians criminalized Indian men and reinforced their own status-whiteness.

Justin R. H. (Apache)

To return to the story that began this chapter, in 1884, a young Apache man named Justin R. H. entered Carlisle at the age of seventeen. On the single index card that affirms Justin's presence at Carlisle that year, officials recorded the following biographical details: he was described as a member of the Mojave band; he had traveled to Carlisle from the San Carlos Agency; his parents were described as deceased; and he had selected carpentry as his vocation.[45] Justin arrived at Carlisle for the second time under an unusual set of circumstances, and documents relating to his return similarly reflect the inscription of settler power.[46] In 1912, at the age of forty-five, Justin was paroled out under Carlisle's jurisdiction to Superintendent Friedman. In fact, when Justin learned that he was to be paroled in this capacity, he wrote to Friedman, expressing that this arrangement was a welcome alternative to being sent back to the San Carlos Agency. "I am in the prison life," Justin explained, "I have been [in] trouble with the Indians about five years ago, but now their try to Parole me out and their try to send me always [*sic*] from the Indians here. I think their send me back to Carlisle, so I ask you to in flavor [*sic*] me to write to Parole Officer Mr. Frank E. McCreary that you want me to come back to Carlisle."[47]

At first glance, Carlisle might seem an odd place for a parolee; but a comment made only three years later by Friedman's successor, Oscar Lipps, reveals that—at least for some public officials—how Carlisle was viewed as the appropriate receiving institution for a man convicted of murder in a US court of law: "Only a few months ago," Lipps wrote in a letter to the superintendent of Sisseton Agency, E. D. Mossman, "I heard of a Judge in some western state sentencing a boy to one year in the penitentiary or to go to the Carlisle Indian School. There is no question but what conditions here have been deplorable."[48]

As Arizona governor Sloan's original proclamation of parole explained, Justin was to be placed under the "protection" of then superintendent Friedman, a word Lipps also used to describe his duties. But there was a punitive dimension to Justin's "protection," which entailed performing continuous labor seven days a week, for fifteen dollars a month, while living in the homes of two Outing patrons: that of Mr. Joseph Palmer, in Edgewood, Pennsylvania, and later, of Ms. Peck, in Tullytown, Pennsylvania. By the time Justin was transferred to Tullytown in September 1914, he was nearly forty-eight years old. Nonetheless, Carlisle officials expected him to comply with institutional rules intended to maintain order among school-aged youth, an arrangement that demonstrates how infantilization figured centrally in Justin's punishment. As Lipps wrote to Carlisle's Outing agent, D. H. Dickey, "I want [Justin] to understand that he is under the control of the school. The Arizona State authorities placed him on parole in the care of the school. If he shows any disposition not to do as the school authorities advise, I shall [communicate] with the Governor of Arizona, who will send officers for him, and he will be sent back to the penitentiary or be placed on parole somewhere in the state."[49] Failure to adhere to Lipps's rules could thus have legal consequences, as Carlisle officials were deputized, in this instance, as parole officers.

Additional correspondence illustrates the extent of Friedman's, and then Lipps's, deputization as agents of the law. A few months after arriving at Carlisle, Justin wrote the Board of Commissioners at the Arizona State Prison to request a pardon for his crimes. In reply, Parole Clerk J. J. Sanders explained, "The Parole Board has nothing to do with pardons. If Mr. Friedman, Superintendent of the Carlisle Indian School, believes you have earned a pardon by your good work at Carlisle, have him write to the Hon. G. W. P. Hunt, Governor of Arizona, Phoenix, Arizona, in behalf of a pardon for you."[50] Just as Carlisle's superintendent assumed total authority over all "students," Friedman was granted the power to act as parole officer and determine Justin's deservingness of a pardon.

The following year, amid accusations of embezzlement and fraud, Friedman's tenure as Carlisle superintendent was terminated and Lipps stepped in. Lipps kept a tighter grip over institutional order than did his predecessor, and Justin and the new superintendent were soon at regular odds. Months after his initial petition for a pardon was denied, Justin sought Lipps's help in writing to the Governor of Arizona. "I will consider [writing to the Governor]," Lipps wrote in reply, "if your conduct continues good. You have done well . . . under the outing although you had some trouble . . . I will ask Mr. Dickey to investigate this trouble which you got into and if you can show that you were not to blame, I will consider your case favorably."[51]

In Tullytown, a small town just north of Philadelphia, Justin likely believed that he labored at Outing patron Ms. Peck's home under relatively autonomous conditions. But Lipps's comment illustrates Carlisle's long disciplinary reach: Lipps inherited and fully assumed authority over Justin as parole officer by virtue of his title. Similarly, Ms. Peck was empowered to scrutinize Justin's conduct on behalf of Carlisle officials, and she had complained to Lipps that Justin continually left the premises without her permission. In an attempt to mitigate this behavior, Carlisle's superintendent in charge wrote to Justin on Lipps's behalf, underscoring that Justin's behavior was misaligned with the responsibilities of (white) manhood: "I am writing to remind you of some of the duties you owe Miss Peck . . . we thought that being a man, you could take the responsibility of the work she requires on her farm."[52] Using the racialized language of indebtedness, the letter called into question Justin's conduct as that of inadequate masculinity, thus illustrating the dichotomous nature of Indigenous infantilization. Conversely, Ms. Peck's whiteness situated her as Justin's racial superordinate and a natural ally of the Carlisle officials. The letter informed Justin, "She is a woman and has her own work in the house . . . we have told Miss Peck that you . . . can take care of her farm for her, under her supervision, of course."[53] Although Peck was "a woman," she, too, extended the prerogatives of the settler society: her deputization as Lipps's proxy helped expand Carlisle's disciplinary reach and, by extension, that of the Arizona penal system.

Justin refused compliance with Ms. Peck's rules and was eventually transferred to the Outing district in Trenton, New Jersey. It is unclear whether he selected Trenton himself, but correspondence shows that he was boarding at the American House and looking for work, and in November 1914, he wrote Lipps repeatedly for a portion of his savings held at the bank in Carlisle.[54] Under Ms. Peck's employ, Justin had earned fifteen dollars a month, the majority of which was re-mitted back to Carlisle—an arrangement required of all Outing members, as Jus-tin was designated.[55] Justin, however, was not truly a member of the Outing; in fact, on at least one occasion in 1913, Justin questioned why then superintendent Friedman continued to treat him as though he were "under the Outing," sub-jecting him to monthly assessments: "I want to ask you about this report every month . . . ," Justin wrote, "I don't understand so I ask to know, I was not a pupil and how is it now this is the pupil report."[56] As Justin's protestations make clear, he was not a student, he was a parolee; Carlisle officials' administration of Jus-tin's finances, which effectively controlled his whereabouts, further underscored his nonstudent status while maintaining his absent presence in Carlisle ledgers.[57] Lipps finally sent Justin some of his money, but Justin soon found that it was not enough to cover basic living necessities in the harsh winter months while need-ing to remit room and board. As a result, Justin explained to Lipps, he was made to choose between his overcoat and eating, and decided to pawn his clothing in order that he might have some shelter and food. Before long, he faced starvation and sent another letter (reproduced in the appendix) pleading for additional funds. Furious with these humiliating and dangerous circumstances, Justin wrote Lipps, this time calling *his* masculinity into question: "You are not a man enough to help me with anythings [sic] . . . O, right my Friend, I see now, you wanted me starving to death."[58]

Soon thereafter, Justin's circumstances worsened. Two weeks following Jus-tin's last letter to Lipps, Dickey visited Trenton and discovered that Justin was "legally married to a colored girl." As a note to Lipps suggests, Dickey felt that the union transgressed the era's racial common sense about miscegenation, but to his dismay, it could not be legally prevented unless under the laws of guardianship.[59] After learning of the marriage, Lipps's first line of action was to report Justin's location to Arizona authorities; now, without Carlisle's paradoxical "protection," Justin's presence in Trenton as an Outing laborer could not be legitimized. Lipps had another concern: he wanted to be released from his responsibilities as Justin's parole officer, and wrote Assistant Commissioner E. B. Meritt to this effect. In reply, Meritt appeared to insinuate that Lipps could blame Justin for the crimes of purchasing and distributing liquor to other Carlisle enrollees who were also "under the Outing."[60] In turn, these charges would enable local police to assume authority over Justin, and Lipps would be freed of any legal liability. A final let-ter from Meritt to Lipps shows that as Justin—and presumably his wife—nearly starved to death, the Indian Office put their plan into action: they notified Trenton authorities of the couple's continued presence in the area and formally relinquished "jurisdiction" over Justin.

When Lipps enlisted Trenton officers to remove Justin and his wife from the local area, he did more than assert his authority as Carlisle superintendent; he also exercised the power implicit in status-whiteness that allowed him to seize, and then relinquish, jurisdiction over a man presumed to be his subordinate. As a Black woman and Indian man in the early twentieth century, Justin and his wife were likely regarded by white citizens as a racial spectacle, and it is probable that the couple was confronted with the ever-present threat of racialized violence in the Trenton area.[61] From Carlisle's brick-and-mortar carceral structure to the penal system and the application of the law, these institutions supported one another in extending the reach of settler power over an Apache man already ensnared in the nation's carceral apparatus, having been convicted of murder in a US court of law and of "interracial assembly" in the court of public opinion.[62] Justin's transfer from the Arizona penal system to Carlisle as a parolee demonstrates the carceral possibilities of the boarding institution, and his subsequent experiences of surveillance and apprehension under Lipps's jurisdiction reveal how numerous public officials and civil servants were empowered to further carry out the work of his criminalization. These facts underscore what Robert Nichols refers to as the "colonialism of incarceration" and show how settler institutions like Carlisle could mold their objectives to exercise carceral control over Indian people.[63] Even as they galvanized the punitive possibilities of coerced labor, US officials and Carlisle employees used incarceration and confinement as a mode of Indigenous elimination. Records relating to George F. highlight similarly unexpected dimensions of adult Indian men's punitive experiences at Carlisle.

George F. (Passamaquoddy)

At midnight on April 21, 1917, George F. (Passamaquoddy, described as Penobscot in Carlisle records), who was then twenty-four, emerged from a house on North College Street in Carlisle and was confronted by two men who had been looking for him. The home was the residence of a white woman, Mrs. Dora Shriver, who had been separated from her legal husband for two months and had been receiving visits from George since that time. That night, George had been neither an intruder nor a thief; neither drinking nor causing a disturbance—only paying a visit to a woman with whom he had a relationship. Though Carlisle superintendent

John Francis Jr. had not approved George's absence that evening as required, he had received permission from another Carlisle official to go into town due to his "most excellent" behavior during the day. But when George had not returned by 11:00 p.m. the following night, Edward Corbett, the night watchman, and Gustavus Welch, the assistant disciplinarian, set out in search of him.[64]

Letters exchanged between Superintendent Francis and Commissioner of Indian Affairs Cato Sells describe how white civilians, public officials, and Carlisle administrators documented George's whereabouts and exchanged information about his behavior, which ultimately led to his apprehension. On April 24, Francis related to Sells that he had had prior knowledge of George's relationship with Mrs. Shriver, whom George had met while attending church services. Mrs. Florence Barron, an acquaintance of Mrs. Shriver and also a Catholic, had been alerted to the developing relationship and was disturbed by what she perceived as the impropriety of the situation. She reported this to Father Francis Feeser, the Catholic priest, who recommended that she inform the "proper authorities."[65] In turn, Feeser reported George's behavior to Carlisle's superintendent. According to the superintendent's letter, the priest "had endeavored to persuade George F. to give up his manner of living."[66] Eleven days later, however, George was missing again, and once Carlisle authorities became aware of his absence, they set out in search of him. A neighboring grocer had witnessed George enter Mrs. Shriver's house, and was able to direct Corbett and Welch to the correct address. According to the officials, they waited under cover of darkness outside Mrs. Shriver's home, and when George emerged, they "placed him under arrest" and transported him directly back to the disciplinarian's office.[67]

Upon George's return to the institution, he must have felt a sense of dread waiting for his punishment; after a few moments of deliberation, Corbett and Welch determined that George would be incarcerated in Carlisle's guardhouse. But as Corbett stepped out of the disciplinarian's office to retrieve the keys, George bolted from the room where they held him. Having escaped one form of institutionalized confinement, however, he was confronted with threat of arrest: as Superintendent Francis reported, "Word was immediately sent out to the local Police and Station Agents. This made it impossible for him to escape, and Sunday night after taps he returned of his own accord to the office of the Disciplinarian and gave himself up."[68]

According to the 1913 "Rules for the Indian School Service," boarding school superintendents were responsible for the "pursuit and return" of enrollees who had "left a school without permission."[69] As indicated by these guidelines, the Secretary of the Interior directed school superintendents to retain pupils of appropriate school age in attendance continuously and authorized superintendents to enlist school employees, and even Indian police, in the apprehension and return of defectors. But Lipps took these directives even further: he facilitated the creation of a complex surveillance network comprised of white men and women, a store clerk, public agents, and a religious official to ensnare George—an action that was not sanctioned, given George's age. These heightened surveillance activities relied on "thousands of eyes posted everywhere," to borrow from Michel Foucault, and they illustrate the quotidian steps local citizens took to prevent Indian people from moving freely throughout town.[70] Similarly, institutional rules, administrators, civilians, and Carlisle police described concentric circles of surveillance within which George was contained, immobilized, and eventually coerced into returning to the institution.

George was ostensibly a Carlisle "student," but he was treated as a dangerous fugitive. His criminalization underscores what Michael Witgen (Ojibwe) describes as white citizens' propensity toward "seeing red," or "the hardening of the race line and the codification of white supremacy" as rule of law.[71] Though police did not arrest George that night, his voluntary return to Carlisle may be interpreted as a deliberate attempt to avoid embroilment within the penal system—George no doubt understood that the probability of being apprehended was high. But having avoided incarceration in the local jail, he was nonetheless punished at the hands of Carlisle officials. In Superintendent Francis's final disciplinary decision, he stated, "[George's] age, the fact that he is a member of the senior class and his rank as a Captain . . . demands exemplary behavior." George was expelled, and left Carlisle on April 30, 1917. Though he had evaded arrest by police, his punishment was steep: Carlisle's superintendent denied him the diploma that he would have received in a matter of weeks and, in so doing, believed he denied George what small advantage would have accrued from graduating from Carlisle.

Indian people who successfully graduated from Carlisle and other off-reservation boarding schools were granted "competency" and eventually United States citizenship. Thus expulsion—for George and others—carried symbolic as well as material heft. It could also mean prolonged punishment, as reservation agents extended Carlisle's disciplinary aims. In one example of this dynamic, in 1914 a twenty- or twenty-one-year-old Chippewa woman named Gertrude B. was being considered for expulsion from Carlisle because officials had determined she was not "profiting" from her opportunity at the institution. As the superintendent of the Red Cliff Agency John Dady assured Lipps, "If the girl does return . . . I will not only charge the parents with the responsibility of taking care of her and protecting her but will charge the constable to see that she is not permitted to run the streets at night after nine o'clock and watch her to see that she does not get into troublethrough [sic] association with the so called 'sporting element.'"[72] Expulsion as a form of punishment was thus not as paradoxical as it may have appeared, as many Indian enrollees who were expelled often returned to agencies that employed methods of surveillance, policing, and incarceration similar to those employed at Carlisle.

Less than one year after George's expulsion, he wrote to Carlisle's superintendent expressing that the cost of "insurance and allotment to mother takes two thirds of my monthly pay," a statement that seemed to announce his determination to provide for his family members, while underscoring how expulsion from Carlisle had not ruined his chances of making a living. He signed the letter—the only extant document in his file written in his hand—"I remain sincerely one of your old students, Geo. A. F, 16th Reg. Engrs Co. C."[73] George's opportunities did not end with his expulsion from the institution. Soon thereafter, as his letter reflects, he joined the 16th Regiment of Engineers in the American Expeditionary Forces stationed "somewhere in France" during World War I.[74] He would go on to become a beloved governor of the Pleasant Point Indian Reservation in Maine.

INDIAN "RUNAWAYS," VIGILANTISM, AND "FACELESS" SETTLER POWER

Like George and Justin, other Indian men were punished for seemingly negligible infractions—including refusing blind obedience to Carlisle's "school rules" and the officials who enforced them. What Friedman envisioned as a solution to the enrollment vacuum thus created another problem, as Carlisle officials were confronted with adult Indian people who did not willingly submit to the demands of white officials.[75] Indian men were especially prone to leaving Carlisle "without permission," and Carlisle officials and local citizens felt threatened by their ability to do so. Disappearing for days and even months on end, these so-called deserters often successfully eluded the authorities tasked with their apprehension and return. A December 3, 1910, report of enrollees who had fled Carlisle up to seventeen months before and who were being dropped from the enrollment ledger reflects gender and age disparities among those who "ran away": of the ninety-one individuals enumerated on this list, only sixteen were under eighteen years of age, while all were between the ages of fifteen and twenty-four; and just one "runaway" enrollee—eighteen-year-old Lillian M. (Chippewa)—was a woman.[76] Ojibwe scholar Brenda Child has remarked on similar dynamics of rebellion and resistance at Flandreau and Haskell from the perspective of Indian youth, and her work shows that many students fled institutional grounds for reasons ranging from loneliness and homesickness to disliking the food served at school.[77] In addition to leaving the institution for similar reasons, older Carlisle enrollees were designated as "runaways" for visiting home, sometimes to care for family members, or for leaving the institution momentarily to tend to other matters deemed to be of personal importance.[78]

Many of Carlisle's disciplinary practices seemed to be at odds with the institution's mission of turning out self-sufficient adults who, as Friedman himself acknowledged in 1911, were already of "mature age and purpose. At Carlisle, the average age of the girls is eighteen years, and the average age of the boys, nineteen years."[79] In fact, from the earliest years of Carlisle's operation until its last, "independence" was touted by various superintendents as one of the hallmarks of a Carlisle education. As early as 1879, Pratt wrote to Commissioner of Indian Affairs Charles Hoyt, describing the likely benefits of labor on the "Florida boys" whom Pratt had transferred as prisoners from Fort Marion to the Hampton Institute, and then to Carlisle. As Pratt hypothesized, by separating the men from one another and assigning them to white households to perform work, "independence, selfreliance [sic] and better English speaking will all be forwarded."[80]

Several years later, Carlisle superintendent Friedman mobilized similar ideas about the assimilationist effects of "independence" in a 1911 article entitled "The Carlisle Plan Makes for Independent Citizenship." As Friedman wrote in response to those who disputed the efficacy of the off-reservation boarding schools, "I maintain fundamentally that at Carlisle, independence is fostered; that paternalism is discouraged; that because of the life the student lives at Carlisle, it is not only the most natural thing for him to go out into the world and strike out independently, but that the record of those who have gone out substantiates and abundantly justified the training of the school, which makes for independent thinking and doing, based on Christian living."[81] Reality, however, somewhat differed from Friedman's lofty rhetoric. Indeed, that so many Carlisle adults were punished for various perceived infractions including "running away" demonstrates the carceral nature of the institution and belies its stated objectives of cultivating independence and autonomy within its "students."

For Friedman, as for his successors, the question was not whether Indian men would find a way out of Carlisle—but how long they would remain away once they had fled and who would bring them back. In fact, "desertion" came to be such a problem for Friedman during his tenure that he began enlisting non-Indian service personnel to assist in the apprehension and return of runaways, deputizing these civil servants as the disciplinary agents of all Carlisle enrollees found outside of institutional boundaries. According to a 1915 article entitled "Stopping Carousals of Carlisle Students" printed in the *Harrisburg Telegraph*, "police, in conjunction with Indian department officials have begun a war on the solicitation evil which it is claimed is a big factor in disrupting the discipline of the school" (fig. 1.1). The article continued, "Orders have been issued to arrest all Indian students found in town without proper passes and other regulations are enforced."[82]

These policing activities were not limited to the Carlisle vicinity, but spanned entire regions. In 1907, eighteen-year-old Lee P. and two other young men, nineteen-year-old Asa A. and seventeen-year-old Weaver D., fled the institution, were arrested by police in Chicago, and were subsequently returned to Carlisle.[83] In 1910, Robert D. and his companion Jesse G. left their Outing homes and were arrested by the police in Patterson, New Jersey, in what Friedman referred to as "an ordinary case of discipline."[84] In fact, so commonplace were the arrest and return of young Indian men that the chief of the Carlisle Police Department knew the balances in their bank accounts, because they would be expected to pay their own arrest fees: "According to an arrangement made by Superintendent Friedman with the Police of Carlisle in which we were to arrest any students found in town in citizen's clothes and without guard passes or in an intoxicated condition and report the same to the School, we have the following fines due from these students. Two dollars from each as per agreement; Jonas P—, Horace P—, Walter A—, John M—, and Fred W—."[85]

All of these "students" were between the ages of twenty and twenty-two, which made their forced return to Carlisle illegal. Two of the men had the outstanding amount paid by the institution—but the three with funds in their accounts remitted their own arrest fees, a fine that appears to have been uniquely applied to Carlisle enrollees detained at the jail (fig. 1.2).[86] As Friedman and his successor, Lipps, authorized local officials to police Indian enrollees and extract a fine for these activities, they encouraged the creation of a race-based surveillance network that profited off patrolling the local vicinity. As this arrangement illustrates in stark relief, policing Indian people paid.

STOPPING CAROUSALS OF CARLISLE STUDENTS

Borough Police and Indian School Authorities Trying to Break Up Disorderly Practice

Special to The Telegraph

Carlisle, Pa., May 4.—By the arrest of two girls, aged 17 and 15 years respectively, local police, in conjunction with Indian department officials have begun a war on the solicitation evil which it is claimed is a big factor in disrupting the discipline of the school. Orders have been issued to arrest all Indian students found in town without proper passes and other regulations are enforced.

According to information which an investigation that has been in progress for some months has brought out, girls, some of them scarcely in their teens, others older, and even some married women of the town meet Indian boys in and about industrial plants in the eastern section of the town and near the junction of the Cumberland Valley and Gettysburg and Harrisburg lines which is but a short distance from the school limits. The girls bring whisky and "parties" lasting far into the night are of almost regular occurrence.

1.1 Newspaper article describing the arrest of Carlisle students found in town. "Stopping Carousals of Carlisle Students," *Harrisburg Telegraph*, 1915, Chronicling America, Library of Congress.

Carlisle officials also incentivized public servants with monetary awards for the return of "runaways" and invested them with real power over Indian bodies— the power of surveillance. In 1915, for example, special officer of the Pennsylvania Railroad Company M. A. Davis wrote Assistant Commissioner Meritt to complain that he had not been fairly compensated for the apprehension and return of eight "runaways"; he had only received payment for two. To illustrate this inequity, he wrote, "I have talked this matter over with my brother officers and they inform me that [they] have received three to five dollars for each and ever [*sic*] run-away Indian pupil they arrested, All I ask for is fair treatment and will welcome a letter from you stating where you stand on this matter."[87]

Davis's request for "fair treatment" is telling; that he felt he was being unfairly compensated for the arrest and return of "runaway pupils" is indicative of the

1.2 The Cumberland County Prison (Jail) at the northwest corner of High and Bedford Streets in Carlisle, Pennsylvania, ca. 1900. Indian men who were arrested by local police were detained here and forced to pay their own arrest fees. Cumberland Valley Railroad tracks are clearly visible and the street is unpaved. The building still stands and has been adapted for other county uses. 467A #03, Cumberland County Historical Society, Carlisle, Pennsylvania.

extent to which this system of remunerative surveillance had become established in the area surrounding Carlisle. As is evident from the above, Davis had had a precedent set for his actions by his "brother officers" whose efforts had been compensated in full. This practice bears out the ways in which non-OIA agents benefited from their participation in Carlisle's punitive regime, which enticed everyday citizens to take part in surveillance activities by compensating them in return. Davis's letter also indicates the extent to which Indian men who managed to transgress the institutional boundaries of Carlisle would be confronted with an expansive surveillance network—"permanent, exhaustive, omnipresent"—of the kind described by Foucault.[88]

Patterns of surveillance and apprehension in the Carlisle vicinity bear striking resemblance to the Foucauldian panoptic schema. Much like the objectives

1.3 The bandstand on Carlisle's grounds, ca. 1879. John Nicholas Choate, "Pavilion (Bandstand) at Carlisle Indian School," 1870–79, Potamkin, PO#01, Cumberland County Historical Society, Carlisle, Pennsylvania.

. . . .

inherent in Carlisle's punitive regime, the intended effect of the panoptic prison structure is the "guarantee of order" in which, as Foucault explains, the "inmate [is in] a state of conscious and permanent visibility that assures the automatic functioning of power."[89] He further suggests that the panoptic principle may be applied to other institutions and achieve similar effects. As Fear-Segal has pointed out, Mariana Burgess, Carlisle's print-making instructor, employed this strategy when she created "Mr. See-All," a phantasm who claimed to witness misbehavior from the centrally located bandstand and reported on these infractions by publishing them in the *Indian Helper*, Carlisle's official newspaper (fig. 1.3).[90]

Yet, the panoptic principle appears to have manifested in a more generalized manner as well. By the turn of the twentieth century, Americans were well accustomed to pastimes that depicted conquest as central to the national mythology. Spectators flocked nightly, for instance, to Wild West arenas to witness the famed Indian scout "Buffalo Bill" Cody vanquish "savage" warriors time and again in reenactments of Indian massacres. This vigilantism also played out in real life, as the enforcement of curfews and the establishment of racialized enclaves, ghettos, and reservations—and the policing of those borders—were woven into the very fabric of American sociality.[91] According to Foucault, the efficacy of the panopticon lies in its ability to alter behavior: "This power [is] . . . like a faceless gaze that transformed the whole social body into a field of perception: thousands of eyes posted everywhere."[92] As these brief examples demonstrate, Americans were active participants in defending settler claims to Indigenous territories. There were many deputies of settler colonialism, and all were invested, in their own ways, in maintaining white hegemony.

The panoptic schema provides a fruitful model through which to understand how race organized power relations across the United States and how white Americans exercised disproportionate and often interchangeable power over Indian people at the institutional, regional, and national level. At Carlisle, the frequently "faceless" nature of white Americans' punitive power made the area surrounding the institution a dangerous place for Indian people, whose skin color marked them as being out of place. For example, in December of 1914, superintendent to the Red Cliff Agency John W. Dady wrote Carlisle superintendent Lipps to request the reenrollment of Adolph M. When he was eighteen, Adolph had been expelled in June of that year for what Lipps described as inexcusable offenses; he explained to Dady that he was "weeding" out "other boys who had behaved in a similar manner" and that he could not justify lenience with Adolph.[93] The perceived offense, it seems, appears to have stemmed from Adolph's ability to pass as white— his light complexion afforded him greater control over his whereabouts, something that many of his peers could not enjoy. For Lipps, however, this was a usurpation of the ability to move freely through society—a privilege that was not Adolph's to exercise. As he put it to Dady, "Adolph is practically white so far as appearances go and he took advantage of that fact by running around Carlisle without permission."[94] Phenotypically "Indian" people were unwanted and unwelcome in town; "practically white" Indian people created surveillance issues—echoing the problems inherent in what Ann Laura Stoler refers to as a "colonial politics of exclusion" based on skin color.[95]

The following month, Lipps would report on Simon S., also under Dady's jurisdiction, in a similar manner: "Simon ran away from the school about two weeks ago. We have been making every effort to locate him but so far have failed. We have heard that he is somewhere not far away and he has been seen several times, but he is practically white and does not look much like an Indian, and so far he has been able to go undetected." The police had been notified, and Lipps was confident that Simon would be located in a few days, and returned to the reservation. By the time police apprehended Simon and returned him to the Red Cliff Agency five months after his initial "desertion," he was nearly twenty years old and thus well past being considered appropriately "school-aged."[96]

In other cases, "passing" as African American could paradoxically serve as protection for men who had fled Carlisle, allowing them to evade notice as an Indian escapee. As a 1913 newspaper clipping (publication unknown) entitled "Indian Deserter from Carlisle Nabbed Here," preserved in Max F.'s (Colville) file, reports,

Max F—, an Indian who is alleged to have deserted from the U.S. Industrial Training school at Carlisle, was arrested last evening by Patrolman Buttorf. [Max] has been working for a number of weeks at one of the industrial plants, where he has passed himself as a negro. Instructions for [Max's] arrest were received yesterday by the police department from M. Freedman [sic], superintendent of the school and an officer will arrive in the city today to take [Max] to Carlisle. [Max], who is twenty-three years old, declares that he cannot legally be kept in the industrial school and does not intend to remain there.[97]

Max's forced return and illegal detention demonstrates how institutional officials worked together to curtail Indian men's ability to freely move about the public sphere to obtain work and earn a living.[98] His experiences similarly demonstrate how white Americans used racial phenotype to determine the "rightful" location of bodies in space, a fact that highlights the role that Indigenous surveillance played in the maintenance of a racially exclusive society. As Saidiya Hartman has observed, the efficacy of fugitive slave acts depended upon ordinary white women and men performing racially discriminatory functions on behalf of the settler state.[99] In the Carlisle context as well, white Americans operationalized an eliminatory logic to purge the landscape of Indigenous people and to defend and preserve their claimed territory.[100] The act of policing Indian people was itself a form of power that could be transferred and traded between settler agents and the institutions under their aegis. As Hernández reminds us, "Settler societies strive to block, erase, or remove racialized outsiders from their claimed territory."[101] Put another way, "Invasion . . . is ubiquitous."[102]

Correspondence relating to Walter S. (Creek), an allotted Carlisle enrollee, further reflects the diversity of those who exerted control over the whereabouts of young Indian men. These records also show how the politics of land shaped some enrollees' experiences of relative mobility and of institutional life. In January 1916, six months before Walter's eighteenth birthday, attorney Harve L. Melton wrote to Lipps to express concern over a recent request Walter had made of his legal guardian, John H. Hill, who was described in correspondence as a "full blood Indian of good habits." As Melton, who was Hill's lawyer, explained, "The guardian of Walter S—. who is in your school has informed me that he has received a request from his ward for $35.00 for clothing. . . . The amount asked for him is the price of his ticket home and we feared that he might be dis-satisfied and might use this money to come home on [sic] so we are sending it direct to you to be given out to him according to his needs." Melton continued, "He is much better off there than at this place. . . . We want to keep him in school as long as possible so he will have enough education to take care of his estate and make a useful citizen. If he comes home, he will be thrown with a class of grafters who will probably get him to drinking, and lead him into bad habits."[103] As seen from Melton's letter, the men suspected that Walter was planning a "desertion" and wanted to ensure that he remained at Carlisle.

In reply, Lipps wrote, "It pleases me that I can state so unreservedly that Walter is doing very well and that we have reasons to believe he will be well cared for during the summer vacation months. . . . I agree with you that our best plan is to keep Walter away from home influences until he is older and I will gladly cooperate with his guardian and you in keeping him at Carlisle regardless of his own wishes in the matter as long as such action meets with the approval of your client."[104] Another letter from Melton elaborated on the concerns of Walter's guardian should he return home, explaining, "As he has considerable money, he would immediately [be] surrounded by a bunch of grafters and whiskey peddlers. I have talked this over with the guardian and with the U.S. Probate Attorney here and we agree that after a year or two more in the east, he might become divorced from his old environment here which was not good." Melton continued, "His property and funds are all under the control of the Indian Agency here but their policy is to turn over this control as much as possible where the Indian is capable and will care for his property. In amny [many] cases an abundance of money has been a positive detriment to the Indian, but we are anxious to make an exception [sic] to the general rule in the case of Walter S——."[105]

Records relating to Walter appear to reflect a genuine concern for his well-being; Carlisle was a safer place, these letters imply, for a young Indian man who might soon hold the title to his allotment outright. Yet, this correspondence also reflects the broader dynamics at play in the lives of Indian people, as well as how the politics of land ownership and the desires of others could shape, dictate, and delineate Carlisle enrollees' mobility.

Conversely, in 1914, twenty-one-year-old Edward J. (Otoe) signed leases on two allotments he had inherited from deceased relatives while enrolled at Carlisle. Shortly after these transactions, he contracted a venereal disease, which rendered him "undesirable" in the eyes of Carlisle officials and the reservation superintendent—a stigma explored in greater depth in the following chapter. As Carlisle's physician quipped in 1914 after examining Edward, "This letter confirms me in my opinion that Edward J— should be dismissed and returned home. It seems to me essential to secure healthy, moral student material here, whereas it appears that Carlisle is considered a Happy Dumping Ground for incorrigibles." It appears that Carlisle superintendent Lipps agreed, for he recommended Edward's expulsion back home to the reservation. Upon learning of these plans, however, superintendent of the Otoe Agency Ralph Stanion protested that "unless [Edward's] term has expired, or it is deemed inexpedient in the interests of Carlisle to return him for the continuation of his term, I would suggest that he be not allowed to return for any portion of the vacation period to the reservation . . . he has no home to return to, and it has been proven by past experiences that his natural proclivities have no other tendencies than to have a demoralizing effect upon him while in the reservation environment."[106] Stanion's comment that Edward had "no home to return to" further indexes the ways in which US officials viewed land ownership and the farming labor associated with it as having a stabilizing effect on young Indian men; because Edward had no allotment and therefore no land to farm, in the eyes of Stanion, he had "no home."

The politics of land impacted Carlisle girls and women as well. In one case, letters of correspondence show that Lipps was prepared to prevent a nineteen-year-old Cherokee woman named Winnie R. from returning home at the request of her father, Andrew. Evidently, six months earlier, Winnie and her father were at odds; Winnie suspected that he had sold off her allotment, which she had inherited from her recently deceased mother. Lipps asked the probate attorney at Stillwell, Oklahoma, to inquire into the matter, and it was revealed that the allotment remained intact. But the conflict illustrates the extent to which Carlisle superintendents were involved with the affairs—financial and familial—of some Carlisle enrollees who were also landowners. Additional correspondence contained in Winnie's file further reflects that Winnie's father was concerned that because Winnie was "of age," if she returned home for summer vacation, he would not be able to compel her to "return East" to Carlisle and finish out her term of schooling.[107] In this case and others, institutional intervention could have very private and personal connotations, as institutional officials and US agents inserted themselves into the intimate dynamics of Indigenous kin and community members, and the complex expectations that Carlisle enrollees navigated in this era. As discussed at greater length in chapter 4, land politics was played out in other settler spaces such as the Canton Asylum for Insane Indians, and the outcomes were often negative; as I examine in that chapter, forced confinement at Canton facilitated the expropriation of Indigenous lands on a small-scale, case-by-case basis.

PUNITIVE POWER AND DOMESTIC DISCOURSE: GOSSIP, RUMOR, AND "WOMEN'S WORK"

As the corollary to the manual labor and farm work that Indian men performed at Carlisle, young Indian women were tasked with domestic chores and placed "out" in the homes of white Americans to serve as household servants and as caretakers of white children. Under the "Outing" system, as this arrangement was called, the white married women of the employment households were understood to have full authority over their domestic servants. As such, they were able to exercise disciplinary power over those who lived and worked in their homes, quietly upholding the racial hierarchies and settler ideals taught at Carlisle within the ostensibly private confines of the domestic sphere. As historian Margaret Jacobs explains of Outing dynamics, "Enlisting white women employers in the project of 'uplifting' and 'civilizing' young Indian women made white women's households more than private homes or workplaces; they became domestic frontiers where colonial relationships continued to play themselves out. As in other colonies around the world, this intimate setting became a significant site for the reproduction and performance of colonial relationships."[108]

On the domestic frontier and in the context of the socially complex domestic networks that comprised Carlisle's Outing system, gossip was a powerful disciplinary tool. In the late nineteenth and early twentieth centuries, reformers sought to remake Indian homes in accordance with Victorian-era standards of puritanical cleanliness and rectilinear order as a way in which to render Indian communities knowable, and thus manageable.[109] As Jacobs has also shown, influential women's organizations like the Women's National Indian Association (WNIA) played a significant role in creating discourses about Indian women as unfit mothers and homemakers, which in turn informed the official child-removal policies that were at the heart of the early assimilationist agenda in the United States. These discourses positioned middle-class, white American women as the standard-bearers of the nation and legitimated their interference in the domestic affairs of Indigenous communities as essential for Indian "progress." Reformers like WNIA founder Amelia Stone Quinton used her connections to powerful statesmen to influence an assimilationist agenda that would evangelize, educate, and "care" for Indian people, while Alice Cunningham Fletcher measured allotments and recorded patrilineal family lines among the Nez Perce and Omaha.[110] Natalee Kēhaulani Bauer has further demonstrated how gendered constructions of "benevolent whiteness" that naturalized white American women's interventions into Indigenous "education" highlight their complicity in upholding racialized and gendered hierarchies during the long nineteenth century.[111]

This "women's work" was as discursive as it was material. As cultural historian Jane Simonsen has discussed, "Creating the illusion of a coherent national identity in this era was a crucial aspect of the cultural work that domestic writers did. The efforts of these writers and reformers to define domesticity as a white, middle-class trait were attempts to assert power over the lives and bodies of those whom they deemed foreign; bad housekeeping became a marker of racial inferiority."[112] While the white American middle-class codified their own domestic ideals in law and culture, domestic discourses and the practice of homemaking thus became an effective means through which to solidify race, class, and gender hierarchies in a diversifying nation.

But for Indian women at Carlisle, domestic discourse could also be an intimate form of discipline. As Superintendent of the Indian School Service Estelle Reel promoted domestic training as liberating to the Indian "race" as a whole, her standardized boarding school curriculum compelled Indian women to accept white American domestic standards as foundational to "civilized" living, proper femininity, and the health and prosperity of their families and communities. Carlisle publications reinforced these ideals, using articles such as "Our Dining Hall,"

1.4 Young Indian women set the dining room tables at the Carlisle Indian School, ca. 1883. Indian girls and women were indoctrinated into gendered forms of labor, such as laundry and cooking, that helped to keep Carlisle running and overhead costs down. Cumberland County Historical Society, CCHS_PA-CH1-077C, Cumberland County Historical Society, Carlisle, Pennsylvania.

. . . .

which described "cheerful" Indian girls setting the tables and preparing the food for Carlisle students, to indoctrinate Indian enrollees into white American norms as well as to compel compliance with institutional authority (fig. 1.4).[113] Carlisle officials similarly enforced these settler mandates through a militarized daily regimen and habituated enrollees to chores, vocations, and routines assigned on the basis of their perceived gender: farming, tinsmithing, and harness-making for "boys" and sewing, cooking, and cleaning for "girls." In this way, Carlisle authorities wedded Victorian-era ideals of maternalism, chastity, and purity with domestic labor as they taught Indian "girls," many of whom were older, to become proper women—in short, to become properly "domesticated" and subordinated to white authority.

This section shifts focus to the private sphere of the American household and the fraught domestic scenarios in which young Indian women placed "under the Outing" found themselves. In so doing, it centers a particular form of domestic discourse—gossip—as an important method of communication and knowledge exchange for the Indian women, Outing patrons, and Carlisle officials who participated in it. Through a close reading of records relating to an eighteen-year-old Cherokee woman, Lucinda R., this section analyzes the specific ways in which "loose talk" maintained and disrupted power relations at Carlisle and beyond.

In the Outing program's early years, patrons were a somewhat homogeneous group: the majority were Quakers who came from middle-class social backgrounds deemed "respectable" in the eyes of Carlisle's superintendent. A few families participated in the program for decades in households across Pennsylvania and New Jersey and, later, New York and even Maryland and Delaware, as the Outing program grew. Some encouraged their neighbors and relatives to join as well, adding another layer of insularity to the system. All families selected for the program regularly attended religious service, a component of the Outing program's mandates, and none of the households contained liquor, which was also a requirement of patronage. As anthropologist Genevieve Bell has explained of Outing patrons' vetting process, "Pratt sought references and recommendations on their patrons: referees were asked whether the patron in question drank or used tobacco, whether he was 'a man of good habits, whether he was kind to employees and paid them promptly, and what class of people he employed.'"[114] Although participation in the Outing program became more routinized as the decades wore on, and, presumably, the selection process of both patrons and "pupils" less rigid as the program expanded, the fundamental mission remained the same: it was an "apprenticeship for civilization."[115]

In the same way that the unpaid and frequently unacknowledged "women's work" of domestic labor supported the patriarchal household and male-dominated political activity in the public sphere, white Americans used gossip, rumor, and hearsay to affirm their authority over Indian women, like Lucinda, who labored in their homes and under their aegis. For white American women, these activities had broader implications beyond the discipline of their Indian workers: domestic discourse expanded their sphere of influence over the semi-private setting of the Outing system, modifying and extending the institutionalized disciplinary structures that were largely under the political purview of white men.

It is important to note that Carlisle women were typically less mobile, physically, than their male counterparts. The nature of their labor—largely unremunerated— kept them indoors and under observation, which made it easy for "country mothers," as the married patrons of these households were sometimes called, to subject their domestic workers to relentless behavioral assessments. Letters of correspondence contained in the colonial archive reflect these dynamics, as white American women wrote to Carlisle officials to report Indian domestic servants for perceived promiscuity, untrustworthiness, or personal failures in morality. Viewed through the prism of white American middle-class notions about "proper" domesticity, gossip emerges as a contested disciplinary phenomenon—a means by which Outing patrons and Carlisle officials could assert race and class solidarity with one another and a process through which white American women and men attempted, with various degrees of success and failure, to discredit and subordinate the Indian women under their "protection."

"UNDESIRABLES": GOSSIP, WHITE POSSESSIVENESS, AND INDIAN WOMEN IN THE OUTING SYSTEM

In the closed, closely monitored environment of the Outing home, field matrons, Carlisle officials, reservation agents, and patrons subjected Indian women to intense scrutiny. In private correspondence, semipublic conversations, monthly visits, and official reports, these white authority figures observed, reported on, and reacted to Indian women's behavior on a regular basis. The documents generated by these disciplinary activities show that the intimate quarters shared by Indian women and white Americans fostered numerous conflicts. These records also show power disparities that were reified in writing: in instances of conflict when Indigenous women challenged Outing patrons, white Americans reported on the Indian women who labored in their homes by referring to them in derogatory terms such as promiscuous, dishonest, incorrigible, lazy, and filthy.

White Americans' criticisms of Indian women overwhelm the archival record in the form of letters of correspondence, institutional reports, and surveys completed by Outing patrons or Carlisle's Outing matron. By comparison, Indian women's impressions of white patrons were not consistently documented. It is evident that radical power discrepancies account for the relative paucity of information about how Indian women felt about these employment arrangements. Had Indian women held positions of power, and had their perspectives been more highly regarded in Outing scenarios, their words might be more prominent in the historical record. Although their written perspectives are relatively few and far between, however, the force of their actions while living and working "under the Outing" speaks volumes. Disciplinary records reflect an array of white Americans' complaints about Indian women based almost entirely on information exchanged between

Outing patrons and white officials to the exclusion of workers' perspectives; they also document Indian women's courageous attempts to direct the outcome of their lives. In this way, the presence, ambitions, and desires of young Indigenous women are both palpable and powerful.

The sheer volume of disciplinary documents reveals the extent to which verbal and written discourse mattered in the communities affiliated with Carlisle. These records are a classic example of what Foucault describes as the school's "field of documentation"—a corpus of knowledge that enabled the teacher's exercise of power; settler power, in this case.[116] The one-sidedness of letters of correspondence and official reports also reveals how dangerous false accusations and misrepresentations could be for the Indian women who were the subject of these totalizing exchanges: punishment, including expulsion or reinstitutionalization in external facilities, was meted out to Indian women based only loosely on white officials' observations. Similarly, Carlisle officials' perceptions of Indian women's behavior were often the product of information exchanged among white members of their own class, and disciplinary records reflect that Carlisle officials accepted hearsay issued from their white peers as valid sources of knowledge. These dynamics reflect instances of what Karen Adkins describes as "invisible gossip," where those in a position of power use their authority to shame, humiliate, discredit, or demean their perceived antagonists, employing the rhetorical techniques of gossip while refusing to recognize their speech as such.[117] Building on this discussion, I adopt a definition of gossip as an epistemologically productive discursive phenomenon. Carlisle authorities, Outing home patrons, and white civilians used evaluative talk as a system of knowledge that categorized and organized white, nonwhite, and Indigenous bodies into racial, class, and gender hierarchies, while attempting to reify their own subject positions as the exclusive arbiters of national belonging, power, authority, and property.

In the Carlisle vicinity, gossip served as an informal means of transmitting and receiving knowledge, but it also made its way into the official record, as US officials cited, catalogued, and organized gossip into formal corpuses of knowledge. In April 1915, for example, during Friedman's superintendency, Indian Service agent J. H. Dortch spent five days at Carlisle at the direction of Commissioner Sells in order to investigate the conditions of the institution, and his writing illustrates how many of his impressions were obtained by word of mouth. Under section 5, "Discipline," Dortch reported, "The chaos which reigned at this school a year ago, and with which you are familiar, was not exaggerated *if the statements of many employes* [*sic*] *are correct.* Nearly all with whom I talked referred to them with a shudder. The girls openly defied the then matron and did not hesitate to order her to shut her mouth in language as picturesque as it was scandalous, to secretly meet the boys of the school, and to arrange means for the boys to enter their sleeping rooms at night" (emphasis mine). He went on, "If the conditions at the girls' building were bad, those at the boys' were inexpressibly so. *I was told* that the boys brought liquor on the grounds, got drunk and 'scrapped,' defying all authority, even hanging the outing agent by the heels from a third-story window; that drunken students would parade the grounds, shooting pistols, and in fact, in true old-time western style 'shoot up' the school" (emphasis mine).[118]

Dortch's report demonstrates that he accepted Carlisle gossip as being more than merely propositional, trivial talk about Indian people. Instead, he treated these anecdotes as reliable testimonies that he accepted and cited as official knowledge-claims. Although somewhat humorous and perhaps hyperbolic, the report indexes how US officials and Carlisle employees welcomed speculation and hearsay from one another as the basis of disciplinary action. "From what I heard," Dortch writes, "I do not believe that conditions were exaggerated in last year's reports. Immorality also was said to prevail almost openly at the hospital, where conditions were said to be almost intolerable."[119]

As a counterpoint to descriptions of the past "chaos," Dortch praised Outing matron Matilda Ewing's dominance over the female enrollees: "Her control of these two hundred and odd girls, mostly young women and many practically white, was simply excellent. Quiet and unassuming, by some psychological power of impressing her individuality upon these formerly wild and said to be unmanageable girls, she has gained a complete ascendency over them."[120] Though Dortch assured Sells that the previously "unmanageable" Indian women had been "dominated," other records show that Carlisle employees relied on external institutions such as the legal apparatus to supplement Carlisle's disciplinary aims. This interrelationship between US institutions demonstrates how disciplinary objectives were interwoven throughout the fabric of the settler state, as ostensibly distinct facilities worked together to police, surveil, apprehend, punish, and disappear Indian people.

Gossip was entrenched in Carlisle's settler vernacular as a mode of everyday speech, and its use highlights the tenuousness and porousness of the established settler order. In some instances, as the following reveals, white Americans' idle chatter about Indian people became naturalized as official knowledge-claims. Records relating to an eighteen-year-old Cherokee woman, Lucinda R., reveal how white patrons used gossip to assert ownership over the bodies and labor of Indian women who worked in the Outing system and under the jurisdiction of Carlisle authorities. Additionally, these records show the extent to which hearsay pervaded the everyday lives of white citizens and Indian people, as evaluative talk registered spatial, personal, and linguistic transgressions. Gossip was used by many in the Carlisle vicinity—white and Indigenous alike—to invoke and resolve tensions produced by the commingling of different bodies, races, and classes in private households.

On January 7, 1915, Superintendent Oscar Lipps sent a letter addressed to James Henderson, the superintendent of the Cherokee Agency in Cherokee, North Carolina, regarding Lucinda, who had been enrolled at Carlisle in 1913 at the age of sixteen. "My dear Mr. Henderson," Lipps explained, "I regret very much to advise you that Lucinda R—, who is enrolled here from the Agency under your jurisdiction, is in a pregnant condition and that I must ask you to co-operate with me in caring for the girl."[121] Lucinda had been a member of the Outing program the summer before and was employed in the home of Alexander Holcombe and his wife Margaret in Cynwyd, Pennsylvania. The Holcombes were white American citizens and Presbyterians who lived near the Johnston household in which Lucinda's friend, Margaret B., was employed as well. As members of the Outing program, Lucinda and Margaret would have been responsible for performing a variety of domestic duties—cooking, cleaning, washing clothes, and childcare—for the families who resided in the homes in which they lived. They would have also been expected to conform very strictly to both Carlisle's and the host families' rules. Occasionally, Lucinda was permitted on Sundays to go across the street to visit her friend, and the two of them would travel together to see another companion, Jane, who lived in the town of Bala where the Presbyterian Church was located.[122]

On one such Sunday, Lucinda arrived at Margaret's house only to discover that Margaret had left for Jane's without her, so Lucinda made the decision to continue on the usual route to Bala unattended. Later, after Lucinda's pregnancy was discovered, she allegedly reported to Carlisle administrators that she had become "intimate" on this unaccompanied walk with a "strange man she met while on her way to visit Jane O— in Bala," but that she could not recall his name and had never seen him before.[123]

Upon learning of this report, Mrs. Holcombe was furious that Lucinda "claim[ed] that it happened before she returned to Carlisle last August" and felt "sure that she [Lucinda] [was] not telling the truth in reference to this."[124] Mrs. Holcombe was insistent on this point and offered the following proof to Lipps that Lucinda was lying: "She never went to visit Jane O— in Bala except in daylight on Sunday afternoons and the walk between the homes is along much travelled streets. She was never allowed to go even to the Post Office except with one or more of our children."[125] In other words, Lucinda was monitored constantly—by passersby in broad daylight, by the Holcombes' white children, and by Margaret Holcombe herself—and so could not possibly have had the interaction she claimed she did.

In the days following this correspondence, Mrs. Holcombe sought to protect her own reputation against the proof—Lucinda's pregnancy—that something illicit had happened on her watch. In so doing, Mrs. Holcombe related to various Carlisle officials via correspondence that she felt that Lucinda had betrayed her trust, and she endeavored to craft a version of events that allowed her to maintain her image as respectable homemaker. In the process, she mobilized rumor against Lucinda, seeking first to discredit the veracity of Lucinda's story.

On January 10, 1915, Mrs. Holcombe wrote Lipps that she had on a previous occasion scolded Lucinda for exchanging "suggestive correspondence with a boy named Harold Gilbert"; Mrs. Holcombe also reported that "she [Lucinda] also was very fond of one of the young men in the foot-ball squad and wrote to me . . . of her delight at having been his selected one to go to the Penn-Indian game in Phila. She did not mention his name."[126] As is evident from this letter, Mrs. Holcombe attempted to deflect blame for Lucinda's pregnancy away from herself and her household by insisting that the father of Lucinda's child might be identified as either Harold Gilbert or the unnamed football player, in whom Lucinda had allegedly had prior romantic interest.

Two weeks after sending her last letter, Mrs. Holcombe wrote Lipps again: "After consultation with my sister who was in our house the last ten days of July I feel that Lucinda has not told the truth as to the happenings on Sunday July 26th. That week my sister took her in company with our three little girls to an amusement park. . . . Margaret B— left the house with her and returned with her on July 26th. . . . We trust that Lucinda has already told you the truth in regard to the matter."[127] In invoking the "truth," Mrs. Holcombe gestured toward what American studies scholar Katrin Horn observes of the duality of containment and exposure inherent in gossip.[128] But in engaging in speculation and the creation of a rumor about Lucinda, Mrs. Holcombe also opened herself up to scrutiny by Carlisle officials.

Letters of correspondence about Lucinda's pregnancy reflect how efficacious gossip and rumor could be in upending seemingly entrenched racial dynamics and power hierarchies. In one example, in response to Mrs. Holcombe's version of events, Carlisle's unnamed Outing manager—likely Nellie Denny, a Sisseton-Wahpeton woman married to Carlisle Disciplinarian Wallace Denny—wrote, "Last evening I had Lucinda over in my room for about an hour, but I failed to get any other story from her, than that which she has already told others. This child adhered to this story in such a way that we cannot doubt her word. She goes to her home in Cherokee, N.C., this afternoon and, I suppose, the truth, if there is any other story, will never be known."[129]

As reflected by this letter, the Outing manager did not unquestioningly accept Mrs. Holcombe's speculations about Lucinda—but she (or he) also seemed loath to place blame squarely at Margaret Holcombe's feet. Reinforcing the uncertain circumstances of Lucinda's pregnancy, the Outing manager's response underscored the fact that the absent referent—the father of Lucinda's child—could be anyone, thereby casting doubt on the Holcombes' ability to maintain authority over the Indian women who labored in their household.

The ambiguity of the Outing manager's identity and gender in letters of correspondence is particularly notable; this unknown information raises the specter of uneven power dynamics between Mrs. Holcombe and the Outing manager, whose official title is a masculine one; the term "matron" was typically used to denote a female and feminized position of employment. Yet, this situation also illustrates how Indigenous people could participate in and complicate settler structures of discipline and punishment: by disguising her identity, Nellie—who was a former Carlisle enrollee—asserted a paternalistic authority over Mrs. Holcombe that would otherwise be unavailable to her. These facts further demonstrate how gossip and rumor could introduce disequilibrium into Carlisle's institutional order, and could disrupt, challenge, and even upend seemingly entrenched racial, gender, and class hierarchies in unforeseen ways.

Records about Lucinda tell us little about how she experienced life in the Holcombe household, what threats to her safety and security she faced, and whether she was able to seek out and find respite with a friend or confidante.[130] As Caitlin Keliiaa (Yerington Paiute and Washoe), Dian Million (Athabascan), and others have observed of similar dynamics, Indigenous women experienced high rates of sexual abuse and were exposed to violence both in boarding institutions and Outing programs across Turtle Island in this, and subsequent, eras.[131] After having been expelled from Carlisle, Lucinda made her way back home to her brother and grandfather, who anticipated her return; at the time of this writing, I have been unable to locate mention of Lucinda or her child in archival repositories that might paint a fuller picture of their lives after leaving Carlisle's institutional grounds. These records do, however, reveal how gossip, rumor, and hearsay played important roles in the negotiation of power, authority, and ownership among Indian women, like Lucinda, and Carlisle officials and Outing patrons who interacted with one another on an everyday basis. Radical disparities in class, gender, education, and race defined the nature of interactions at Carlisle and in the Outing system; but the archival record also reveals that Indian people told stories about white Americans to effectively refute entrenched racial and power dynamics. Some of those stories had significant consequences—although not all rumors were equal, nor did they circulate evenly.[132]

In the flurry of activity related to the discovery of Lucinda's pregnancy, on January 3, 1915, Lipps sent another letter to Mrs. Holcombe suggesting that Lucinda's pregnancy could be attributed to Mrs. Holcombe's neglect. He wrote, "[Lucinda's] confession reveals the fact that she became thus while living under your care and protection last summer."[133] As is evident from Lipps's note, Mrs. Holcombe was under scrutiny herself by Carlisle authorities, who expected her to fulfill her civic duty to tend not only to her family but also to the Indian woman who labored in her household. Lipps's suggestion thus went beyond the possibility of Mrs. Holcombe's tarnished reputation; his remark also alluded to her failure both as a homemaker and as a woman tasked with the oversight of a domestic servant who figured as an extension of the Holcombe household, and thus, as a "white possession": as an Indian woman, Lucinda was presumed to be a legal ward of the US government and, by extension, of the white Americans under whose "care and protection" she labored.[134]

As a white American woman, Mrs. Holcombe was expected to be self-possessed and in control of her private domicile; as Horn reminds us, "domestic privacy" could be threatened from within, by being "too crowded (with family members, for the poor) or too 'invaded' (with servants, for the rich) to function as a true sanctuary."[135] Lucinda's pregnancy, and the illicit circumstances implied in this scenario, thus defied the settler order; in becoming pregnant by an unidentified man, her body was rendered opaque and therefore threatening. The fact of her pregnancy represented Indigenous women's ability to reproduce their nations while suggesting the frightening, dual possibilities of white *dis*possession and Indigenous sovereignty, bodily or otherwise. The archival record bears little concern for or mention of Lucinda's safety and well-being in her Outing setting.

It's difficult to know for certain why this issue was the topic of significant correspondence for so long, but just over one full year after Lucinda was expelled from Carlisle, an irate Alexander Holcombe (Margaret Holcombe's husband) wrote a letter to Lipps which illustrated the potential power of Indigenous women's counter-rumors. In this correspondence, he referenced Eva (Seneca), an eighteen-year-old Carlisle enrollee, who had replaced Lucinda as the Holcombe's domestic servant. Holcombe fumed,

Dear Sir:-

It is impossible to express our annoyance and surprise at learning from [Eva J—] that it is now being rumored that our son is the father of the child born to Lucinda R— last year. We can not understand how such a maliciously false tale could be started except as an indirect result of the absolutely false and rotten story which we learn has been told by Eva [J—].... Our son is an active boy of 16 years who leads his class in High School and whose spare time for several years has been spent in the work of the Boy Scouts.... It is a perfect outrage that irresponsible people should circulate such false rumors against us in a way from which we have no defense. Mrs. Holcombe and I have always taken a great deal of interest in the girls you have sent us.... We have tried to treat them not as servants but as helpers in our home and they have been allowed as much as possible to share in our family pleasures. Eva [J—] however was so filthy about her person that our children did not wish to be near her. We were much grieved last year to learn of Lucinda's trouble but we cannot feel that it was brought about by any carelessness in our observance of the rules of the Outing System. It seems so unfair after all this time to allow malicious rumors to be given credence.... You, who have sons of your own, can readily understand our desire to shield our boy from such absolutely false and unfair accusations which are being made after all this lapse of time.

Very truly yours,

A. H. Holcombe[136]

Holcombe's letter of outrage reveals a great deal about the destructive capacity of gossip for white citizens, as well as the racial common sense present in the Holcombe household. As seen from this letter, Holcombe was indignant that his son was rumored to be the father of Lucinda's child, and in rushing to his son's defense, painted himself and his family as morally superior to the Indian women he employed. That this letter was sent so long after Lucinda was expelled from the Carlisle vicinity also points to the potential severity of the rumor's impact—a rumor Holcombe felt certain was started by Eva. It is possible that, for the Holcombe family, the rumor contributed to a damaged reputation among their peers, which could have significantly affected their standing in their community. As such, Holcombe's letter underscores the efficacy with which young Indian women could wield gossip as a form of retribution.

It is difficult to glean what prompted Holcombe to write to Lipps at this time, but it is evident that he felt it was necessary to defend his family against what he characterized as a "maliciously false tale." While he does not accuse Lucinda directly of spreading the rumor, he does cite Eva, a symbolic stand-in for Lucinda, as the source of his grief. But in detailing the ways in which his children "did not wish to be near [Eva]" because she "was so filthy about her person," he sutures Eva's racialized body to her status as a servant in their household in a process of dehumanization that is central to the architecture of white supremacy.[137] In so doing, he reiterates the ways in which Eva's Indianness—as well as that of Lucinda and other Indian women who labored in his household—was her defining feature, which rightfully placed her in a subservient position to himself, his wife, and his family.[138] There is only one extant letter in Lucinda's Carlisle file that is written in her hand, dated June 7, 1914, six months before her pregnancy was exposed. "Dear Sir," she wrote to reservation superintendent James Henderson from the Holcombe household in Cynwyd, "As I am in need. I must ask for a part of the money left that which I was to receive . . . in 1912. I did not get my share. So I will ask if you will kindly send me about half of the money. Not for pleasure uses but to pay the expenses for the work done on my teeth. . . . I can pay the other half from my spending money. I do not wish to spend on the earning [from Outing] so far I have not drawn any and am saving it."[139]

In addition to documenting the discrimination that Indian women encountered in the homes of white Americans, records relating to Lucinda's experiences reveal how the Outing system assisted in the subordination of Indian women to men and white Americans under state-sponsored, institutionalized structures of patriarchal colonialism. Indian women who labored "under the Outing" in American homes were expected to perform (but could never attain) a version of (white) womanhood predicated on docility, compliance, and agreeableness. American historians describe these characteristics as a product of the cult of "true womanhood," a social system that dictated gender relations among the white middle and upper classes; women of color and immigrants were excluded from "true" womanhood on the basis of race or ethnicity.[140] Like the Holcombes, American families who employed Indian women expected them to perform a racialized, subservient version of femininity while striving to attain a more perfected form of (white) womanhood. Holcombe's reference to "irresponsible people" in his letter thus points to the racial and gendered expectations of the Indian women he employed in this volatile domestic setting while revealing the destructive potential of the privileged information they held about the Holcombe family. As cultural historian Kyla Tompkins explains, Black, Irish, and Indian domestic workers possessed intimate knowledge of white Americans' tastes, preferences, and weaknesses as domestic laborers and as such could stage what she refers to as "kitchen insurrections"—a notion of duplicity that Holcombe drew on in his letter to Lipps, as well.[141] Nonetheless, that Holcombe felt it was necessary to defend his son against rumors started, as he suggests, by Eva, indicates that Indian women could also use gossip as an effective form of discursive resistance, or even revenge against their Outing patrons.[142]

That there was a young man around Lucinda's age in the house at the time of her pregnancy does not definitively indicate that Holcombe's son fathered Lucinda's child. But the fact of the young man's presence does call into question Lucinda's reported inability to identify the "strange man" she met one Sunday afternoon, and Mrs. Holcombe's insistence that Lucinda had previously been scolded for "suggestive" behavior when it came to young men. Lucinda's statements perhaps suggest that she was intentionally trying to conceal the identity of the "strange man," either because he was no stranger at all or because he was the wrong kind of stranger— one with relative power over her. While we cannot tell from Lucinda's file whether she was being abused at the hands of her Outing patrons, the documents about her pregnancy point to the ways in which young Indian women of childbearing age who were placed in similar domestic scenarios were at risk for pregnancy, abuse, and sexual violence—a risk that Carlisle administrators also privately acknowledged.[143] In a similar vein, writing of a Unangax̂ internment camp in Killisnoo in the mid-twentieth century, Iñupiaq historian Holly Miowak Guise has meticulously described how sexual violence toward Indigenous women has historically been used as a colonial tool to silence their voices.[144] That so many Indigenous women were exposed to the fraught domestic environments of Outing households underscores the need for a Truth and Healing commission in the United States.

Gossip and rumor were not inconsequential: they were useful tools in Carlisle's architecture of settler colonialism and white supremacy, and they resulted in material repercussions for Indian women and, on some occasions, white American citizens. At the local level, letters of correspondence about Lucinda and other Indian women demonstrate how the Outing system supported the institutionalized disciplinary structures at Carlisle that labored to "domesticate" Indian people by subordinating them to white authority figures. These documents also show that the Outing system enabled white Americans to reinforce race, class, and gender hierarchies by exercising punitive power over the bodies and psyches of their domestic "helpers." Gossip, rumor, and hearsay furthered these objectives, as Indian women were often denied recourse to accusations that circulated among Carlisle officials and Outing home patrons. Yet, as records relating to Lucinda also demonstrate, this uneven dynamic was not totalizing; Indigenous women in Outing households exchanged information about their patrons with one another as well, and as Eva's counter-rumor illustrated, this information exchange could exact small instances of revenge—and do so successfully, as seen from Holcombe's fury. In many ways, evaluative talk between and among Indigenous enrollees, Outing patrons, Carlisle employees, and others mediated, resolved, and produced conflict at Carlisle and beyond—a dynamic that expands our understanding of Carlisle's disciplinary regime and the means by which Indian people resisted it.

⋮

Carlisle attendees are regarded with esteem within their communities, and for good reason: this polysemic institution altered the lives of over ten thousand Indian people, a fact that highlights its "dizzying" historical significance (fig. 1.5).[145] For many adult enrollees, Carlisle was not a school at all; the routinized practice of adult punishment highlights the subtle and overt conflicts that resulted from challenges to the entrenched settler order. Indian women and men who enrolled at Carlisle were often already self-sufficient, and they demonstrated this in myriad ways: by enrolling at the institution of their own accord, seeking out romantic and sexual partnerships, leaving the institution to attend to matters of personal importance back home, and asserting their autonomy and identities as Indian people. Similarly, some adult enrollees were in full possession of the titles to their allotments and were thus also, in some sense, US citizens.[146]

Yet, as adult Indian people enrolled at an institution that claimed to prepare Indian people for self-sufficiency and eventually citizenship, it is white Americans who often profited in the most obvious ways, as they accrued power and sometimes

1.5 Carlisle's graduating class of 1917. Fewer than 10 percent of all enrollees graduated from Carlisle; the author's maternal relative Sarah Fowler (Choctaw) is pictured here in the top row, far left. Photographer unknown, "Graduating Class of 1917," Winnishiek, WK-27-02, Cumberland County Historical Society, Carlisle, Pennsylvania.

. . . .

prestige as deputies of the settler order. From railroad employees and town gossips to nosy neighbors and local pastors, the commonality often shared by the disparate historical actors who policed Indian people was their status-whiteness. These facts complicate Carlisle's false promises of Indigenous uplift and shed light on the legacy of this punitive racial regime; they also illuminate the historical implications of white Americans policing Indigenous people at the United States' most notorious Indian residential facility and in other institutions of the settler state—a pattern of deputization that continues to play out in America today. Records relating to Indian enrollees at Carlisle document the determination and fortitude of Indian women and men who found remarkable ways to navigate a complex institutional regime of discipline and punishment. As their actions illustrate, they did not easily or willingly submit to the demands of institutional officials, and they used all the resources at their disposal to establish methods of resistance and to carve out moments of independence and, perhaps, joy. The following chapter shifts to other Carlisle enrollees' experiences of labor, training, and employment in Carlisle's Outing system and the many ways Indian people negotiated institutional authority within the private labor sector.

"HOE HANDLE MEDICINE"
MEDICINAL LABOR AT THE FORD MOTOR COMPANY
AND LANCASTER GENERAL HOSPITAL

On June 11, 1886, an article entitled "Hoe Handle Medicine" appeared in the *Indian Helper*, the official publication of the Carlisle Indian Industrial School. "On a bright summer morning," the narrator began, "a young man with a silk handkerchief around his throat and a very sad, sick looking face knocked at the doctor's door. A lady came to the door and told the man that the doctor was out in the garden hoeing corn. He went where he was told."

"Well, sir, what is the matter?" the doctor asked.

"Doctor," cried the ailing man, "I feel sick all over. My head aches, I can't eat. I am weak. I want medicine."

"Yes, I see. Let me look at your tongue. Ah! Yes. Now your pulse. Yes, sir," said the doctor, "you must have some medicine, or you will die. But, this corn must all be hoed before 10 o'clock, and now I have to go to see a sick person, down street; so while I am gone, you hoe my corn for me. You know how to hoe?"

"Yes," the sick man replied, "my father was a farmer but I don't have to work. I have enough money to hire my work done."

"Very well," said the doctor, "this will not hurt you, so go on hoeing till [*sic*] I come back."

The doctor left, and the sick man picked up the hoe and got to work. When the first row was complete, he took off his handkerchief, and before long he had hoed all six rows of corn, just in time for the doctor's return.

"Well! Well! My young man. How are you feeling now?"

The sick man did not say anything, but kept looking for a bottle of medicine he thought the doctor was going to get for him.

"The work hasn't hurt you? Has it?" asked the doctor.

"Oh, no." said the sick man.

"I thought not. Let me feel your pulse again. Splendid! Now go home, and take this medicine two times every day. Do it faithfully, and be honest about your eating. Don't use tobacco, and this medicine will cure; Give me one dollar for this medicine."

"One dollar?" asked the astonished sick man.

"That is all I charge, when sick people come to me. If I have to go to them I charge more."

"But in mercy's name! What is it for? Where is your medicine? I did not take any medicine?"

"My dear young friend," the doctor explained, "I gave you my hoe to work with. I gave you hoe-handle medicine, and let me tell you the truth, sir. You are rusting out. Going to pieces, dying, because you do not exercise."

The young man paid the dollar. He was a little angry at first, but when he thought more about it, he felt sure the doctor was right, and went back and thanked him. He took exercise every day," the story concluded, "and grew to be a strong, and healthy man."[1]

⋮

"Hoe Handle Medicine" was written two decades before the Office of Indian Affairs (OIA) would acknowledge that their own indifference had produced health crises at off-reservation boarding institutions, but it presaged developments that would have a lasting impact on Indian people and their communities.[2] This chapter takes up those changes to examine how the concept of "hoe handle medicine," or medicinal labor, served as a powerful guiding logic within the Indian Office and in settler spaces of labor that Indian people traversed in the early twentieth century.

After the turn of the century, US officials, reformers, and other self-styled "friends" of the Indian had largely abandoned the notion that Indian people could be fully assimilated. Industrial and domestic labor was prescribed in the spirit of "improvement" in the hopes that hard work would transform "idle" Indian people into productive American citizens, as the parable above suggests. Much of this "improvement" was to take place in formal labor programs such as the Outing program, first established at Carlisle in 1879 under Captain Richard Henry Pratt, and later duplicated at other schools. In the years following its implementation, Carlisle's Outing program underwent significant shifts that reflected the changing objectives of the federal boarding school system and the increasing specialization of vocational programs at large, off-reservation schools. Following the implementation of new directives under Commissioner of Indian Affairs Cato Sells, by 1916,

Carlisle superintendent Oscar H. Lipps had established automotive and nurse training "partnerships" with the Ford Motor Company at Highland Park in the Detroit area and the General Hospital in Lancaster, Pennsylvania. With the establishment of these partnerships, Indian women and men ostensibly had new avenues of self-sufficiency and upward mobility open to them—but the etiological chaos of the early twentieth century created new opportunities for anti-Indian racism to be expressed as scientific "fact," and these shifts were contested in surprising ways by the Indian people who labored in white-dominated spaces of employment.

This chapter turns to the experiences of Indigenous people in the private labor sector. In so doing, it reads across the grain of disciplinary records relating to Indian women and men who sought to become automotive mechanics and nurses and enrolled in Carlisle's training partnerships with the Ford Motor Company and the General Hospital. These records reveal how white American discourses about Indigenous health seized on laboring Indian bodies and how inequitable labor environments attempted to fortify existing racial hierarchies, subordinate Indian workers to white authority figures, and maintain Indian people as second-class laborers. As wages rose and Western medical knowledge became more sophisticated in the early years of the twentieth century, white Americans began to enjoy better working conditions, increased health, and longer lifespans.[3] Simultaneously, reservation communities faced increasingly widespread epidemics, high rates of poverty, and an ongoing lack of employment opportunities on reservations and in major metropolitan areas across the United States. Despite improvements in medical knowledge and health care for the general American population, as well as increased access to education and options for gainful employment, the OIA often promoted labor—rather than medicine—as the cure for disease in Indigenous communities. Disciplinary records relating to Indian women and men who trained at the Ford factory and General Hospital reveal how both institutions extended the punitive objectives of the Carlisle Indian School. As seen from the enrollees' experiences, both the factory and hospital fused discourses about work with the attainment of health in attempts to compel Indian people to accept their status as racialized menial laborers. Analyzing the use of medicalized language in these labor scenarios, this chapter highlights contested patterns of Indigenous pathologization and proletarianization in the American workforce.

⋮

As the twentieth century wore on, Indigenous populations endured widespread health crises on the reservation and in spaces of close interpersonal contact, such as large boarding institutions like Carlisle. Although Western medical and scientific communities made unprecedented strides in the treatment of infectious diseases in this era, these advances were largely ignored by the OIA, which routinely failed to improve health conditions for Indian people at boarding schools and, often, on reservations. As Jean Keller, Clifford Trafzer, Preston McBride, and other boarding school historians have demonstrated, it was not until the end of the first decade of the twentieth century that the OIA implemented any systematic medical care of boarding school populations, who suffered high rates of tuberculosis, trachoma, influenza, measles, and other infectious diseases.[4] Although high rates of illness in Indigenous populations stemmed in large part from federal mismanagement, the Indian Office persistently identified Indigeneity as both a literal and symbolic source of pathology and contamination. As revealed by OIA investigative reports about contagious disease in Indian communities, US officials characterized Indigenous lifeways as inherently pathological; to many white American citizens, illness was Indian peoples' natural and permanent state of being.

Simultaneously, boarding school officials continued to derogate select elements of Indigenous lifeways as backward and pathological, while incorporating other traditional Indigenous practices into what K. Tsianina Lomawaima (Mvskoke) and Teresa McCarty have termed the curricular (and ideological) "safety zone."[5] In addition to immersing enrollees in Christianity, English instruction, and hierarchical power structures with US officials at the top, Carlisle officials also sought to compel Indian enrollees to make themselves constantly productive by subjecting them to tightly regimented daily schedules and manual labor around the clock. As one component of this Western educational regime, the Outing system formalized manual labor as a learning opportunity and civilizational ritual. Outing patrons, school employees, and OIA agents measured the effectiveness of the program by the degree to which Indian laborers successfully performed assimilation to Euro-American norms and standards. In this context, labor was curative; US officials promoted medicinal labor as the key to the successful "uplift" of Indian communities.

These beliefs played out in Carlisle's Outing program and its expanded training "partnerships" with the Ford Motor Company in the Detroit, Michigan, area and the General Hospital in Lancaster, Pennsylvania. Indian women and men who enrolled at Carlisle were encouraged through OIA discourse and boarding school propaganda to work hard, and they were promised new avenues of self-sufficiency as they trained to become nurses and automobile mechanics. Yet, those who entered these employment arrangements often faced intensified forms of anti-Indian discrimination that they resisted and challenged—in many cases by working harder and more diligently toward their goals. These records showcase ingenious methods of Indigenous resistance; they also reveal how the ideology of medicinal labor dictated Indian peoples' constant productivity under white authority figures, an arrangement that benefited the settler society by extending its punitive reach into private spaces where Indigenous people were employed. As Carlisle officials granted employment supervisors at Ford and the General Hospital near-total authority over Indian laborers, white Americans transferred and traded power among themselves laterally, fortifying the settler order.

Indigenous labor had profound medical and moral connotations that US officials and employment supervisors mobilized in attempts to manage and control the Indian people who labored under their aegis. The interrelated ideas that Indigenous lifeways were inherently pathological and that labor was curative benefited the settler society; it reaffirmed the idea that white bodies were healthy and normative, a phenomenon that Jessica Cowing refers to as settler ableism, and which I, Traci Brynne Voyles, Susan Burch, and others have expanded on. Similarly, these ideas extended patterns of Indigenous labor exploitation established in the earliest years of colonial incursion.[6] Far from "curing" Indian people of illness or unemployment, the ideology of medicinal labor maintained the objectives of the settler society by exacerbating racial inequities in white-dominated spaces, in some cases worsening health and employment outcomes for Indian people. Examining the dynamic experiences of Carlisle enrollees in two employment settings, this chapter argues that "hoe handle medicine" is an apt metaphor for diffuse settler labor that "cured" by exploiting Indian women and men in the homes, factories, and fields of white America.

MEDICINAL LABOR: HEALTH AND WORK IN NATIVE AMERICA

The late nineteenth and early twentieth centuries were a period of intense debate in American and European medical communities, as the "new bacteriology"—characterized by the appearance of isolation hospitals—spurred novel questions about the nature of disease that would dramatically alter the practice of medicine and inform the public health campaigns of the early 1900s.[7] By 1900, according to the US Centers for Disease Control, "the three leading causes of death in the

United States were tuberculosis, pneumonia, and diarrhea and enteritis, which (together with diphtheria) caused one third of all deaths."[8] In addition, between 1890 and 1920, more than one million Americans succumbed to typhoid and paratyphoid fevers.[9] As Western medical communities sought to contain the spread of infectious diseases, changes in the practice of medicine had slowly begun to reorder public conceptions of health and illness in the United States. In 1890, Robert Koch announced his discovery of tuberculin, derived from tubercule bacilli, which he believed prevented the proliferation of bacterium in animals. His discovery proved ineffective as a cure for tuberculosis, but it paved the way for tuberculin to be used as an effective diagnostic tool and led to a better understanding of the way tuberculosis spread among human populations.[10] The diphtheria antitoxin was also introduced in the mid-1890s, which improved mortality rates for a highly contagious illness that infected the mucous membranes of the nose and throat and could lead to paralysis and death. These developments brought about huge strides in the treatment, control, and understanding of contagion and the epidemics that tore through densely populated areas unchecked; as medical historian Jacob Steere-Williams notes, by the turn of the twentieth century, American bacteriologists were "armed with knowledge of many microorganisms responsible for the spread of infectious diseases . . . [and] follow[ed] three commands: identify, isolate, and disinfect."[11]

Advances in Western medicine were not always beneficial for Indigenous or other nonwhite populations, however. As the practice of medicine became professionalized and fell evermore under the exclusive purview of elite white men, epidemiological developments in the United States served the interests of a white population that was fearful of contagion and clung to beliefs about nonwhite communities as being particularly disease-ridden.[12] These prejudices resulted in significant health disparities between white populations and those of color: for instance, just as tuberculosis was in decline among white citizens, at 1.73 deaths per 1,000 incidences, the death rate from tuberculosis hovered at 4.85 per 1,000 for Black Americans and at 5.06 per 1,000 for American Indian people.[13] As historian Samuel Roberts Jr. writes of this discrepancy in African American communities, "For most of the first half of the twentieth century, tuberculosis ranked among the top three causes of mortality among urban blacks. In 1900, 1920, and 1940, pulmonary tuberculosis accounted for 15.0 percent, 12.8 percent, and 8.4 percent of African American mortality, respectively."[14] "Modern tuberculosis," Roberts explains, "always had a socioeconomic and political profile. The majority of tubercular disease cases originated in the airborne travel of the tubercle bacillus to the lungs, thereby making conditions of poor housing what public health scholars today would call a 'fundamental cause' of tuberculosis. So, too, were poor nutrition, stress, and overwork."[15]

As Western medical practitioners devised explanatory frameworks for widespread illness in urban populations and communities of color, public health discourses seized upon American Indian people in complicated ways. Tuberculosis and trachoma were significant causes of morbidity and mortality on Indian reservations; as medical historians have demonstrated, Indigenous people were often active participants in the preservation and protection of their communities from these and other contagious diseases, utilizing both traditional and Western forms of medicine to address acute and chronic health crises. As Juliet Larkin-Gilmore has shown, Mojaves regularly asserted medical autonomy in this era by soliciting care from specific traditional healers or Western medical practitioners of their choice, sometimes traveling significant cross-border distances from the Colorado River Agency to locales such as Needles, California, in order to access care—as did two Mojave siblings named Alice B. and George M., who had tuberculosis.[16] As Larkin-Gilmore argues, the steps Alice and George took to access the care they deemed best for George were acts of bodily autonomy and tribal sovereignty. Other tribes similarly established their own practices and facilities to care for the sick or infirm, such as the Choctaw Nation's sanatorium, opened in 1916, in Talihina, Oklahoma. In the early twentieth century, the Cherokee Nation was also involved in securing health care for ailing tribal members by leveraging the resources of "health drives," or caravans of field matrons and other Indian Service officials, who traveled through Oklahoma to provide rudimentary assistance to tubercular tribal citizens.[17] Brianna Theobald, Clifford Trafzer, David H. DeJong, and other scholars have similarly documented how Indigenous people made their own informed choices about the health of their families and nations at the turn of the twentieth century.[18]

It was difficult for Indigenous families to assert similar influence over the abysmal conditions of boarding schools, however, and nowhere did contagious disease spread as quickly as it did within the confines of residential institutions. Despite knowledge of the conditions that Indian boarding school enrollees faced, the OIA ignored advancements in the fields of medicine and science that could potentially ameliorate the suffering of thousands of Indigenous youth and their communities while criminalizing tribes' use of traditional healing practices. In fact, it wasn't until 1908 that Commissioner Francis E. Leupp implemented a systematic approach to student health at boarding institutions, and before Leupp's appointment of Dr. Joseph A. Murphy as medical supervisor in 1909—one of his final acts as commissioner—the Indian Service had no government agent tasked with the administration of medical care at all.[19] By 1904, however, tuberculosis had reached such epidemic proportions in Indian communities that this disease alone forced the OIA and Commissioner William Jones to acknowledge the crisis and cultivate a sense of urgency about the eradication of this and other infectious diseases.[20]

In a tacit acknowledgment of the deteriorating conditions among reservation and boarding school populations, Congress ordered the Public Health and Marine-Hospital Service to help fulfill OIA treaty obligations by conducting a systematic investigation of health conditions on reservations and within Indian communities. According to the preface of *Contagious and Infectious Diseases among Indians*, the final report that issued from this campaign, Congress authorized the investigation on August 24, 1912, and appointed the head of the Division of Scientific Research, Assistant Surgeon General J. W. Kerr, to spearhead the effort; alongside Kerr, Surgeon Taliaferro Clark and Past Assistant Surgeon J. W. Schereschewsky acted as reporters.

From September 28, 1912, to December 30 of that same year, Kerr oversaw a systematic study of Indian peoples' bodies at each Indian agency. All Indian boarding schools, day schools, sanatoria, asylums, and other institutions of confinement, as well as individual Indian homes, were included in the investigation.[21] There was more at stake, the report argued, than a better understanding of disease in Indian communities—given the increasing frequency of interracial mingling, along with increased white encroachment on Indian lands and territories, the investigators believed the illnesses that Indian people contracted posed a potential public health crisis for the general public, as well.[22]

Many of Kerr, Clark, and Schereschewsky's observations about Indigenous illness and disease codified assumptions about the inherent pathology of Indigenous lifeways into policy recommendations. For instance, the following was reported: "The factors which facilitate the dissemination of trachoma are . . . the conditions which prevail wherever human beings are closely crowded together as in tenement houses, hovels, schools, and insanitary institutions." The authors continued, "The careless personal habits and unhygienic conditions characteristic of ignorance and poverty, the use of the common towel and washbasin, and the agency of the fly, create conditions which could obviously favor the spread of trachoma as they would that of any infectious disease."[23] As demonstrated by the authors' language of deficiency, US officials were quick to blame Indigenous people for their own suffering and loath to acknowledge the role that federal mismanagement played in the spread of infectious disease.

This refusal was reflected in comments about environmental causes of the spread of contagious disease as well: "The sanitary conditions on reservations were found on the whole unsatisfactory.... [The Indians'] personal and social habits favor the spread of disease, as they are careless about spitting and the disposition of human and household waste." Characterizing social relations within tribes as a primary contributing factor to the spread of illness, the authors continued, "Their fondness of visiting, together with dances and social gatherings which are attended by the sick and the well, afford opportunity to spread any communicable disease which is present." Even beyond attributing the spread of illness to Indigenous ways of relating, Kerr, Clark, and Schereschewsky argued that inborn characteristics led to illness among Indian populations: "Owing to their improvidence and racial indolence and poverty, their food supply on the whole is scanty and inferior, thus lowering vital resistance and increasing the predisposition to disease."[24] This callous assessment minimized the US government's failure to provide adequate medical care to tribal communities; it also suggested a correlation between Indigenous people's poor health and adherence to traditional lifeways.

In another example of this line of thinking, in reference to an investigation of trachoma rates on the White Earth Reservation in Minnesota during which it was found that of 1,323 Indian people examined, 272, or 20.56 percent, had active trachoma infections, Kerr and his assistants reported the following: "Wherever the primitive Indian is found in contact with civilization, childlike in his conception of responsibility, accepting the vices of the white man but eschewing the good things, there the heaviest trachoma infection has been found. On the other hand, the more nearly he approaches the surrounding white population in manner of living, as in the case of the Indians of the Fond du Lac Reservation, there little trachoma is found."[25]

As this report illustrates, the investigators believed that Indigenous behavior held implicit clinical value as a likely predictor of pathology; as Indian people more nearly approached white American norms in comportment, morality, and day-to-day relations, incidences of illness would recede from view. Yet, historian Jean Keller compares rates of illness at off-reservation Indian boarding schools in the school year of 1911–12, and her findings paint a bleak picture of what conditions were like in these supposedly "civilized" environments. In Southern California, the Sherman Institute admitted a significant 36 percent of its demographic body to the infirmary in that year, while 78 percent of the Carlisle Indian School's population was admitted to the institution's infirmary in the same time period. At Haskell Institute in Lawrence, Kansas, that number climbed to 92 percent.[26] Consequently, Keller argues, cultivating and maintaining a healthy institutional population increasingly occupied boarding school superintendents, replacing "assimilation" as the sole goal of these environments.[27] As Keller suggests, the indoctrination of Indian people proceeded for decades without consideration for the physical, mental, or spiritual well-being of boarding school enrollees. McBride also observes that "systemic neglect contributed to students' poor health [at boarding school]. [Dr. Joseph] Murphy's inspections of Carlisle, Sherman, and Haskell made him ponder if the nation 'had not been guilty of criminal negligence' at these institutions."[28] Historian Mikaëla Adams similarly notes that in 1918, over a third of Haskell's population fell ill with a particularly virulent strain of influenza and was hospitalized, with more than seventeen enrollees dying from this epidemic.[29] As these examples demonstrate, boarding school environments—ostensibly civilized spaces—were hotbeds of contagious disease, a lethal consequence of Indian Service officials' indifference to Indigenous health.

By the time Kerr, Clark, and Schereschewsky issued their findings, US officials had long promoted the idea that Indigenous "uplift" could only be accomplished with the guidance of white Americans—a notion that was reflected in the 1913 report, as well. In the first recommendation of a twelve-point list of changes to be made in the interest of bettering health conditions on Indian reservations, the investigators wrote, "Improvement in [economic status] is necessarily directed toward causing the Indian to become self-supporting so that at all times his food supply will be regular and sufficient." "The Indian, therefore," the recommendation continued, "should have closer and more practical supervision and encouragement in the tilling of his land and the raising of his crops."[30]

The suggestion validated white intervention into Indigenous affairs (or what Elizabeth Esch has described as "white managerialism") and reflected the idea that the cultivation of agricultural land and crops would be critical to the improvement of Indigenous health—a well-worn trope promoted in boarding school curricula, as well. In the authors' last recommendation, they stated, "The physicians to the Indians should be so organized as to insure adequate medical and sanitary supervision."

That medical intervention came last in the report's recommendation of ways to improve health outcomes revealed a seeming paradox; labor, rather than medicine, would be the cure for Indigenous illness.[31] White intervention into Indigenous affairs already permeated virtually every aspect of life on the reservation and had often failed to improve health outcomes, economic status, or living conditions among tribal nations. As these and similar OIA efforts illustrate, health took work. For Indian people, health would be the reward for hard work and obeisance to white authority.

The prevailing notion among US officials that Indian people were idle or somehow averse to productivity was both incorrect and rooted in an ongoing settler desire for Indigenous labor. In one example of the fundamental importance of communal labor to Indigenous cosmologies, the Ojibwe of Minnesota continue to harvest wild rice, or manoomin, in the late summer months; manoomin is regarded as a sacred food and is inherent to their creation story. In a similar vein, seasonal rhythms of harvesting, periods of abundance, and traditional gender and kinship roles are reflected in the Choctaw calendar, originally divided into thirteen months that corresponded with phases of the moon. Chafo Iskitini Hvshi, or October, translates to "Little Hunger Month," for instance, while April, or Tek Ihvshi, refers to "Women's Month," in honor of Choctaw women who were regarded as life-givers, and were thus primarily responsible for the nation's agricultural crops.[32] As these few examples illustrate, Indigenous cosmologies reflected and continue to assert the healing, ceremonial, and sacred practice of communal work in accordance with the needs of the People and the rhythm of changing seasons. But because Indigenous practices of labor reflected and reinforced an intimate understanding of their environments and tribes' sacred relationship to the land, these practices were targeted for destruction by settler powers who sought to reconfigure Indigenous lifeways in the image of Euro-American norms.

Beyond the centrality of communal labor to many tribal nations' lifeways, Indigenous labor was also foundational to the establishment of early colonial economies in the United States and, later, to the development of other major American enterprises.[33] As historians Alice Littlefield and Martha C. Knack have observed of the Great Lakes region in the middle of the nineteenth century, "Indians there entered commercial extraction industries, such as fishing and farming, and sold such traditional products as maple sugar and wild rice. Many also sold their labor to non-Indians in logging, railroad construction, copper mining, farm work, shipping, tourism, and domestic labor."[34] Indian women and men entered the US labor economy both voluntarily and as a result of external factors, spurred by shifting colonial power dynamics, the depletion of once-abundant natural resources, and a concerted effort by US officials to eradicate the seasonal rhythms of traditional trading, hunting, and gathering.[35] These efforts were, in some ways, effective; by the last decade of the nineteenth century, the Southern Paiutes relied primarily on participation in the wage labor economy, washing clothes, digging irrigation, and harvesting potatoes and other crops to meet their needs.[36]

Yet, Indigenous people also viewed the wage labor economy as an opportunity for self-reliance, as Wailacki and Concow historian William Bauer Jr. writes of Native peoples' adaptation to shifting economies on the Round Valley reservation in California. As he explains of the Yukis, they "understood the unreliability of government resources and the reality that only by combining job opportunities could they ensure their subsistence."[37] By the 1870s, Round Valley tribes had established migratory patterns that took them away from the reservation to tend flocks, shear sheep, and perform other farm work for white squatters who paid them cash.[38] Rather than demonstrating a resistance to work, the Yukis, like other Indigenous tribes, seized opportunities to supplement inadequate government support with wage work, incorporating new patterns of self-sufficiency into the fabric and rhythms of reservation life.

In subsequent decades, opportunities to earn a cash wage proliferated elsewhere with the establishment of dozens of federal Native American boarding institutions and the expansion of the Outing system in major metropolitan areas, such as Los Angeles, Phoenix, and the San Francisco Bay Area.[39] Historian Kevin Whalen has assiduously described Sherman Indian School enrollees' participation in the Outing system in Southern California and the surrounding region and the ways in which it afforded students from diverse tribal and communal backgrounds an opportunity to secure a semblance of stability in a heterogeneous urban landscape.[40] Despite providing increased opportunities for work, however, expanded employment options for Indian people remained largely menial, and carried punitive connotations in some urban contexts. As Kelly Lytle Hernández has demonstrated, for example, colonial powers used labor as punishment for vagrancy and other infractions. After California was granted statehood in 1850, Hernández explains, one of the first acts the state legislature passed stipulated that Natives could be arrested and imprisoned "on the complaint of any reasonable citizen" and subjected to degrading work designed to expand the infrastructure of a fast-growing Los Angeles.[41]

Despite the fact that Indigenous people had long participated in traditional forms of work as well as Euro-American enterprises and wage labor economies, white officials continued to promote hard work within Indian communities well into the twentieth century as though labor was a foreign concept for Indigenous people. In part, these discourses were informed by renewed efforts within the Indian Office to compel Indian people to become the enthusiastic farmers of land allotted to them under the General Allotment Act and subsequent legislation aimed ultimately at territorial acquisition for white settlement.[42] Much of the land assigned to Indian people under these conditions was inarable or otherwise undesirable and yielded little in the way of subsistence. Nonetheless, Indian commissioners persisted in their characterizations of "unproductive" Indigenous bodies as crude and uncivilized, while making bold pronouncements about what they perceived to be Indian peoples' deficiencies—their laziness and tendency toward waste—along with the need for heightened white intervention. As Indian Commissioner Leupp remarked, for instance, about per capita payments made to Indian people in alignment with treaty obligations, "Many payments are made at such seasons as seriously to interfere with the best interests of the Indians. For example, at one agency the Indians leave their homes in the middle of the planting season and absent themselves for several days in order to draw an annuity of a few dollars; at another they receive their money in the part of the year when they need it least, and, with their usual improvidence, it is gone before severe weather begins."[43] Although Leupp was incensed by what he interpreted as a demonstrated lack of financial acuity among Indian people, his comment affirmed the rightness of US officials' interference into Indian affairs; his words were somewhat reproachful, but he clearly believed that it was officials' duty to increase their oversight and administration of the land, labor, and resources of their Indian "wards."

For Indian people enrolled in Carlisle's training "partnerships," a similar style of "white managerialism" was also a prominent everyday reality. Archival documents about the adult Indian women and men who labored at Ford and the General Hospital reveal how the ideology of medicinal labor served the interests of a white population that sought to manage Indian workers and maintain them at the bottom of the racial and class hierarchy in white America. The historical record attests to the complex realities of Indigenous experience in the private labor sector in an era of increased opportunities to earn a wage. Disciplinary records similarly demonstrate how spaces of labor were significant sites of Indian-white conflict in the early twentieth century, as Indian people sought to achieve their goals and were met with intensified forms of racism, pathologization, and institutionalized white supremacy that they challenged and negotiated in myriad ways. The following pages examine these experiences in greater detail.

"INDIANNESS" AS ILLNESS AND LABOR AS PANACEA: INDIAN MEN AT THE FORD MOTOR COMPANY

In 1915, an article entitled "Ford 'Original Americans'" appeared in the February issue of the *Ford Times*, published monthly by the Henry Ford Motor Company and circulated to would-be consumers. This brief article discussed twenty-five "students," Indian men over twenty-one years of age, who were enrolled at Carlisle under the Outing program as employees at the Ford automobile plant in Highland Park, Michigan, just outside of Detroit (fig. 2.1).[44] The article began by suggesting that the men were still students at Carlisle and, after listing each employee by tribal affiliation, concluded, "These Indian students are splendid types of the Ford workman, and have proved themselves worthy representatives of their alma mater and of the principles which the United States Government has inculcated through its courses."[45] Designating the Carlisle men first as students and later as employees, the article symbolically extended the men's "student" status into the space of the factory. "Ford 'Original Americans'" illustrates how Carlisle and the Ford Motor Company worked together to define the Carlisle men as members of the economic underclass and keep them in a prolonged period of tutelage, which prevented them from exercising full financial independence and individual autonomy as adult workers.[46]

Two years before the US War Department repossessed the Carlisle barracks for use as a wartime hospital, Carlisle superintendent Oscar Lipps established a blacksmithing course as a supplement to Carlisle's vocational training curriculum, an offering that was meant to be a precursor to apprenticeship at Ford. Ostensibly, Indian men could enroll in the blacksmithing course at Carlisle and, having successfully completed it, petition to be nominated for the training school in Detroit—a program that in some ways, at least on paper, duplicated the Carlisle regimen of a half-day split between labor and learning.[47] The arrangement was, in theory, a symbiotic one. According to a 1917 letter to Commissioner Sells detailing the Carlisle-Ford partnership, enterprising Indian men would train first at Carlisle and later at the factory, where they would work an eight-hour day and then, in the evenings, attend courses in mechanical drafting and automobile engineering. The idea was that after completing night school classes and successfully

2.1 Aerial View of Ford Motor Company Highland Park Plant, 1923. 84.1.1660.P.833.34974. From the Collections of The Henry Ford. Gift of Ford Motor Company. Image from the Collections of The Henry Ford.

· ·

demonstrating mechanical competency, the Indian men would be hired outright as Ford employees—and enjoy the "five-dollar day" that became a hallmark of early Fordism and symbolic of Henry Ford's progressivism in the marketplace.[48]

For the Carlisle men, there were very real opportunities to be had by working at the Ford plant. In the sprawling Detroit metropolis, they would have enjoyed relatively increased autonomy over their whereabouts; they were relinquished from the scrutinizing gaze of Carlisle administrators, and they earned far more even at the apprenticeship rate of $2.72 a day than they would have as a farmhand in one of Carlisle's Outing districts.[49] But despite these relative advantages, the training arrangement at Ford could also be highly punitive and infantilizing. Although the Carlisle men had already received preliminary training in automotive mechanics before their arrival at Ford, correspondence suggests that they were enrolled in the "student corps" as apprentices alongside boys and young men between the ages of twelve and fifteen.[50] It is not difficult to imagine how this arrangement might have been humiliating, given that the mandatory age for graduation from the apprenticeship school was eighteen, an age which most of the Carlisle men had far surpassed by the time of their transfer to Ford.[51] By maintaining the Indian men in this liminal, unnecessary apprenticeship status and preventing them from being promoted to regular workers, the company thus avoided paying higher wages to the Indian mechanics and reified the discriminatory employment practices that typified Indigenous laborers' experiences in this era.

The racial overtones of the arrangement were clear. Because most Ford workers could be adequately trained in under two days, few jobs required extensive periods of apprenticeship—a fact that suggests that the blacksmithing course at Carlisle would have been more than enough to prepare the Indian men for work as regular laborers at the factory.[52] As factory work became more routinized and deskilled, Ford was able to bypass the problems associated with a labor force in which nearly 40 percent of its workers did not speak English, and the introduction of the assembly line in 1913 would eventually increase productivity on an unprecedented scale, revolutionizing mass production around the world (fig. 2.2).[53] Indeed, the rapidity with which Ford could train new workers has been described as one of Henry Ford's greatest contributions to American industry and mass production. The Indian men's prolonged trainee status thus would have added a dimension of infantilization, along with that of the mandatory attendance in mechanical drafting courses alongside boys in their late adolescence and early teenage years, and contributed to what some of the Indian men described in letters of correspondence as a racially hostile work environment.[54]

Georgios Loizides similarly describes how labor at the factory was assigned on the basis of race, so that Ford's "Americanization" project was also necessarily an exercise in racial stratification within the laboring population. American Indian workers are absent from Loizides's discussion, but his analysis of race relations at Ford illustrates the dynamics that the Carlisle men navigated while working in Motor City. As Loizides explains, managerial policies at Ford were predicated on racist conceptualizations of differing physical ability, so that racial hierarchies were reinforced within the theoretically democratic factory—a space populated by interchangeable laboring bodies.[55] Anti-Black racism at Ford was an ugly affair, as indicated by the type of labor assigned to Black laborers: "Whether relegated to the Foundry department or not," Loizides writes, "Black workers were given the worst jobs."[56] Moreover, Esch makes the forceful claim that Ford's "'ethos of the assembly line' was put to work in the service of white supremacist ideas and racial-segregationist practices at Ford and via Ford as the company built its self-described empire through the 1930s."[57]

2.2 Magneto Assembly at the Ford Highland Park Plant, 1913. 84.1.1660.P.833.167. From the Collections of The Henry Ford. Gift of Ford Motor Company. Image from the Collections of The Henry Ford.

· ·

In the early years of the twentieth century, Ford's production line was considered by many Americans to be relatively desegregated. Securing a job at Ford was a possibility for European immigrants and men of color, especially Black men, who were otherwise closed out of other spaces of lucrative labor, industrial or otherwise—a fact that historian Kyle T. Mays notes as well.[58] By 1914, Henry Ford himself had promised that all laborers would receive the same compensation for their work—five dollars a day—compensation that would have made jobs at the factory highly appealing to men who had few opportunities to earn similar wages elsewhere.[59] For the same reasons, however, racism was pervasive at the plant. As researcher Robert Mansfield remarked after a visit to the factory in 1926, "Mr. Ford owes a great deal to his negro workers for the work they are willing to do. In other words, he would have a hard time finding white workers enough who would do it and do it so well. I think in Ford's the negroes were doing 'the hardest, roughest, and dirtiest work' in many instances. . . . Young white foremen in charge of some of these men certainly did not think kindly of the work. Only 'n—ers, wops, and dagos' would do it, said one."[60] Historian Frederick Hoxie similarly describes a situation that would have been very familiar to Indian laborers in the early twentieth century; as "[Commissioner of Indian Affairs Robert] Valentine reminded a dissatisfied Colorado beet farmer in 1909, 'If you were hiring white labor to do this work, in all probability you would have to pay them more wages than you do the Indians.'"[61]

Henry Ford is credited with revolutionizing American industry with his five-dollar day, moving assembly line, and Model T (fig. 2.3). But less is known about how Ford's assimilationist agenda toward immigrant and other nonwhite populations intersected with the US Office of Indian Affairs' efforts to "civilize" Indian people. The article featured in the 1915 *Ford Times*, "Ford 'Original Americans,'" demonstrates that intersection; it also gestures toward the ways in which employment at Ford extended the paternalism of the US government over Indian workers by attempting to deny them autonomy and authority over their whereabouts and resources. In some cases, the partnership between Carlisle and Ford appears to have benefited Indian men in material ways. In others, archival evidence demonstrates that the arrangement was an easy way for Ford to extract labor from the Carlisle men, who did not retain full control of their wages. In many instances, archival records show that while white laborers were described as "splendid workmen" for exhibiting ambition, dedication to their work, and attention to detail, Indian men who similarly displayed an excellent work ethic were denied autonomy and respect at the factory. Routinely, Ford overseers attached negative connotations to Indian men's independence in a process that pathologized their bodies and labor and refused them the "upward mobility" that was held out as a reward for hard work and company loyalty.[62]

Letters of correspondence relating to Indian men who worked "out" at Ford document a pattern of pathologization and labor exploitation in Detroit. These records also reflect the peculiar ways in which the ideology of medicinal labor impacted the Indian men's experiences of physical illness. As was the case at Carlisle and back home on the reservation, white officials at Ford also sought to manage ailing Indian bodies—a dynamic that reified the overseers' authority and hearkened back to the hierarchies endemic to the slave plantations and mission systems of earlier eras. In so doing, these factory officials promoted the idea that labor was medicinal and health took work—settler-ableist notions that denied

2.3 Ford Model T Assembly outside the Highland Park Plant, ca. 1914. 84.1.1660.832. From the Collections of The Henry Ford. Gift of Ford Motor Company. Image from the Collections of The Henry Ford.

· ·

Indian people rest, affirmed eugenicist beliefs, and further contributed to punitive practices that exacerbated existing racial inequities for the Indian men at the plant in Highland Park. As the following reveals, however, the discriminatory attitudes of their supervisors did not deter Indian men in their career ambitions, nor in their pursuit of agency and autonomy over their lives.

Grover M. (Pottawatomi)

Grover M. (Pottawatomi) was twenty-three years old when he arrived at the factory in 1915. Like the other Indian men sent to Ford, he would have completed the blacksmithing course at Carlisle and been designated as a student-apprentice upon his arrival in Detroit. As correspondence from the head of Ford's Sociological Department, Mr. Wagstaff, indicates, Grover and the rest of the Carlisle men were enrolled in the trade school during the day while working night shifts. According to a 1916 letter from Wagstaff to Carlisle superintendent Oscar Lipps, the Carlisle men evidently disliked this arrangement and appeared to have successfully avoided it, which highlights how the Indian men experienced greater freedom than they did at Carlisle and less direct oversight while working at Ford: "The Indian boys have been very fortunate in escaping night work but there is no good reason why they should be favored in this respect. We do not concede school work as an excuse as there are day classes for night workers. I have always liked the spirit with which these boys have tackled anything they were put at, and am a little surprised that a brand new one should raise an objection."[63]

By 1916, Grover's file reflects that he was being treated for a venereal disease by a physician at Ford and had chosen not to disclose this information to his supervisor. It is possible that Grover believed he would be dismissed from Ford if his illness was discovered. Venereal diseases carried significant social stigma in this era, and were viewed as physical and moral contagions. As historian Allan Brandt has observed, "Venereal diseases provided a palpable sign of degeneration, as well as a symbol of a more general cultural crisis. . . . Indeed, Progressive physicians were quick to suggest the relationship of social pathology to medicine."[64] Similar beliefs were also reflected in records relating other Carlisle men, including Otto T., discussed below.

Grover was unable to keep the matter of his illness private for long; eventually Wagstaff learned of his physical condition and wrote Lipps to that effect. In reply, Lipps mused that Grover's condition might be explained by inborn characteristics of racial admixture, and he encouraged Wagstaff to discipline Grover in whatever manner he saw fit: "If you feel that it is necessary to send him away," Lipps explained, "do not consider our feelings regarding the matter. While a student here, Grover was a good sort of a fellow and seemed to be interested in his work. However he shows traces of a poor quality of white blood and very little, if any, of Indian blood and it may be his present low inclinations are the result of the lack of good family and early training."[65]

Wagstaff agreed; he similarly attributed Grover's illness to heredity. As he explained to Lipps, "Our factory medical department sent [Grover] to the hospital because treatment did not progress favorably while he was working, swollen conditions interfering. . . . He has always worked along willingly and I think should be given a further chance. We can't blame him if he was unfortunate in his selection of parents. His experience will likely be a lesson to the other boys."[66] Echoing eugenicist discourses such as that published by Madison Grant in the same year, Grover's "bad blood," according to Lipps and Wagstaff, undermined his racial and social betterment at the factory.[67] However, the two men felt that Grover should be given another chance, expressing a belief in the idea that poor heredity could be overcome with hoe handle medicine: hard work and white oversight.

Grover's second chance was short-lived, for in January 1917, he was up for dismissal once more, his physical health again being called into question. As the head of Ford's Educational Department, G. W. Griswold, wrote to Lipps, "We are pulling this man's record as a quit. He has been absent for about two months, claiming to have been due to eye trouble. Examination by our Medical Department a month ago, failed to reveal any particular cause for this trouble. . . . We do not feel that he sufficiently appreciates a job here to warrant out [sic] taking the matter up with him and are consequently pulling his record as a quit."[68] A month and a half later, however, Griswold withdrew this threat. On February 28, 1917, he again wrote Lipps, this time with a change of heart: "This young man on presenting further proof to our Medical Department that he has been physically unable to work, was given one last chance and is being reinstated to the Student's Course." Grover's illness, likely trachoma, had been "proven," and in the eyes of Grover's supervisors, this legitimized his continued employment and perhaps even necessitated it, as the Fordist ethos promoted the curative and assimilationist effects of labor on all nonwhite, noncitizen factory employees. As a *Ford Times* article from 1916 entitled "Real Ownership" put it, "Do you want Health? Work for it."[69] In another example, that same year, a *Ford Times* article entitled "Doing Nicely, Thank You!" suggested that hard work could be a kind of salve for Indian people: "Mr. A. B. Hutto is one of the native Indians who are working as agricultural instructors among their own people . . . and he has found the Ford car an able assistant in the work of redeeming the Indian through labor."[70]

By the time Griswold wrote Lipps in February 1917, Grover was twenty-five years old—well past being considered appropriately "school-aged" by the Office of Indian Affairs. In a reflection of this reality, his "Outing" card shows that he was dropped from the Carlisle rolls on January 3, 1917; as a handwritten note remarked of his dismissal, "Did not behave himself. Have not been able to keep track of him."[71] Evidently, Grover refused subordination at the hands of Carlisle officials; as an adult, he was far beyond the disciplinary grasp of Carlisle authorities and was capable of directing his own life. Despite these facts, however, Griswold sought to maintain authority over the factory worker: he suggested to Lipps that Grover's reinstatement at Ford should come with the caveat that he be reenrolled as a Carlisle student—and forced to remit a portion of his pay back to Lipps, "as is done with the other boys."[72]

In addition to reflecting the belief that the Indian men were incapable of transacting their own affairs, Griswold's proposition also presumed the Carlisle men's status as wards of the United States government, which further legitimized their inequitable treatment while working at the factory. Grover's reinstatement at Carlisle enabled Carlisle and Ford officials to maintain control over his resources and mobility while at Ford, an arrangement that would have aligned with Carlisle's policy of requiring all enrollees—regardless of age—to remit a portion of their Outing wages back to the institution. Other arrangements similarly illustrate the ways in which officials at Carlisle, Ford, and the Indian Office reinforced institutional paternalism and authority over the Indian men. George M. (Kiowa) for instance, was twenty-three years old when Lipps threatened to write George's "commanding officer" at Ford over a ten-dollar debt he allegedly owed Carlisle.[73]

In another example, in 1917 or 1918, Ford worker Andrew B. (Oneida) was approximately twenty-two years old when he was made to sign an "Agreement" between himself and the Carlisle Indian School—an agreement that was typewritten on US Department of the Interior letterhead. In signing the document, Andrew "agreed" that "it is quite necessary also that the Ford Motor Co. suspend or expel boys of ill repute, in order that we keep a clean industrial supply of boys. Those who have weaker characters will go from bad to worse and drag down those who otherwise would make good." The "Agreement" went on to explain that in such instances, "It might be well to recall him to [Carlisle] for discipline, placing a more desirable boy in his position, or it might be well to reprimand him, whereas in severe cases he should be expelled at once, however, his wages should be retained in order to meet any debts that might appear." Another stipulation of employment at Ford contended that "Indian youths have not the knowledge of spending money in legitimate ways, therefore, it seems necessary that they be guided in their savings."[74] As these documents illustrate, Carlisle superintendents, Ford supervisors, and US officials supported one another in maintaining the Indian workers in the subordinate status of dependent wardship, an arrangement that was legitimated by discourses about Indian peoples' lesser abilities and supposedly inborn characteristics of idleness, criminality, or thriftlessness.

Many of the Indian men who sought employment at Ford did not view themselves as students, apprentices, or youths in need of such patronizing oversight. In fact, as a 1916 letter from Lipps to commissioner of Indian Affairs Cato Sells reflects, Indian men had been increasingly inquiring into the possibility of enrollment at Carlisle expressly for the purpose of obtaining meaningful work at Ford: "The inquiries," Lipps explained, "are a result of an offer that has recently been made to a number of young men thru Supervisor Dagenett's office in Washington and are from young men who have been in attendance at this and other nonreservation schools. In the majority of cases they are over 21 years of age."[75] In response to this increased interest in factory work, Lipps's correspondence further indicates that he sought "general authority" from the Indian Office for the enrollment of Indian men "over 21 years of age and . . . those who are more than 24 years of age if it is shown that they are taking our preparatory course for work in an automobile and other manufacturing establishments where special instruction is a part of the work that is given."[76] Indeed, it appears that Sells did grant "general authority," because by 1916, twenty-five Indian men were working "out" at Ford.[77]

Other letters of correspondence reflect that Indian men sought work at the Highland Park plant for a variety of reasons—some complicated, others seemingly straightforward. In 1917 a twenty-two-year-old Mescalero man and former Carlisle enrollee named Pablo H., discussed in the introduction, wrote to Lipps to ask his advice. Pablo's letter illustrates how some men viewed opportunities for work via Carlisle or Dagenett's office pragmatically: as a means to earn a wage and help one's family. Pablo's letter reflects that after leaving his position as disciplinarian at the Greenville Indian School, he took up a job in Prescott, Arizona, as a clerk at the Head Hotel. But, as Pablo explained to the Carlisle superintendent, "owing to certain conditions at home, I am compelled to go to work again; I am here at presscott [sic] Ariz [sic] working and waiting for a good opening." Pablo continued, "If you happen to hear of a place as Disciplinarian, please see if you can get me in. I think that if I can get a place as Assistant in Phoenix or other place I can attend night school. . . . If I do not enter the service I would like to go to the Ford Factory if I can get in."[78]

As reflected by this letter, Pablo sought more lucrative opportunities due to "certain"—perhaps diminished—circumstances back home on the reservation. His letter similarly indicates how some former Carlisle enrollees cultivated and maintained enduring relationships with Carlisle superintendents, as well as the ways in which many former enrollees were acutely aware of—and sought to leverage—the power and authority Carlisle officials could wield. In fact, Charles Dagenett (Peoria) was himself a former Carlisle enrollee, having been appointed under Commissioner Leupp to the position of Supervisor of Employment within the Office of Indian Affairs. In 1905, Dagenett had established the original agreement with Ford for the training and employment of other ambitious Indian men across the country, many of whom used work at the factory to improve their lives and the living conditions of their loved ones back home.[79]

A letter written to Lipps by David B., a twenty-three-year-old Eastern Cherokee man who was working at Ford in 1916, reflects the use of factory labor as a means of familial aid. David explained, "I received a letter from home the other day asking me for a little so I would be very thankful if you would send them on to [my father] Jeff [A—.] twenty five dollars as they said they need the money. If you require that I make that amount up again I will be only to [sic] glad to do so."[80] In reply, Lipps wrote, "I have your letter saying that you want to give Twenty Five Dollars to your home people. I am always glad when the boys want to help the folks at home. This shows a step in the right direction." Lipps's response offers a glimpse into moments of understanding with the Carlisle men, while illuminating how Indian Service officials could look favorably on those who used their earnings to improve the circumstances of their families. As historian Douglas Miller has similarly pointed out, Indian laborers were not "hapless victims"; many seized on wage work in urban settings as a means to secure their economic futures.[81] Indeed, the Indian workers at Ford may be viewed as among the first cohort of Indian people, prior to the formalized federal Indian policy of relocation in the 1940s and 1950s, to venture away from the reservation to metropolitan centers in search of better opportunities.[82]

For men like Grover, Pablo, or David, then, labor at the Ford factory was often an expression of self-sufficiency—expressions that were sometimes met with unnecessary oversight and periods of tutelage that diminished autonomy over their whereabouts, resources, and wages. As another Indian worker's experience reveals, labor at Ford could also duplicate the punitive connotations of manual labor at Carlisle, as Carlisle officials used the factory as a place in which Indian men could be disabused of "undesirable" traits as if those characteristics were pathologies to be eradicated.

In 1913, a twenty-year-old Chippewa man named Otto T. was being considered for expulsion from Carlisle after having contracted syphilis. As Carlisle's physician smugly reported, "I regret to report that Otto T— is afflicted with primary syphilis. Joseph S— presented himself this morning with a glorious dose of gonorrhoea [sic]."[83] Joseph was slated for expulsion and fled the institution before receiving punishment, but Otto was not as fleet-footed. As Superintendent Lipps wrote to Walter Dickens, Indian agent to the Red Lake Agency, "In view of the fact that Otto's condition is a menace to the other students as well as of undesirable moral influence I would thank you to advise me at once how you can co-operate with me to effect his return home. If he has any funds to his credit with you it may be possible to arrange so that he can be placed in some Hospital for treatment." In response, Dickens objected, "Otto has no funds on deposit to his credit at this Agency. He has an uncle within the Cross Lake District, but this man has no funds either, and I am entirely at a loss to know what to advise in the premises. As you know we have no hospital at the Red Lake Agency though we anticipate the construction of one during the current fiscal year. Could not this young man be placed in some of the sanatoriums throughout the United States?"[84] Otto was passed off both by Carlisle officials and those back home; he was being considered for confinement in a sanatorium. Instead, however, he was placed under the "Outing" and then subsequently at Ford, illustrating the ways in which officials viewed the factory as an assimilationist, disciplinary space.

Once in Detroit, Otto was determined to use the avenues available to him to improve his employment outlook—efforts at independence and autonomy that landed him in hot water with his Ford supervisors, despite being aligned with the stated aims of the Carlisle-Ford training partnership. According to a 1917 letter sent from Griswold to C. V. Peel, Carlisle's acting superintendent in the absence of Lipps, Otto was often absent from the apprentice's course in which he was enrolled at Ford, due to taking a commercial course in an automotive school in downtown Detroit. As punishment for this chronic truancy, Griswold thus resolved to "hold up" Otto's timecard in order to force him to attend Ford's night classes. As Griswold explained to Peel,

> We told him that we would give him another chance providing he would promise to present himself each and every time he was served with a notice to come to class unless he had some further good reason for being absent. He has refused to comply with our request and stated that he would just as soon have a job somewhere else, that the Ford Student Course did not mean much to him.
>
> In view of his attitude we arranged to hold his card up until such time as he would comply with instructions. If he does not comply . . . we will pull his card as a quit. We suggest that in co-operating with us, you refrain from sending him any money until such time as the case has been finally disposed of.[85]

Griswold viewed Otto's ambitions as threatening; Otto's enrollment in an advanced course in automotive mechanics, outside the purview of Ford oversight, represented a rejection of his assigned role as unskilled laborer at the factory. Otto's aim of becoming an expert mechanic similarly rejected Ford's efforts to decouple factory work from intellectual labor, and in an attempt to force Otto to limit his goals, Griswold again suggested that Carlisle withhold financial resources from the Indian men.[86]

In the following weeks, Otto sent his own letters of appeal, detailing the disagreement with Griswold—evidently younger than Otto, who was then twenty-two—from his perspective. As indicated by a letter sent from Otto to Lipps in early January 1917 (reproduced in the appendix), Otto believed that as a Carlisle man, the school should be inclined to assist him in his difficulties while working "out" at Ford. As he explained to Lipps, "You cannot understand the cause of my release from the students' course until Mr. Griswold explains it to you because I never stated in the telegram. . . . I was called up to the office of Mr. Griswold on the 5th of January. He then commenced to ask me why I don't attend the students' meeting held every day up at the Educational Dept." He continued,

> I told some of the reasons why I can't go every meeting. He commenced to say some of the things that I didn't feel like hearing which is as follows:
> "There are five hundred men behind you, looking for a chance to get in the factory as students; waiting for you to get out if you don't follow the rules of the students' course.
> "Don't you know that it is the only reason why you are working for the Ford Motor Company is simply because you are a student, there is nothing else."[87]

In pleading his case, Otto explained that he was determined to learn about the different makes of cars, taking advantage of his location in the heart of the burgeoning automobile industry, so that he could better his chances at securing gainful employment—a fact that Griswold resented. Otto went on to explain that he sought this additional training because he felt that the education he received at Carlisle and at Ford was inadequate: "A student finishing the course in the Ford factory does not know much about automobile[s]. Think of the many different kinds of cars. A man willing to run a garage business want to be able to handle any car that comes to his shop besides Ford car. To do this a man must have training in the place where they teach the automobiles in the proper way. My next step is this. The only thing I will ask from the school is to send all my money, and let us see what I can do in the automobile world."[88] He closed, "I really thought that there is [no] use for me to stay with a company where they offer no encouragement, after

I learned the opinion of Mr. Griswold toward the Indian students. But you know that yourself, when a man has a little office and some authority, that he would talk as though he is going to run over that fellow he is talking to, and this was the case of this young man when he didn't give me sufficient time to reason with him."[89]

Otto was denied autonomy over his own earnings, and he returned to Ford's student course to finish his certification. But correspondence dated a mere two weeks later reflects that Ford transferred Otto to the assembly plant in Chicago—a solution possibly devised as a way to avoid further disputes between Otto and Griswold.[90] Some of the last documents contained in Otto's file reflect that he was no longer considered a member of the Outing and was, in his words, on his "own way." But after being released from the gaze of Griswold and Carlisle officials, the balance he had on deposit at the bank in Carlisle was transferred to Ford's Educational Department at the Chicago plant—a fact that suggests that he was not unconditionally granted independence from his liminal apprentice and student status. Otto's experiences of subordination, self-advocacy, and resistance showcase the obstacles Indian men encountered at Ford; similarly, his letters register his broad awareness of the structures of supremacy he negotiated as a Chippewa man, while also reflecting his sheer determination to direct the outcome of his life.[91]

In a similar vein, correspondence related to Carlisle enrollee and Ford worker Joe Gilman (Ojibwe) reveals the many ways in which white managerialism extended into the lives of even those Indian men who far exceeded the racialized expectations of US officials and employment supervisors (fig. 2.4). In 1915, Gilman, who had earned notoriety for his record-breaking assembly of a Model T (two hours and fifty minutes), wrote to Lipps to ask for assistance in accessing some of his earnings. "I am going to ask you for a 'Recommendation,'" Gilman explained, "in regards to my work, my habits, my general conduct, and ability to make proper use of my funds, etc. I have some money at Leech Lake agency and I have put in a request for Three hundred Dollars ($300.00) for the purpose of getting furniture."[92] As demonstrated by his request, Gilman needed Lipps to attest to his financial responsibility so that the agent at Leech Lake would release his earnings, which he intended to use in order to make a home for himself and his wife, Lydia, whom he had recently married. In reply, Lipps agreed to write the recommendation—and stated that he would be closing out Gilman's account at Carlisle, as well.[93] Although Gilman was twenty-three years old, had achieved superior mechanical abilities, and was newly married—a status that was used to measure Indigenous adherence to white norms—the Indian agent required Gilman to seek a recommendation from Carlisle's superintendent in order to access his own earnings. Lipps provided the recommendation and released Gilman's funds from institutional administration, but it is hard to imagine a scenario in which the same would be required of a white man of comparable age and achievement.[94] Joe's and Otto's differing experiences of financial independence and presumed wardship similarly demonstrate the paradoxes, contradictions, and inconsistencies that Indian workers faced while navigating bureaucratic and paternalistic structures of oversight.

Ford officials operationalized a logic of Indigenous deficiency: in order to achieve their full potential, Indian bodies required hard work conducted under white observation and management. As apprentices, the Indian men occupied a liminal status; they were neither regular employees nor entirely students, and they were promoted only after officials' recommendations. But as regular workers, Indian men continued to be subjected to oversight at the hands of white authority figures, an arrangement that illustrates in stark relief differing expectations for white and Indian laborers. As the above experiences demonstrate, this dynamic of perpetual Indigenous oversight at Ford enhanced and augmented white officials' authority while contributing to inequities for the Carlisle men and other men of color, including immigrants, in Detroit. Although archival records document the ways in which Indian men had varied and heterogeneous experiences in the private labor sector, in many cases these records also reflect a common pattern of unnecessary and inapplicable interference into the lives of Indian workers. These experiences illustrate how the ideology of medicinal labor was complex and contradictory, resulting in practices that often reified white officials' power over Indian workers while spurring Indian men to find creative ways to retain autonomy over their lives. Similarly complex policies, practices, and attitudes impacted the Indian women who worked "out" at the General Hospital.

NURSES-IN-TRAINING: RACE, GENDER, AND LABOR AT THE GENERAL HOSPITAL

As the corollary to the training partnership at Ford, in 1916, Carlisle superintendent Oscar Lipps established a nurse training program at the General Hospital in Lancaster, Pennsylvania, fifty-eight miles east of Carlisle (fig. 2.5). Much like the challenges to individual autonomy encountered by Indian men working at Ford, the arrangement at the General Hospital created similarly fraught dynamics

2.4 Joe Gilman (Chippewa) and wife Lydia Douglas in 1915. Some Indian men like Joe enrolled at the Carlisle in order to participate in the training "partnership" at the Ford Motor Company in Detroit. In 1916, Gilman set the record for the fastest-ever build of Ford's Model T, clocking in at two hours and fifty minutes. "Joe Gilman Student File," photograph, 1915, National Archives and Records Administration, RG 75, series 1327, box 98, folder 4290. Image courtesy of the Carlisle Indian School Digital Resource Center, Dickinson College, Carlisle, Pennsylvania.

. . . .

for the Indian women who lived and worked on the ward. While there, those in training were expected to perform general caretaking labor at the hospital and were evaluated by the head nurse, Miss Taylor, according to gender-specific criteria about proper conduct. Documents relating to Ozetta B. and Emerald B., two young women who trained at the General Hospital in 1916, demonstrate how hospital supervisors similarly assumed disciplinary authority over the Indian women under their oversight. As was the case at the Ford factory in Highland Park, institutionalized racism and inequitable power structures created formidable obstacles for Indian women striving to attain nursing certification. In the regimented space of the hospital ward, medicinal labor took on a very literal connotation: not only would the Indian women receive Westernized medical instruction; it was hoped that they would go on to practice this kind of medicine in their own communities.[95] This arrangement thus was intended to serve the dual purposes of replacing traditional Indigenous healing practices with Western protocols and creating a new generation of Indigenous medical practitioners within their

2.5 A postcard of the General Hospital in Lancaster, Pennsylvania, ca. 1915. From the author's personal collection.

own communities—a complex dynamic that Clifford Trafzer has described as "medical colonialism."[96] As was the case with the Indian men who worked at Ford, the Indian women who lived and labored at the General Hospital did not accept the ideology of hoe handle medicine unquestioningly.

The Carlisle women admitted to the General Hospital's program would have been expected to perform general caretaking tasks on the ward and study training manuals or other medical literature under the tutelage of a head nurse or physician in charge—a standard program of study in nurse training programs across the United States. Few materials have been preserved about the specific routines expected of the Indian women in Lancaster, but a pamphlet for the German Hospital in Brooklyn, New York, which also accepted some Carlisle women into its program, offers insight into what a typical course of instruction offered. Aspiring nurses in Brooklyn were trained in elementary physiology, hygiene, domestic economy, and the foundations of the profession, including bacteriology, the proper cleansing and bandaging of wounds, the administration of anesthesia, and the prevention of communicable diseases.[97] The nurse trainees would have also been assigned individual shifts, lasting roughly nine hours, and expected to ad-here to a strict code of behavioral and professional conduct. In exchange for their care of patients, the women received room and board, laundry services, textbooks when required, and uniforms. Personal time for rest and recreation was limited to part or all of Sunday, and perhaps one other afternoon during the week. Under ideal circumstances, the women were told that they would emerge from their training with certification in nursing. Certification in hand, they would thus be eligible to undertake a civil service exam and secure a coveted position in an in-creasingly critical field as the United States entered the First World War.

In Lancaster, two Carlisle women—Ozetta B. and Emerald B.—found them-selves in an arrangement similar to the one described above.[98] In addition to the standard oversight that was a component of any nurse training program, however, the women in Lancaster faced strict scrutiny by Head Nurse Taylor, as well as Carlisle's Outing matron, Lida M. Johnston, who made regular visits to the hospi-tal to check in on their progress. Implicitly and explicitly, these visits were meant to ensure that the women were progressing racially as well as professionally, thus duplicating the same kind of racialized surveillance that Carlisle enrollees en-dured while living on institutional grounds.

During one of Johnston's visits, in 1916, it was revealed that Nurse Taylor had punished Ozetta (Pottawatomi), who was nearly twenty-one years old, for what was perceived as an inexcusable breach of behavioral expectations. At issue was the fact that Ozetta had her photographs made—an offense that was viewed as serious enough to be reported to Carlisle superintendent Oscar Lipps. Indeed, as a letter from Lipps to Ozetta reflects, he too did not consider the infraction to be a small one; her reputation, he explained in coded terms, would be perma-nently marred as a result. As he wrote to Ozetta, "I am sorry to have to file with your permanent record here at the school, the report and photographs of you which Miss Johnston [the Outing Matron] has given to me. Neither I am sorry to say, is a very great credit to you."[99]

Given the times, the photographs in question (figs. 2.6 and 2.7) underscored Ozetta's relative independence and indifference to the gendered dicta of the era. In particular, one of the photographs (fig. 2.7) might have been interpreted as being suggestive of a relationship between two women in an era in which homosexuality was viewed as a psychiatric disorder. Coupled with the fact that the domestic, mar-riage, and kinship relations of Indian people were sites of ongoing conflict at this time, Ozetta's photographs would have documented a challenge to the domestic teachings of the era as well.[100] As K. Tsianina Lomawaima has argued, federal Indian boarding school curricula sought to inculcate Indigenous women like Ozetta into Victorian-era dictates of chastity and feminine "decency"—dictates that Indigenous enrollees found clever ways to resist.[101] In one example of the subtle and overt ways Indian girls and women refused these teachings, Lomawaima recounts a "bloomer story" told by Maureen, a fourteen-year-old Choctaw girl who was enrolled at the Chilocco Indian School in 1931. As Maureen explained, "We wore gray sateen bloomers and black cotton stockings and GI [government-issued] shoes the first year I was up there. Well, when we went to the dances, we could wear what we called 'home clothes' [the personal clothes that the girls brought from home], but if we put home clothes on over those big old sateen bloomers, it looked terrible."[102] Maureen went on, "So all the girls hated that and some of them would get brave. . . . They pulled their home pants on and then put their bloomers over them so when we had inspection . . . we'd raise our dresses and show we had our bloomers on. Then when we'd get out of the building we'd pull those bloomers off."[103] In a similar vein, Ozetta's photographs document a playful but powerful rejection of the gender norms to which she was meant to be assimilating.

In the first image (fig. 2.6), Ozetta's posturing rebels against the demure self-styling expected of women in the early twentieth century. Her pants alone would have been a fashionable statement of defiance in any context, but as a nurse, her choice of clothing additionally bucked the expectation that she dress in the sober cap and gown that marked her as an aspiring, chaste, and moral member of the profession. Her crisp, white pants and shirt mirrored the aesthetically sterile environment of the hospital, but it was improperly masculine—intentionally so—and thus a radical refusal of the gendered hierarchy to which she was subjected as a nurse-in-training and, above all, as an Indian woman. In the second image (fig. 2.7), Ozetta leans against an unidentified friend who is dressed in attire that would have been considered more properly feminine. Reaching her hand in through the heavy cape that adorns her companion's narrow shoulders, it is difficult to tell whether Ozetta extends her arm in a hug or embraces her friend at her waist; her forearm disappears into the folds of her companion's cape, and along with it, the viewer's satisfaction of knowing where her hand has landed. While there are many aspects of the photograph that could potentially raise the objections of Ozetta's supervisors—the sheer audacity of having her photograph made being one of them—it is also possible that the opacity of the women's relationship was

2.6 "Ozetta B—., ca. 1916." National Archives and Records Administration, RG 75, series 1327, box 106, folder 4506. Image courtesy of the Carlisle Indian School Digital Resource Center, Dickinson College, Carlisle, Pennsylvania.

2.7 "Ozetta B—. and Unidentified Female, ca. 1916." National Archives and Records Administration, RG 75, series 1327, box 106, folder 4506. Image courtesy of the Carlisle Indian School Digital Resource Center, Dickinson College, Carlisle, Pennsylvania.

the greatest offense of all, along with the obvious pleasure that they derived from being in one another's company.

These fleeting moments of joy between Ozetta and her companion, captured in the medium of photography, register multiple refusals. The images suggest a degree of privacy stolen by the two women, and because surveillance was a constant reality for Indian enrollees at Carlisle and other boarding institutions, Ozetta's enjoyment of herself away from the prying eyes of authority figures would have been an exceptional, and threatening, moment of relative freedom. As Cutcha Risling Baldy (Hupa, Yurok, Karuk) points out, US officials have historically monitored the most intimate aspects of Indian girls' and women's lives—including their monthly menstrual cycles—guided by the belief that Indian people and their children were more prone to sexual activity that needed to be regulated.[104] Lipps's letter to Ozetta similarly demonstrates a vested interest in the regulation of Indian women's sexualities, even from afar. After receiving the complaint from Nurse Taylor with Ozetta's photos enclosed, Lipps wrote to her to remind her that he had the power to destroy her good name along with her chances for gainful employment. "The record you are making now," he explained, "will count either in your favor or against you when you apply for work in the future . . . so you see how very important it is that you watch every action of yours and make your record clean every day."[105]

At a time when photography was becoming more accessible to the general public, Ozetta's images—taken in private but made public by the head nurse—disrupted what cultural historian Laura Wexler has called the settler-national "domestic sublime" or the "ideal of domestic peace" that photographic technologies promoted, created, and maintained in turn-of-the-twentieth-century America.[106] Indeed, not long before Ozetta had her photographs made, Carlisle founder Richard Henry Pratt enlisted photographer John Choate to document the civilizational progress being made at the institution, which further illustrates the potency of the photographic medium in the Carlisle context.[107] To Lipps, the photographs thus provided documentary evidence that Ozetta was "unclean," a pathologizing word with significant racial overtones, especially for an Indian woman pursuing her nursing license. Given these facts, Ozetta's co-optation of this colonial technology was subversive—a refusal of the "regulatory violence" that Tanana Athabascan scholar Dian Million has described in the context of settler surveillance.[108] Similarly, Lipps's confiscation of Ozetta's photographs demonstrates how powerful and threatening the images were as artifacts that enabled Ozetta to identify herself as "the interlocutor of [her] own experience" beyond the gaze of the white authority figures who sought to control her.[109] Reclaiming the photographic medium as a source of pleasure and power, Ozetta's images threatened Lipps's settler logic of Indigenous deficiency and medicinal labor, while making loud claims to Indigenous authorship.[110] Other archival records reflect that Ozetta was a strong and capable nurse, who was determined to secure a position in the civil service. At the conclusion of her nurse training program, however, Ozetta made the decision to travel to her brother's home in Sharon, Oklahoma, to care for her sister-in-law, who was very ill. "I am sure if I can be of any help to them," she explained to Lipps of her decision, "I am willing to give up my plans for working in Lancaster [in the Outing program] this summer. My brother is in a position where he cannot be with [his wife] all the time, and there is no one whom they really can depend on. I feel I would not be doing right to refuse to go when I can go."[111] Soon after putting her nursing skills to the test, Ozetta's sister-in-law improved, and Ozetta made arrangements to take the civil service exam. As she wrote in a letter to Lipps on June 29, 1916 (reproduced in the appendix), "I expect to go to New Mexico on a visit to my father in August some time. And would like to start work in September, if such can be the arrangements. I will be ready to take them [the exams] about the middle of July or any time the arrangements can be made."[112] Much like her photographs, Ozetta's words reflect an independent and confident young woman who was determined to succeed—characteristics that were somewhat incongruous with the expectations and limitations white officials placed upon her and other Indian women in this era.[113]

Documents relating to the punishment of eighteen-year-old Emerald (Chippewa), a nurse-in-training along with Ozetta, reveal other gendered dimensions of the Indian women's experiences at the General Hospital, and they show how feminine ideals intersected with dominant ideas about race and labor in profound ways. At twenty-one and eighteen years of age, respectively, Ozetta and Emerald were adults and thus no longer legally subject to the oversight of Carlisle officials. However, as was the case with the Indian men at Ford, Lipps's authority over Ozetta and Emerald was implicit and could be transferred from one set of institutional authorities to another. Letters of correspondence contained in Emerald's file document the harsh treatment the Indian women received under Nurse Taylor, who assumed disciplinary authority over Ozetta and Emerald as they were removed from one white-dominated space to another. These records also show that this lateral transfer of disciplinary power enabled institutional authority figures to stand together in solidarity over and against the Indian women under their jurisdiction and, through that solidarity, fortify their own racial standing in the institutions of the settler state.

A letter dated May 9, 1916, sent from Carlisle Outing matron Lida Johnston to Lipps, demonstrates how supervisory complaints against Emerald were largely unrelated to her professional abilities, and were instead about Emerald's obvious rejection of her subordinate status as an Indian woman. For Emerald, these dynamics created an intolerable atmosphere, which led her to flee the hospital altogether on May 8, the day before Johnston's report was written. After visiting the hospital to investigate the conflict, Johnston reported, "Miss Taylor took charge of the nurses in February of this year. New rules were put into effect. Emerald seemed to resent the new order of things. Whenever a privilege was given her, she took advantage of it and went just a little further. She remained off duty for every little ailment."[114] After detailing Emerald's period of recovery after tonsillitis surgery and subsequent illness and Emerald's apparent unwillingness to follow the doctor's order to take bed rest—another gendered remedy that differed from Indian men's experiences of illness at the Ford factory—Johnston continued, "Miss Taylor further reports that Emerald had a pleasant cheery disposition and was well liked by the patients. As a nurse she was a hard worker—was not a loafer, but she was not thorough. She was inclined to slick things over. She spent money freely, had too many clothes, was the best dressed girl in the institution, was always receiving boxes by express, flowers, etc."[115] As Johnston's report reveals, Nurse Taylor felt that Emerald was a competent nurse and well-liked by her patients, but she resented her expensive tastes. In the tightly regimented space of the hospital ward, Indian women, evidently, were not allowed to hold the title of "best dressed."

Like Ozetta, Emerald was regarded as a hard worker and capably performed her duties. She had demonstrated her abilities as a nurse and was well on her way to achieving professional certification—accomplishments that appeared, at least on paper, to align with the OIA's views of the "benefits" of labor for Indian people. Despite these evident successes, however, Emerald remained in poor standing with her supervisor, which illustrates the paradoxes inherent to the Indigenous women's circumstances. In many ways, it is hard to tell whether Nurse Taylor wanted Emerald to succeed in her training, or whether she wanted to compel Emerald to accept her "proper" place on the ward at the bottom of the hospital's social hierarchy. The letters and reports that Emerald's supervisors exchanged described a young Indian woman who took pride in her appearance and work performance, but whose personal conduct was misaligned with the demeanor of obeisance that Nurse Taylor, Lida Johnston, and other authority figures believed Emerald should exhibit. As a result, Emerald soon found herself under intensified scrutiny as she went about her work—leaving little time to participate in the "leisure culture" and opportunities to socialize, which, as Jacobs has discussed, enticed some young Indigenous women to take up jobs in major metropolitan cities.[116] It is evident, however, that Emerald was serious about finishing her training and embraced the opportunity; as she wrote to Johnston on June 4, 1915, shortly before beginning her training at the hospital, "I received a letter from Miss Wardell of the Lancaster hospital and I am to report for duty Sept. 1st '15 . . . I am so anxious to enter as it means so much to me."[117]

Letters of correspondence exchanged between institutional authorities additionally reflect that Emerald was subjected to private assessments of character and conduct in much the same way that domestic servants were the subject of Outing patrons' gossip and idle chatter, as described in chapter 1. Yet, Johnston's report also includes details about Emerald's behavior that reveal that she, along with Ozetta, found ways to resist Nurse Taylor's racialized and gendered expectations.

As Johnston's report further elaborated, "After [Emerald's] tonsillitis operation and time was given her to recover, instead of caring for herself she got up and went automobiling. In fact, she went automobiling at every opportunity. The party with whom she went most frequently is a Mr. Hall. I learned that this young man has no definite employment."[118] As seen from this disapproving report, Emerald evaded heightened scrutiny intended to limit her mobility and prevent sexual partnerships from forming, which the act of "automobiling" with Mr. Hall materially and symbolically rejected.[119] On May 8, 1916, the day she fled the hospital, Emerald wrote Lipps: "I feel as tho I have done you a wrong because you have been so good to me. I have been sick on and off for quite a while, Miss Taylor, our Supt. says it is due to my 'running around.' . . . Well I entertained my company once a week," she continued, "and I can hardly see what harm is in that. It agreed with the rules of the hospital. . . . As for Miss Taylor I intend to expose her mistreatment of the nurses. I'll remain here till I receive further orders from you. I'll do anything you wish except return to the hospital and I guess she wouldn't have me now anyway."[120]

Four days later, on May 12, Lipps sent a response that was unforgiving: "I have miss Johnston's report of her visit to you, also your letter. I feel that you have acted very unwisely. You have not lived up to the rules of the Hospital as you should. You have not taken the advice or even orders from your superior officer in the manner you should. You did not consult me but took matters into your own hands and left the Hospital." He continued, "Your chief aim seems to be to have a good time and you are willing to sacrifice your training, your health and your general welfare in other ways, to get this good time."[121] He did not advise, he explained, a return to the hospital; instead, he would send her back to her home, to reside "in the care of [her] own people."[122] In closing, he made it clear that he felt she was ill-suited for nursing, rejecting Emerald's accounting of her actions: "I hope that you will in time see the mistake you have made in not finishing your training at the Lancaster Hospital and I trust that when you have fully regained your health, you may again take up the work in a profession for which you have a natural aptitude."[123] What Lipps thought that profession might be, he did not say, but that was beside the point; Emerald would not be allowed to resume her training, as punishment for "having a good time." Emerald, much like Ozetta, refused to take this hoe handle medicine; and, like other Indian workers who refused subordination to white authority figures, she threatened the many hierarchies—racial, professional, gendered, and classed—in which she was to play a subordinate role.[124]

As demonstrated by the experiences Indigenous labor examined above, Indian women and men were not limited in their ambitions; they actively sought out opportunities for employment, and their punitive experiences illustrate the obstacles they encountered while trying to complete training, obtain meaningful work and labor opportunities, or support their families back home. As I explore in the following chapter, dominant ideas about Indigenous deficiency, pathologization, and limited capacity created conditions that rendered Indian people vulnerable to forced confinement in the many facilities that comprised the settler society's nebulous apparatus. Chapter 3 turns to one such facility—the House of the Good Shepherd in Reading, Pennsylvania—and the experiences of Indigenous women who were confined there after breaching the boundaries of "acceptable" conduct. Chapter 3 also illustrates global dimensions of forced confinement and historical intersections between labor, incarceration, and social reform in the United States—and beyond.

SISTERS MAGDALENE
ENTWINED HISTORIES OF "REFORM" AT GOOD SHEPHERD HOMES

In 1914, at least three young Indigenous women were sent from the Carlisle Indian School to the House of the Good Shepherd in Reading, Pennsylvania, as punishment for various perceived behavioral infractions. In the context of Native American history, the House of the Good Shepherd is a lesser-known facility—characterized in Carlisle superintendents' correspondence as a convent or a reform school—located eighty miles east of Carlisle and in operation under Catholic sisters from 1889 to the early 1970s, when the building was razed.[1] Examining the little-known relationship between Carlisle and the Good Shepherd home, this chapter follows Ojibwe historian Brenda Child's pathbreaking essay in which she asks, "Is the boarding school experience overly remembered? Is it remembered at the expense of other significant events, tragedies, and practices of settler colonialism that also dramatically shaped American Indian people's lives?"[2] At first glance, the relationship between these two ostensibly distinct "schools" is seemingly straightforward: Indigenous girls and women who breached the boundaries of "acceptable" conduct were transferred from Carlisle to the Good Shepherd home to be subjected to individualized "care" under the tutelage of Catholic sisters. Upon closer examination of archival records relating to those who were sent from Carlisle to Reading and who remained there involuntarily for months on end, however, it is evident that the Good Shepherd home was more than an institution of "re-education": it was a carceral place of Indigenous disappearance, and its existence directly benefited the settler society (fig. 3.1).

What might the Indigenous women's experiences of forced confinement in the Reading facility illuminate about the shifting objectives of settler colonialism at the turn of the twentieth century? In answering this question, this chapter argues that the Good Shepherd home and other "reform" institutions played an important, but overlooked, role in the apparatus of the US settler state in the Progressive Era, akin to the role of Magdalene laundries in what historian James Smith refers to as Ireland's "architecture of containment."[3] At stake is a better understanding of the relationship between Carlisle and auxiliary institutions, such as the Good Shepherd home, and the significance of these relationships for

3.1 Postcard of the House of the Good Shepherd in Reading, Pennsylvania, postmarked September 8, 1909. From the author's personal collection.

. . . .

survivors of the US federal boarding school system and their descendants. According to a 2022 US Department of the Interior report, the Good Shepherds also administered at least two federally funded "industrial schools" for Indian people in Denver, Colorado, and Wauwatosa, Wisconsin, in the nineteenth and twentieth centuries.[4] In light of the Interior Department's ongoing federal investigation into the legacy of the boarding school system, it is critical that all institutions that intervened into the lives of Indian people be identified and come under scrutiny. Building on the insights of the previous chapters, this chapter makes the case for expanding discourses about the federal "boarding school system" in the United States to encompass and accommodate settler institutions that do not neatly fit the definition of a "school."

Indigenous people who attended off-reservation boarding schools at the turn of the twentieth century are often regarded, and regarded themselves, as being "away from home"—located in a place far away from and opposed to the condition of being within and among their families and tribal nations. Yet, in addition to recalling experiences "away from home," enrollees' letters of correspondence and remembrances of their time "at school" are frequently marked by experiences of moving from place to place—a phenomenon that disability studies scholars and social scientists refer to as *transinstitutionalization*, or the transfer from one institutional context or locale to another, oftentimes involuntarily.[5] This chapter describes the significance of this pattern within the context of US settler colonialism.[6] Enrollment at Carlisle was often entrance into a rhizomatic network of noneducational settler institutions—a fact further illuminated by the Indigenous women's forced transfer from Carlisle to the Good Shepherd home in the second decade of the twentieth century.

The Good Shepherd Sisters are a French Catholic order infamously associated with Magdalene laundries in Ireland, the purposes of which have been well established. The Good Shepherd Sisters operated facilities that served similar carceral objectives in the United States as well, targeting "wayward" or "erring" girls and women who were often committed by the courts, or sent from other institutions, as punishment for various crimes of morality.[7] US Magdalene laundries were contemporaneous to those in Ireland: the first Good Shepherd home in the United States was founded in 1842 in Louisville, Kentucky.[8] Over the next several decades, fifty-nine Good Shepherd homes and schools would take charge of "wayward" girls and women of varying cultural, educational, and social backgrounds until 2001, when the last facility was closed.[9] Despite these parallels, however, Magdalene laundries in the United States are rarely discussed or acknowledged in national discourse; when they are described contemporaneously or in academic works, they are often subsumed under histories of religious education or social reform.[10] The relative silence about this history in the United States is pervasive: the general public remains mostly unaware that Good Shepherd homes in the United States resembled the Magdalene laundries of Ireland, and few people know that American Indian women were forcibly confined to this kind of place in the early years of the twentieth century.[11] Placing these histories into conversation with one another, this chapter further illustrates how Indigenous people uniquely experienced confinement as a tool of US settler colonialism at the turn of the twentieth century.

What shall we make of these histories of forced institutionalization that run parallel to one another in more ways than one? Michelle Jones and Lori Record, two women incarcerated in 2014 at the Indiana Women's Prison, argue that Good Shepherd homes were Magdalene laundries—and were also the first women's prisons in the United States.[12] They write, "To answer the question of whether these Magdalene Laundries were the first prisons for women in the United States, we need to ask first what constitutes a prison. . . . If a prison is defined as a place of confinement for crimes and of forcible restraint, and if the persons committed to these places cannot leave when they want to and are, in fact, confined against their will, it becomes irrelevant whether the place is called a prison—or, instead, a refuge, correctional facility, house, penitentiary, or even laundry—if it operates as a prison."[13]

As Jones and Record explain of this carceral designation, Good Shepherd homes were "prisons in all but name." Yet, the authors do not explicate the facilities' first designation as Magdalene laundries, which is this chapter's primary objective. Good Shepherd homes, including the one in Reading, housed "penitents" referred to as Sisters Magdalene, and these institutions sustained themselves through the unremunerated domestic labor of confined women.[14] Placed within a broader history of settler colonialism and social reform in the United States, this chapter thus emphasizes the Reading home's characteristics as a Magdalene laundry—a carceral place of coerced labor to which young Indigenous women were sent from Carlisle to wash away their "sins."

The first section provides an overview of Magdalene laundries, or asylums— these terms will be used interchangeably—and the purpose they served in Ireland. Building on this discussion, the following section shifts to an examination of archival records relating to the Indigenous women sent from the Carlisle Indian School to the Good Shepherd home in Reading, Pennsylvania, in the second decade of the twentieth century. These records reveal that US officials used the Reading facility as an alternative to the prison—a pattern that benefited the settler society by removing "troublesome" young Indigenous women from white Americans' claimed territory and a process that was challenged by the women and their families. This section also discusses the history and characteristics of Magdalene laundries which emerged alongside broader social reform efforts, as well as the silences that pervade master historical narratives about these facilities in the US settler-national context. The third and final section discusses gendered distinctions in the punishment of Indigenous women and men who were enrolled at Carlisle and regarded as behaviorally "incorrigible," which further illustrates the use of carceral auxiliary institutions, such as "reform schools," as tools of US settler colonialism. Together, these contested patterns of Indigenous institutionalization reveal punitive connections between Carlisle and the Good Shepherd home that furthered settler objectives of Indigenous elimination and resource appropriation. The extralegal relationship between the two institutions points to underexamined dimensions of the federal "boarding school system" in the United States—a relationship which holds contemporary relevance for the survivors of settler institutions, their descendants, and their tribal nations.

MAGDALENE LAUNDRIES AND IRELAND'S "ARCHITECTURE OF CONTAINMENT"

The history of the Magdalene laundries in Ireland stretches back to the middle of the eighteenth century, when Lady Arabella Denny, a Protestant, founded the first institution for Irish women considered "fallen" in Dublin in 1767.[15] In the years following the devastation of Irish potato crops by blight (1840s onward), the Catholic Church began to exert unprecedented power over Irish social life, exercising a heightened ability to define the standards of "respectability," proscribe female sexuality, and demand women's compliance, obedience, and subordination to male authority. Concurrent with shifting gender, class, and religious dynamics under an empowered Catholic Church, Catholic religious orders came to dominate the administration of charitable organizations that multiplied in Ireland in the postfamine years. Over the course of the following century, Protestants and Catholics were extensively involved in the "salvation" of Irish women—unwed mothers, prostitutes, women with intellectual or physical disabilities, victims of abuse—who were regarded as failing to live up to patriarchal standards of morality (fig. 3.2). Simultaneously, the Sisters of the Good Shepherd, a French Catholic order that would come to have a particularly prominent presence in the Irish cultural lexicon, established their footing in Limerick in 1848—a stronghold that would last for a century and a half. With the passage of the Reformatory Act of 1858 and the Industrial Schools Act of 1868, Catholics soon outpaced Protestants in their control over asylums, hospitals, and orphanages in Ireland.[16]

As Irish historian James Smith notes, by the end of the nineteenth century, there were twenty-two asylums in operation in Ireland, half of which would remain under Catholic operation beyond the turn of the twentieth century.[17] Within these facilities—ostensibly charitable institutions—"fallen" women were subjected to grueling physical labor scrubbing, folding, and ironing garments in order to "wash away their sins." Entry into the laundries was on a supposedly voluntary basis; "women religious" did not have the legal authority to keep

3.2 Irish women perform in a play at the Sisters of Our Lady Charity of Refuge Convent and Magdalene Laundry, Gloucester Street (now Seán McDermott Street), Dublin, Ireland, ca. 1930s. Footage shot by Father Jack Delany. Father Jack Delany Collection: Communion Processions, Irish Film Institute. Image courtesy of the IFI Irish Film Archive. Reproduced with permission of Irene Devitt.

Irish women forcibly confined, but as historians of these institutions have amply demonstrated, institutionalization was coerced and thus often indefinite.[18] Many women entered the laundries and stayed for life.

According to Smith, by the early 1920s, Magdalene laundries were part of an elaborate institutional network that was supported by the Catholic Church and the nascent Irish Free State, both of which acted as the "self-appointed guardians of the [Irish] nation's moral climate."[19] Prior to 1900, under British colonialism, the laundries announced themselves as philanthropic enterprises created to respond to and curb prostitution: "Closely associated with the moral reform and spiritual conversion of fallen women in the city . . . [twenty-two] asylums operating in Ireland by the end of the nineteenth century, provided shelter for women considered likely to end up on the street."[20] Protestant-run institutions largely ceased operation by the early twentieth century, allowing Catholic facilities to predominate; but after 1900, as Smith argues, industrial schools, mother and baby homes, reformatories, and hospitals functioned in concert with one another as a carceral network that punished a heterogeneous group of Irish women by removing them from society.[21] Together, hegemonic discourses about female morality and brick-and-mortar structures comprised Ireland's "architecture of containment"—one that "helped to engineer widespread public consent . . . while [keeping] the . . . institutional response to sexual practice . . . shrouded in secrecy."[22]

According to the scholars behind Ireland's Justice for Magdalenes (JFM) political campaign and research initiative (founded in 2009), by 1922, ten laundries continued to operate under the Catholic Sisters of Mercy, Sisters of Our Lady Charity, Sisters of Charity, and Sisters of the Good Shepherd in disparate parts of Ireland. Many of these facilities would remain in operation throughout the next several decades. In 1996, the last of the laundries—an institution located on Seán McDermott Street in Dublin—was shuttered. The JFM scholars also note that the Good Shepherd Sisters operated an industrial school in Limerick that regularly recruited "wayward" girls for confinement and religious conversion in their four facilities, with additional locations in Cork City, Waterford, and New Ross, Ireland.[23]

Intake processes at the laundries strongly resembled those of American Indian boarding schools like Carlisle in the last decades of the nineteenth century—a fact that highlights commonalities between institutional objectives as well as national attitudes toward devalued populations. Upon arrival at the laundries, Irish girls and women had their hair shorn; they were forced to replace their clothing with stiff work uniforms and assigned new names—along with a number—in a process of deindividuation intended to erase their identities. Survivor testimonies reveal that the women experienced these facilities like prisoners would a prison: they were carceral institutions in which "penitents" were subjected to physical abuse, as well as unrelenting isolation from friends, family, and even children for years on end, and oftentimes, indefinitely. As JFM scholar Claire McGettrick and colleagues note, "Figures relating to the three Dublin Magdalene convents at the end of 1983 reveal that nearly a quarter of the women confined had not seen their siblings since entering the institution; most had not seen other relatives or friends, and while just over half of the women had children, approximately 6 per cent of those Magdalene women who were mothers saw their children after incarceration."[24] Other details illustrate the extreme austerity of these environments: "The girls and women rose very early in the morning and went to Mass and then worked without pay, usually six full days a week at laundry or needlework. They also had general chores relating to the running of the institution. All the survivors

3.3 Irish women at the Convent of Our Lady of Charity on Gloucester Street (now Seán McDermott Street) in Dublin, Ireland, ca. 1933. Footage shot by Father Jack Delany. Father Jack Delany Collection: Communion Processions, Irish Film Institute. Image courtesy of the IFI Irish Film Archive. Reproduced with permission of Irene Devitt.

describe how the work was endless, repetitive, compulsory, forced and unpaid" (fig. 3.3).[25]

In recent decades, Irish Magdalene laundries have received increased attention in part as a result of the Justice for Magdalenes campaign, comprised of Irish survivors and their families, along with activists, allies, and scholars.[26] Thanks to their tireless work, in 1996, a memorial honoring the Magdalenes was established at St. Stephen's Green in Dublin, and in 2013, Taoiseach Enda Kenny offered a formal apology, on behalf of the Irish state, to the women, children, and families impacted by this history.

This is just one small step toward justice.

Nonetheless, survivors who were interviewed shortly after this historic event often described how significant it was to receive a formal apology from Ireland's

Prime Minister.[27] As fifty-seven-year-old survivor Martha remarked in an interview with JFM scholar and professor Dr. Katherine O'Donnell after Kenny's speech: "We clapped [inaudible] you know, it was just a *wonderful, wonderful* . . . it was what I needed, it was . . . because for the first time then, the child wasn't wrong . . . I've no shame! The shame is on you!"[28] Similarly, seventy-year-old survivor Bernadette stated in reference to Kenny's apology, "We were elated! We couldn't believe. No, I just could not believe, because we were looking for this day and to be honest we never thought it would come. And the things he said were nice things. . . . And now all we hope is . . . [that] it's going to be a happy ending."[29]

In 2015, the Irish government established the Magdalene Restorative Justice Ex-Gratia Scheme; to date, 32.8 million euros have been administered to 814 survivors, a fraction of the 11,000 individuals impacted by confinement in the twelve Irish facilities that fall under the purview of the redress scheme.[30] At the time of this writing, all four religious orders—the Sisters of Charity, Sisters of Mercy, Sisters of Our Lady Charity, and Good Shepherd Sisters—have "declined" to contribute to the survivors' fund.[31]

⋮

A century before the Taoiseach's apology and nearly three thousand miles across the globe, in 1914, four Indigenous girls and women were cleared by the medical examiner for transfer from the Carlisle Indian School in Carlisle, Pennsylvania, to the House of the Good Shepherd in Reading, Pennsylvania (fig. 3.1). Ranging in age from fourteen to twenty, Agnes W. (Menominee), Carrie P. A. (Red Cliff Chippewa), and Gertrude B. P. (Standing Rock Sioux) were sent from one alien environment to another, reinstitutionalized as punishment at the direction of Carlisle Superintendent Moses Friedman; Myrtle (or Muryl) S. (Omaha) was also given a physical examination and cleared for removal along with the young women named above. Other letters of correspondence reflect that in 1914 and 1915, respectively, Friedman and his successor, Oscar Lipps, were making arrangements to send two other Carlisle enrollees, Charlotte C. (Chippewa) and Lillian C. (Pine Ridge Sioux), to the Good Shepherd home as well. At the time of this writing, the archival record is unclear as to whether Myrtle, Charlotte, and Lillian were sent to the Reading home, or whether, for unknown reasons, they remained at Carlisle until the expiration of their terms of enrollment. Additionally, a seventh woman named Edna R. (tribal affiliation, if any, is unknown), who claimed to be a Carlisle affiliate, was sentenced to the Reading facility by the Cumberland County Court for the crime of prostitution in 1927, nearly a decade after the Carlisle barracks were repossessed by the US War Department and the institution had ceased operation. It is possible that other Indigenous girls and women not named here were sent from Carlisle to the Good Shepherd home, as well.

The Reading home was founded in 1889 and operated by the Catholic order of the Sisters of the Good Shepherd, one of dozens of similar facilities across the United States. In fact, beginning with a home founded in 1843 in Louisville, Kentucky, the Good Shepherd Sisters administered no fewer than fifty-nine facilities in major metropolitan areas such as Brooklyn, San Francisco, Kansas City, and Dallas, many of which they characterized as places of education. According to Nancymarie Phillips, "The Good Shepherd Sisters began as a social service congregation and not a teaching order. However, they added the provision of education to girls in their care because of changing social needs and legal requirements regarding the education of minor children."[32] In correspondence exchanged between Carlisle superintendents and US officials, the Reading home is similarly characterized as an institution of learning and reform.

The turn of the twentieth century saw a significant expansion of facilities dedicated to the "care," reform, punishment, or education of marginalized populations in the United States.[33] As discussed in chapter 1, the institution itself was society's answer for dealing with populations such as the enfeebled, infirm, or elderly, and those criminalized or deemed to be a a burden upon or a danger to an increasingly heterogeneous citizenry. Historian David Rothman has argued that the prison was central to US citizens' imagining of themselves; it was part and parcel of Americanness in the post-Jacksonian era, and it was essential for reconciling the idiosyncrasies of the criminal with the citizen and, out of chaos, promising order.[34] Similarly, as historians Estelle Freedman and Regina Kunzel have demonstrated, the mass warehousing of female populations defined as "degenerate" or otherwise threatening to the national polity was thought to mitigate those characteristics, and incarceration helped define and redefine the meanings of gender, sexuality, and criminality, and their interrelationship with one another.[35] As institutions dedicated to the Christian "re-education" of young women who ostensibly required "special attention," Good Shepherd homes thus fit into a larger landscape of facilities that extended US citizens' understanding of the place of the institution—and the significance of the inmate—in American society. While historians have often described the establishment of the American welfare state as a primarily elite, Protestant enterprise, Catholic "women religious" and the working class also exerted significant influence over the shape and character of "charity work" at the turn of the twentieth century, as historian Maureen Fitzgerald has demonstrated.[36]

It is unclear how the relationship between Carlisle and the Good Shepherd home was established, but it is evident that the Reading facility appealed to Carlisle officials who believed that heightened oversight and hard manual labor—"hoe handle medicine"—would have a curative effect on the Indian women they deemed to be "undesirable." A letter from Carlisle superintendent Oscar Lipps to the superintendent of the Pine Ridge Agency, John Brennan, explains the ostensible benefits of the "convent": "Our experience in dealing with incorrigible girls here is that it is not best for many reasons to place them in regular reform schools. . . . Last summer we had three wayward girls with whom we could do almost nothing. It was suggested to me that I place them in a Convent. This I did with remarkably good results." He continued,

> The girls are carried on our rolls as outing pupils and we furnish them with clothing and other necessaries supplied by the government, and keep in close touch with them. The Sisters in charge are very kind but firm. The girls attend school part of the time and work a part of the time, as they do here. They are taught music and have their own little Orchestra and Chorus in the Home . . . if placed in this Home . . . [the girls are] under constant observation and training and only [their] good traits and characteristics encouraged to predominate.[37]

Although Lipps characterized the environment at the Reading home as an innocuous extension of Carlisle's disciplinary regime, his letter reveals how the "convent" functioned as a holding pen for young women who were unwanted by Carlisle officials, but whose presence—at least on paper—was needed for statistical purposes. The clerical practice of carrying the Indigenous girls and women on Carlisle rolls demonstrates how the institution's officials created absent presences: those sent to Reading were listed as "outing pupils"—a catch-all designation that disguised processes of transinstitutionalization while ensuring the continued allocation of federal treasury funds for the "upkeep" of all Carlisle enrollees.[38] Far from being a neutral practice, this arrangement was monetarily beneficial for Carlisle. One survivor's account of her time spent in a Good Shepherd home in Indiana similarly contradicts Lipps's benign description of Good Shepherd homes.

⋮

Minnie Morrison was ten years old in 1907 when she was removed from an orphanage to a Good Shepherd home in Indianapolis, and her testimony, published in 1925, provides invaluable insight into the conditions of these facilities in the United States.[39] Minnie writes,

> I only got one clean dress a month, and underwear every two weeks. . . . One morning when I looked at my dress, and tried it on, it did fit me better than any of the others did, but it was torn in the neck. I saw some of the girls pinning their dresses, so I thought I would pin mine, and I did, but when we went to work, we turned them down because it was so hot. At noon when we got through dinner, and were marching out, Mother Priscilla jerked me out of line, and turned me around and tore my dress completely off of me. Of course I did not like this at all. She made me walk in front of the other girls, and had them laugh at me and shame me. I did not want to go back to work that afternoon, so I hid in the upper laundry.[40]

Minnie also shared details about the "education" she would be receiving: "After breakfast Mother sent for me to come and told Regina to take me up in the ironing room. I asked her if I was not going to school, and she said, 'Yes, this is an industrial school.'"[41] Minnie continued, "She took me upstairs and over to the ironing room. There were about thirty girls in this room. All were older than myself, and each one was standing behind an ironing board. Each girl had two irons and a small stove for heating them. . . . Mother took me over to an ironing board, and said, 'Why does Sister send me these small girls?' I could just see over the top of the board, so Mother gave me a wooden box to stand on."[42] Other details about the labor regime at the Indianapolis Good Shepherd home are shared in Minnie's account as well, including information about the horrific experience of having her left fingers amputated after a Sister pressed a hot poker to Minnie's fingers as punishment for wearing rings on them (fig. 3.4). As Minnie recalled of this devastating ordeal,

> [Mother Priscilla] took me to the engine room. The engineer who had charge of the furnace was standing there when all at once Mother took hold of my right arm and strapped it to the water pipe which runs from the engine room upstairs to the ironing room. When I saw her do this, I began to try to get away, but my struggles were all in vain. The Engineer caught hold of me around the waist and held me so tight I could not get away. While he held me, Mother

took a red hot poker from the furnace, took hold of my left arm, and said, "You will never wear rings on these fingers again." She put the red hot poker against my rings and melted them from my fingers. At the sight of the red hot poker, and the awful pain when she put the iron on my fingers, caused me to lose consciousness.[43]

Following this traumatic event, Minnie suffered through forced labor in the laundry for nearly a month before being admitted to St. Vincent's Hospital, where her fingers were amputated in March of 1915. She remained there for six months before the Sisters of Charity, who provided care at St. Vincent's, "persuaded" her into returning to the Good Shepherd home.[44]

As Minnie's testimony reflects, these environments caused genuine suffering; but the nature of the domestic labor performed at the laundries enabled Good Shepherd homes to bill themselves as educational institutions that offered "wayward" girls and young women a chance at redemption and future employment, a fact which further underscores how US officials believed that remedial labor could also correct perceived moral shortcomings.[45] Indeed, between 1857 and 1957, Phillips estimates that over thirty thousand young women between the ages of thirteen and twenty-one experienced institutionalization—typically between eighteen months and two years in duration—in Good Shepherd homes.[46]

Young women came to these facilities by a number of means: some were committed by the courts for crimes such as petty theft and prostitution; other women were destitute, immigrants with few job prospects, or victims of abuse or neglect. Good Shepherd homes rarely admitted pregnant girls and women or unwed mothers; facilities in Cleveland, Ohio, and Peekskill, New York, were the only two locations known to do so.[47] The young women confined in Good Shepherd homes were thus viewed and understood differently from other subjects of rescue; as Kunzel has documented, Protestant mother and baby homes such as those run by the Crittenton society existed contemporaneously with Good Shepherd homes and were successful in promoting narratives of unwitting seduction that helped garner pity and understanding for young women who "got into trouble."[48] By comparison, the girls and women who spent time at Good Shepherd facilities were not considered to be as deserving of public sympathy or redemption.

At the Reading facility, the Carlisle women were regarded as similarly "incorrigible" and likely performed dangerous, unremunerated work akin to that described by Minnie. According to Phillips, the majority of the Good Shepherd

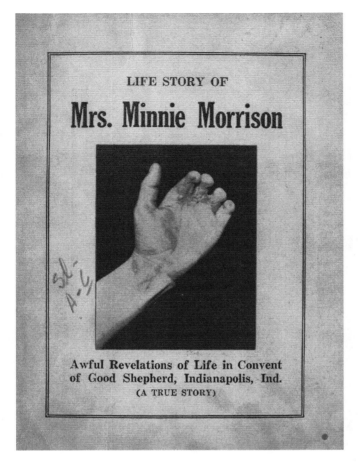

LIFE STORY OF

Mrs. Minnie Morrison

Awful Revelations of Life in Convent
of Good Shepherd, Indianapolis, Ind.
(A TRUE STORY)

3.4 Minnie Morrison was ten years old when she was sent to a Good Shepherd home in Indianapolis, Indiana. She escaped from the convent in 1921 at the age of twenty-four, and four years later published her life story. At the age of eighteen, Minnie suffered a catastrophic injury to her left hand when a Sister pressed a hot poker against her fingers as punishment for wearing rings. In an effort to conceal this abuse, while Minnie was convalescing in the hospital after having her fingers amputated, Good Shepherd Sisters coerced her into signing a statement saying she caught her hand in a laundry mangle due to "carelessness." The preface to her testimony states, "[Minnie] trusts that this book will soon be in every American home, and may be the means of saving many other girls from the cruelties which Mrs. Morrison has suffered." "Life Story of Mrs. Minnie Morrison: Awful Revelations of Life in Convent of Good Shepherd, Indianapolis, Ind.: A True Story." Toledo, Ohio, 1925. University of Hawaiʻi, Manoa, Social Movements, Archives and Manuscripts. Image courtesy of University of Hawaiʻi, Manoa.

homes in the United States supported the maintenance of their institutions by forcing "inmates" to do commercial laundry and embroidery as part of their "re-education."[49] For Indigenous women, however, domestic labor carried explicitly racial overtones. Historians of this era have extensively documented how domestic settings were contested sites of Indigenous struggle at the turn of the twentieth century, as American reformers—especially white women—sought to remake Indigenous lifeways in the image of Euro-American standards.[50] Beth Piatote (Nez Perce), for example, has argued that domestic settings—the homes of Indigenous families in particular—constituted a new frontier in the United States' assimilationist campaign toward Indian people.[51] Similarly, historian Cathleen Cahill has described federal efforts to inculcate Indigenous families into Euro-American norms of domesticity and has shown how this paternalistic agenda intersected with the stated objectives of many large, off-reservation boarding institutions such as Carlisle, the Haskell Institute in Lawrence, Kansas, and the Hampton Institute in Virginia. In each case, the efforts of white women reformers spanned public and private domains; closed, elite organizations, such as the Women's Christian Temperance Union and Women's National Indian Association, as well as public agencies such as the United States Indian Service and field matrons, were all deeply invested in disparate elements of "Indian affairs," which illustrates the scope and robustness of the resources that could be marshaled in the name of Indigenous "uplift."

Rarely were reformist efforts solely about the "improvement" of Indigenous peoples' lives, however. As US officials and reformers promoted the adoption of Euro-American forms of domesticity as key to the "civilization" of Indigenous communities, they also targeted Indigenous women's practices of homemaking as inadequate, uncivilized, or unsanitary. In one prominent example, in 1916, Commissioner of Indian Affairs Cato Sells implemented the "Save the Babies" campaign, ostensibly intended to reduce infant mortality rates on reservations. As Emily Harrison has pointed out, the campaign was "waged through infant indigenous bodies, but not for indigenous lives"—a reality reflected in the Office of Indian Affairs' pathologizing directives that further legitimated white managerialism into Indigenous affairs.[52] As Commissioner Sells proclaimed on January 10, 1916, "The crux of the matter is this: We must, if possible, get rid of the intolerable conditions that infest some of the Indian homes on the reservation, creating an atmosphere of death instead of life."[53] He continued,

This campaign for better babies, for the rescue of a race, calls for redoubled energy and zeal throughout the service, for it means personal work and tireless patience. . . . I believe that the high aspirations and missionary spirit generally prevailing among our field employees are a guaranty of substantial and lasting achievements, and I hope and believe we shall have the quickened cooperation of all denominational agencies, religious missionaries, and mission schools having special interest in the Indian's spiritual welfare and whose priceless labors, luminant with self-sacrifice and religious fervor, have done so much for the red man. We shall all, I am sure, exert an irresistible union of effort.[54]

As Sells targeted Indigenous women, bodies, and homes as objects of rescue and improvement, he echoed and extended the eugenicist philosophies that played out in the "Better Babies" campaigns elsewhere in the United States.[55] Similarly, when Sells called on disparate officials and the institutions under their aegis—field employees, religious missionaries, and mission schools—to assist with the preservation of Indigenous life, he drew on a well-established network of settler agents who viewed white interference into Indigenous communities as an appropriate expression of zeal and "concern" for Indigenous communities.

In one of the purest manifestations of settler interference into Indian affairs in this era, enrollees at Carlisle and other boarding institutions were encouraged to participate in the "Outing" program, an exploitative system of labor devised by Carlisle founder Richard Henry Pratt in 1879 (discussed at greater length in chapter 2). The philosophical foundations of Outing were simple; Pratt believed that by placing Indigenous people in the homes of prosperous, white American families to perform domestic work and farm labor, that "civilization" would be rapidly accomplished—it would simply rub off (fig. 3.5). Carlisle's Outing was widely regarded as a success and similar programs were implemented at Indian residential institutions across the United States; but Outing often did much to affirm existing racial hierarchies, even if it somewhat improved economic or employment outlooks for the Indian people who participated in this system.

Prior to their confinement at the Good Shepherd home, Agnes, Carrie, and Gertrude had been domestic workers in Carlisle's Outing program, where they performed unremunerated labor in the homes of white Americans under the auspices of racial "uplift." As members of Carlisle's Outing program, these young women would have been expected to conform very closely to their patrons'

3.5 Jennie T—. (Seneca), "under the Outing" with Mrs. Winnifield Scott Davidson in Newville, Pennsylvania, while enrolled at the Carlisle Indian School. 1893. "Jennie T—. Student File," Cumberland County Historical Society. ᴄᴄʜꜱ_13A-23-01, Cumberland County Historical Society, Carlisle, Pennsylvania.

expectations of "proper" feminine conduct, which often meant acting with total deference to the American citizens in whose homes they lived and labored.

Archival records indicate that these households could be extremely dangerous; they exposed Indigenous women to physical and sexual abuse at the hands of Outing patrons, which included male heads-of-households and their sons—as was the case with eighteen-year-old Lucinda R. (Cherokee), who in 1915 became pregnant while she was working "out" in the home of Alexander Holcombe in Cynwyd, Pennsylvania.[56] As discussed in chapter 1, records relating to Lucinda and her expulsion from Carlisle reflect that she refused to identify the paternity of her child and reveal that the Holcombes' teenage son, who also lived in the household, was rumored to be the father.[57]

In addition to being vulnerable to physical and sexual abuse, Indigenous women placed in these precarious domestic scenarios were also regarded with suspicion and accused of wide-ranging behavioral infractions—from generalized "disobedience" and petty theft at one end of the spectrum of perceived transgressions to alleged "attempted murder" at the other. As demonstrated by these examples, Outing households were characterized by radical power disparities that could result in Indigenous women's removal from the Outing program and return to Carlisle, or outright expulsion. In some cases, these fraught circumstances could also result in Indigenous women's removal from Carlisle's jurisdiction and incarceration in external facilities, as the women's confinement at the Good Shepherd home demonstrates.

Like the Ford Motor Company's "apprenticeship" program discussed in the previous chapter, similarities between the Good Shepherd home and Carlisle's regimens of a day split between labor and learning made the laundry appealing from the perspective of Carlisle superintendents who wanted to eliminate young women deemed too "troublesome" to remain at school. Records relating to the Indigenous women being considered for confinement at the Reading home reflect that some of them had previously had trouble with Outing patrons or Carlisle authorities who were tasked with their "oversight." In seventeen-year-old Gertrude's case, her enrollment card reveals that she ran away from her post in Lansdowne, Pennsylvania, at least once; she was returned to Carlisle and, several months later, sent to the Reading facility on July 31, 1914.

In fact, it appears that all four of the young women were transferred from Carlisle to the Good Shepherd home on the same day: a letter from Carlisle's physician to Superintendent Friedman reflects that Gertrude, Agnes, Carrie, and Myrtle had been given physical examinations and cleared for removal on July 31, 1914.[58] Although Myrtle's father wrote Carlisle's superintendent at least twice to demand that Myrtle be sent back home, she was nonetheless subjected to an invasive medical assessment and declared "fit to go."[59] In each instance, the young women were maintained as absent presences within Carlisle's ledgers. Additionally, as discussed, Carlisle officials referred to the women sent to Reading in ledgers and correspondence as being "under the Outing," which suggests that institutional authorities viewed the Indigenous women's confinement in the laundry as a natural—if extreme—extension of the labor they performed at Carlisle. The administrative designation of being "under the Outing" thus disguised the young women's true location at the laundry in Reading while obscuring the carceral nature of their confinement—a practice that constitutes an example of what Douglas Miller refers to as "settler custodialism," or another form of settler "custody and control in Native American history" that falls outside of prison walls.[60]

The Indigenous women's experiences intersect with multiple histories of institutionalization, incarceration, and "reform" in the United States; but they are also distinctly representative of the settler state's efforts to eliminate challenges to its sole sovereignty and its extralegal attempts at territorial expansion. As mentioned at the outset of this chapter, Jones and Record argue in a 2014 article that Good Shepherd homes were the first women's prisons in the United States.[61] Indeed, the government-sponsored report on "Benevolent Institutions" for 1910 refers to the women confined at the Reading home as "inmates," which further underscores the explicitly carceral nature of this facility.[62] Yet, the partnership between Carlisle and the Good Shepherd home illustrates in stark relief how institutionalization helped further settler objectives of white ascendancy and territorial dispossession by removing Indigenous women from society and re-institutionalizing them deep within the settler state. As Patrick Wolfe has famously observed about the logic of settler colonialism, "The primary motive for Indigenous elimination is not race, but access to territory. Territoriality is settler colonialism's specific, irreducible element."[63] Put another way, as historian Kelly Lytle Hernández has powerfully argued, "Mass incarceration *is* mass elimination" (emphasis mine).[64] As revealed by letters exchanged by US officials and white citizens about the Indigenous women confined in the Reading house, settler agents worked together to establish profitable punitive relationships between the brick-and-mortar structures used to contain, reform, or punish Indian people in this era.[65]

Records relating to a young Sioux woman named Lillian C. illustrate how Superintendent Lipps viewed the Good Shepherd home as an alternative to the prison—an extralegal means of incarcerating Indigenous women deemed threatening to the hierarchies in which they were situated at the bottom. In 1915, Lillian was accused by her Outing patrons of nearly causing the "double murder" of their twin infants and was slated to be sent to Reading as punishment. As one Carlisle official described Lillian's actions, it was "the most fiendish attempt to commit a crime that has ever been perpetrated . . . [at Carlisle]."[66]

Allegedly, Lillian had placed a tapeworm in one of the infant's napkins in an attempt to be sent back to Pine Ridge—a powerful strategy of intentional misbehavior that others with similar aims also employed.[67] Historians Brenda Child (Ojibwe) and K. Tsianina Lomawaima (Mvskoke) have extensively documented subtle and overt acts of Indigenous girls' and women's resistance at boarding school, ranging from running away to wearing "home clothes" rather than the schools' bland uniforms.[68] These facts showcase the determination of Indigenous students to shape their environments and highlight important efforts to exercise and preserve agency over their identities as Indian people. It is possible that Lillian was utilizing similar strategies of rebellion in order to be released from Carlisle's jurisdiction and sent back home. The extreme nature of the allegations against Lillian point to the severity of her living environment. Her correspondence similarly indicates that she hated her Outing home and was homesick; as she wrote in a letter to her father Andrew, "I am getting very poor because I am sick. . . . I am very lonesome out in the country, . . . I never to [sic] stop thinking of you."[69] Given Lillian's profound heartache and longing for home, it seems possible that her actions were an act of rebellion in the hopes that she might be returned back to her community. Rather than releasing her back home to her father Andrew, however, Lipps wanted to transfer Lillian to the Good Shepherd home, where labor under the Catholic sisters would be prescribed as her "cure."

Letters of correspondence exchanged between US officials reflect the explicit logic of Indigenous elimination that motivated their desire to incarcerate Lillian, and how they conspired with one another in a bid to keep Lillian from returning to her tribe and community—a departure from other instances in which "troublesome" Carlisle enrollees were expelled. As Pine Ridge Indian agent John Brennan wrote to Lipps, "It came nearly being a double murder, and I believe the discipline of your school and the hideousness of the crime will justify [her confinement]."[70] In this exchange, Brennan also appealed directly to Lipps's shared sense of power over Indian people. He wrote, "Your civil authority could take the evidence of all concerned and pass sentence, which would seem legal to the parents of Lillian."[71] It is unclear whether this scheme worked; Lillian's father attempted to have his daughter released, but her enrollment card reflects that she remained on Carlisle rolls for another two years before being sent home in 1917, at the age of seventeen.[72]

In another example of confinement the prior year, Carlisle superintendent Friedman removed seventeen-year-old Carrie P. A. (Chippewa) from Carlisle in 1914 and incarcerated her at the Reading home as punishment for being a "menace" and "incorrigible."[73] "I don't ever know if I'll go home," reads one of Carrie's letters, "but I hope I'll be a good girl when I get out."[74] In another instance, Friedman committed Gertrude B. P., who was Lakota, to the Good Shepherd home because she was a "bad influence upon others."[75] She was under eighteen, and so permission for her transfer should have been obtained from her legal guardian, Thomas F., but it is evident that this was not done. Letters of correspondence reflect that Carlisle officials kept Gertrude "on the rolls" at the school, and thus continued to receive federal funds on her behalf while she was confined at the Good Shepherd home. In each case, these letters reveal that Carlisle authorities exercised tremendous authority over Gertrude's freedom and resources—a fact further demonstrated by the ease with which Carlisle officials successfully arranged for a portion of Gertrude's per capita payment to be sent from Standing Rock to the laundry to pay for her ongoing incarceration until she was released in November of 1915.[76]

During Gertrude's confinement, her brother John wrote Friedman's successor, Lipps, at least once to request an update on her whereabouts, as did Gertrude's legal guardian, Thomas. In each of these letters, familial concern is palpable. As John wrote to Lipps in correspondence dated February 6, 1915, "I would like to know how my sister Gertrude is making it at school. I haven't heard from her for nearly four months and I am feeling bad over it because she never writes home telling how she is, at school."[77] Another letter sent from Standing Rock agent Claude Covey to Lipps in September of 1915 reveals that Gertrude's guardian Thomas had demanded that she be sent home immediately: "He has heard that this girl now wishes to become a Catholic sister," Covey reported to Lipps, "and he is very much opposed to this and wants the girl sent home at once."[78] As Thomas and John had clearly not consented to Gertrude's removal from Carlisle, this correspondence documents in heart-wrenching detail how settler agents used the Good Shepherd home as a place to which Indigenous women could be disappeared, often with impunity.

In another example of profitable confinement, a twenty-year-old Menominee woman named Agnes was sent to Reading and forced to make a monetary contribution for her "maintenance." Like Gertrude and Carrie, Friedman and his successor Lipps kept Agnes on the Carlisle rolls—a pattern that illustrates the explicitly remunerative nature of the partnership between the "school" and the laundry.[79] Although Agnes was nearly twenty-one years old and thus well past being appropriately "school-aged," both Carlisle and the Good Shepherd home continued to receive payments on her behalf for a total of sixteen months. As Outing Matron Lida Johnston explained of this extended term of confinement, the Sisters felt that "[if Agnes were] to leave the institution now, she would land in a disreputable house in Reading."[80] According to letters of correspondence contained in Agnes's file, the Good Shepherd Sisters characterized Agnes as promiscuous and untrustworthy; I read her actions as bold. She regularly received "letters from boys in Panama," although she was never allowed to read them, and was allegedly "always planning to 'get out'"—which I take to be a powerful trace of her resolute defiance. As Agnes wrote to Lipps in a letter from August 1914 (reproduced in the appendix), "Well, Mr. Lipps I have made up my mind to be a good girl[.] I am very sorry for what I've done in the past."[81] Confronted with the possibility of her escape, a speculative reading of archival materials bearing Agnes's name wills her to succeed in securing her freedom.

Historians Chris Finley (Colville Confederated Tribes) and Camilla Townsend describe this practice of "momentary fiction" as a methodological imperative when confronted with evidence of abuse in the colonial archive. Writing of a similar dilemma in connection to boarding school student Hezekiah Calvin and the one-sidedness of the historical record ("He left silence in his wake"), Finley and Townsend ask, "What are historians to do? Shall we leave our mentions of Hezekiah Calvin and similar figures brief? . . . Shall we strive to be mindful of his sufferings and explore the possible reasons? In doing so, we risk misinterpretation; silence is notoriously hard to read. What is the ethical choice?"[82] Records relating to the Indigenous women who were considered for confinement at the Reading facility present similar dilemmas; the archival record is incomplete and often bears few traces of their perspectives during or after confinement at the Good Shepherd home. As Indigenous scholars know well, the colonial archive is always already imbalanced; to borrow from Tanana Athabascan feminist theorist Dian Million, we must be cognizant of the conditions under which Indigenous women spoke, when they spoke at all.[83]

What does one make of these traces, with the stories that are too errant for the colonial archive to hold? I have attempted to address the limits of the archive by placing Indigenous and Irish women's experiences of forced confinement into conversation with one another and by giving name to the silenced history of Indigenous confinement in the Good Shepherd home. As Linda Tuhiwai Smith reminds us, naming, reclaiming, and bearing witness are entwined processes that are often rooted in expressions of tribal-national sovereignty.[84] In the context of the Good Shepherd home's history of Indigenous incarceration, this issue of naming and categorization is especially critical; the silences that permeate the history of the US Magdalene laundries similarly underscore what Black feminist theorist Saidiya Hartman, philosopher Michel-Rolph Trouillot, and other scholars have theorized as the settler state's investment in historical amnesia.[85] That this global history of forced confinement in Magdalene laundries intersects with other state-sanctioned efforts to eliminate Indigenous lifeways through the government-funded boarding school system further highlights the importance of intervening in this silencing of the past.

GENDERED PUNISHMENT AND TRANSINSTITUTIONALIZATION

In a reflection of differing societal expectations of women and men at the turn of the twentieth century, there were significant gendered distinctions in the treatment of "wayward" Indian women and men at Carlisle. Indian men who ran afoul of "school rules" were often incarcerated, expelled, or sent back home, as reform institutions typically refused to admit men over the age of eighteen. By comparison, Indian women who were deemed "undesirable" were frequently subjected to heightened surveillance and reinstitutionalization in external facilities like the Reading home, regardless of age. These facts highlight what Steven Ruggles has pointed out about the interrelationship between institutions in this era: "Institutions influence each other both because of the direct transfer of inmates and because the managers are aware of each other's methods and policies"—a pattern also evident in records relating to Carlisle enrollees.[86] Gendered distinctions in patterns of Indigenous confinement also reveal important differences in the role of the carceral institution as a mechanism of settler control, as Luana Ross (Confederated Salish and Kootenai Tribes) has observed.[87]

In one example of the disparate ways in which "incorrigible" Indian women and men were punished by Carlisle superintendents, John M. (tribal affiliation unrecorded) and John B. P., a nineteen-year-old Sioux man who was the brother of Gertrude B. P., were removed from Carlisle in April 1914 as punishment for the alleged "crime" of entering the girls' dormitory. A letter sent from Friedman to the superintendent of the Standing Rock Agency reads, "I transmit herewith for your information a copy of 'Proceedings of a Court-Martial' that was convened on April the 6th to try John B——. and John M——. for the crime of having entered our Girls' Dormitory. On April the 10th I was authorized by the commissioner of Indian Affairs to have the young men placed in a State Reformatory or expelled from this school. Both young men have reached an age where it would be a difficult matter to have them sentenced to a Reformatory, so it has been decided to expel them from this school."[88]

Similarly, in 1914, twenty-one-year-old Grover A. (Kickapoo) was expelled from Carlisle following court-martial and a term of confinement in the institution's guardhouse.[89] As a letter sent from Carlisle's acting superintendent to the superintendent of the Kickapoo Agency states, "Under date of April 10th the Office approved the findings of the court and authorized me to have [Grover] placed in a State Reformatory. As such an arrangement is hardly practicable because of Grover's age it has been decided best to expel him and to send him to his home."[90] In another case of failed transinstitutionalization, in 1915, Superintendent Friedman sent a letter to Charles L. (Eastern Band of Cherokee), a twenty-two-year-old former Carlisle enrollee, telling him to "stay out of this section of the country."[91] Evidently, Charles had sought reenrollment at Carlisle in order to find work, but was denied reentry; additional letters of correspondence reflect that ableist beliefs undergirded this decision. Carlisle officials had deemed Charles "mentally incompetent"; they considered him a vagrant and had at one point tried to confine him in the state reformatory but, for reasons that are unclear, were unable to do so, perhaps due to his age.[92] Another letter from Carlisle's superintendent to the superintendent of the Cherokee Agency, James Henderson, shows that in light of the reformatory's refusal to admit Charles, the men agreed to actively work together to prevent him from returning to Carlisle's "section" of the country.[93]

In chapter 1, I demonstrated that Indian men who "ran away" from Carlisle were captured and incarcerated at the local jail and forced to pay their own arrest fees—a fine that appears to have been uniquely applied to Indian detainees. As Carlisle superintendent Friedman and his successor Lipps authorized local officials to police Indian "runaways" and extract a fine for these activities, they encouraged the creation of a race-based surveillance network that profited off patrolling the local vicinity. These racially discriminatory actions reveal US officials' coordinated attempts to restrict Indian men's ability to move freely throughout the country and showcase the role of individual settler agents in the maintenance of existing racial—and gendered—hierarchies. That reform institutions generally refused to accept Indian men—typically eighteen and older—further highlights how the institution itself also played a critical part in shaping, mediating, and reinforcing dominant views about the relationship between Indigeneity and criminality. US officials regarded Indian men as insubordinate; they were too old and too dangerous to be reformed.

While some Indian men who ran afoul of Carlisle's "school rules" were jailed or sent back home, Indian girls and women, regardless of age, were often reinstitutionalized in external facilities as punishment for breaching acceptable modes of conduct. Hannah K. (identified both as Mohawk and Onondaga in Carlisle records), for example, was seventeen years old when she was committed by the Cumberland County Court to the Glen Mills reform school, also known as Sleighton Farm. According to her "student file," Hannah had been convicted of the crime of fornication and around June 1914 was remanded to Sleighton Farm unbeknownst to her grandmother, Christine S., for a one-year sentence; it is unclear who Hannah's sexual partner was and whether that person was also imprisoned.

Upon learning of this news, Christine wrote Carlisle's then superintendent Friedman demanding her release (her letter is reproduced in the appendix). She said, "I would like to have my grand-daughter back home. It seems to me as if they have stolen my child when they sent her to the Reform school without informing me. I am in poor health and I certainly will be glad if I can see her face again before I die. I think it would have been better if they have notified me before sending her there."[94] Correspondence contained in Hannah's file reflects that upon expiration of her term, she would be placed on parole "in the charge of Miss Mary T. Scheurman, of Waterbury, Connecticut, Secretary of the Organized Charities," rather than being sent back home.[95] Her file does not reflect whether she was paroled out in this manner, but the suggestion illustrates how experiences of forced confinement rippled across Indigenous lives to disrupt kinship networks, as disability studies scholar Susan Burch has observed in her community-centered study of the Canton Asylum for Insane Indians in Canton, South Dakota (the institutional subject of the following chapter).[96] At least one Carlisle enrollee appears to have been sent from Carlisle to Canton—a pattern of transinstitutionalization discussed in chapter 4, as well.[97]

One of the last documents contained in Hannah's file is an amazingly restrained letter written in her own hand, evidently after having been released from confinement:

"Dear Sir," she addressed Lipps, "Would it be any bother to you to have the 'Arrow' sent to my present address. It has been sent to Sleighton Farm and I never get them unless I go out there—and I never go except once a month."[98] Hannah's letter documents the severity with which some Indigenous women were punished for breaching dominant expectations of proper conduct and sexual propriety, while highlighting her determination to direct the outcome of her own life—including her desire to remain current on happenings at Carlisle. Underscoring her relative freedom of mobility, Hannah's words are a powerful instance of what Mishuana Goeman (Tonawanda Band of Seneca) refers to as "(re)mapping," or a potent example of "Native narratives that mediate and refute colonial organizing of land, bodies, and social and political landscapes."[99] Disciplinary records about other Carlisle girls and women similarly reflect the highly gendered nature of forced confinement as well as the ways in which they challenged their comparative lack of rights under US law in the early twentieth century.[100]

Irish women's testimonies also reflect subordination to men and to state authorities under Irish law and describe contested experiences of transinstitutionalization. As an Irish laundry survivor named Katherine explained to her interviewer, in the 1960s, she was repeatedly transferred between a Good Shepherd laundry in Waterford and St. Otteran's, a psychiatric institution. Her interviewer, Claire McGettrick, asked, "So you were sent sort of back and forth?" "Yeah, yeah," Katherine replied, "Because they knew there was nothing wrong with me. . . . See my mother was in the mental hospital, they had my mother's history and they probably thought I was mad too. . . . My mother wasn't mad at all, there was nothing wrong with my mother."[101] Other women sent to Irish Good Shepherd homes also recount how male family members, religious authorities, and state officials rationalized their confinement as a necessary extension of their mothers' medical histories or perceived moral failures. These fraught realities demonstrate how forced confinement has historically dovetailed with the rise of eugenicist movements and philosophies across the globe and point to the ways in which institutionalization has been used in different cultural and national contexts as a powerful method of reproductive suppression and social control—a practice addressed at greater length in the context of the Canton Asylum for Insane Indians, in the following chapter.

:

The colonial archive rarely tells the story we expect it to tell. But in other instances, the stories told are "tragically predictable."[102] In seeking community guidance and input on this research, I have learned that although tribal members may not be familiar with this history, they are not surprised by it either. Menominee Tribal Historic Preservation Officer David Grignon remarked that he was not aware of the Reading home, but he noted that repatriation efforts are ongoing at the Canton Asylum, which, at the time of this writing, may be classed as a settler institution alongside Magdalene laundries and federally funded boarding schools. "There's a lot of red tape," Grignon said.[103] These lacunae and interconnections are a critical part of the story as told from an Indigenous perspective; writing of Indigenous adoptees and survivance, Ho-Chunk historian Amy Lonetree (reading Margaret Jacobs) notes that "the moral of the story depends on who is telling the story." "The surveillance of our families," Lonetree further asserts, "was a common occurrence for Native people in the twentieth century, and it is a story that certainly needs to be told from the perspective of those who have lived through it."[104]

Several questions remain for future research. How was this carceral partnership between Carlisle and the Good Shepherd home established? The Reading facility was Catholic and private, and therefore seemingly incongruous with a government-run boarding institution rooted in the mores of Protestantism.[105] But a similar relationship between industrial schools and laundries existed in Ireland as well, as young women deemed likely to fail were forced out of one institutional context and into another. Moreover, according to the 2022 report issued by the US Department of the Interior about the federal boarding school system, at least two federally funded American Indian boarding schools in Colorado and Wisconsin appear to have been administered by the Good Shepherds. As the Interior report explains of these types of arrangements, "The United States at times paid religious institutions and organizations on a per capita basis for Indian children to enter Federal Indian boarding schools operated by religious institutions or organizations. As part of the Federal Indian boarding school system, the Department contracted with several religious institutions and organizations including the American Missionary Association of the Congregational Church, the Board of Foreign Missions of the Presbyterian Church, the Board of Home Missions of the Presbyterian Church, the Bureau of Catholic Indian Missions, and the Protestant Episcopal Church."[106]

It is important to note, however, that the Good Shepherd home in Reading was not under the oversight or scrutiny of the Indian Service; it was autonomous and independent but served a critical carceral function in the settler apparatus as a place to which Indigenous women were disappeared. As Thomas Biron (Ojibwe), boarding school survivor and former Truth and Reconciliation Commission coordinator at the Native Justice Coalition, pointed out to me in a private conversation, this history of disappearing Native women may also be understood as an antecedent to the Missing and Murdered Indigenous Women crisis.[107]

Did other American Indian boarding schools have informal partnerships with similar facilities? How many Indigenous women perished behind asylum walls? "Prisons in all but name," Magdalene laundries are absent from discussions of settler colonialism and the carceral institutions that comprised the United States' nebulous settler apparatus.[108] As the extralegal arrangements examined above make clear, however, Indigenous institutionalization at the Reading laundry directly benefited the settler society. Like "thousands of eyes posted everywhere," to echo Michel Foucault, records relating to the Indigenous women's experiences reveal a heterogeneous network of settler agents comprised of religious figures, reservation officials, boarding school superintendents, Outing patrons, and field matrons who worked together to police Indian people and to preserve white hegemony.[109] And like Ireland's "architecture of containment," this history highlights the interlocking and interchangeable nature of Carlisle, the Good Shepherd home, and other settler facilities, such as local jails—parallels that have ongoing relevance for tribal nations today.

There are many similarities in the circumstances of the Indigenous and Irish women's experiences of institutionalization, but there are important distinctions as well. Historically, the US government and other settler-colonizer powers have worked assiduously to undermine tribes' statuses as sovereign nations, a reality that distinguishes Indigenous peoples' experiences of forced institutionalization in the United States from those of other populations. Carlisle enrollees entered the institution for many reasons, and some were sent to external institutions by US officials illegally and against the wishes of their families—a fact that showcases how Indigenous people uniquely experienced institutionalization as a tool of settler colonialism, but one that has not been sufficiently addressed or acknowledged in national political fora. Although Carlisle and the US government did not formally contract with the Reading home, Indigenous women were confined there—which suggests that the scope of this carceral network of settler institutions is more expansive than officially reported and publicly understood.

These silences obfuscate the global impact of Magdalene laundries. They also obscure the interconnected experiences of disparate, targeted populations in the United States and the importance of histories of forced confinement for analyses of world-historical processes of imperialism and settler colonialism alike.[110] As McGettrick and colleagues point out and as is the case in the US context, British colonialism frames the development and implementation of Ireland's practice of confining society's most vulnerable members.[111] Similarly, Brenda Child offers another perspective on the legacy of settler invasion and of colonizers' "civilizational" campaigns. She writes, "Our problems and tribulations as Indian people did not end with the decline of the government boarding schools. . . . After I concluded a presentation on a college campus about boarding school history, an Ojibwe woman in the audience commented that her mother had been forcibly sterilized in a reservation border town in Minnesota." Child continues, "At first glance, boarding school history and the more recent history of forced sterilization of Indian women . . . are not necessarily intertwined, unless viewed as part of a broader pattern of colonial violence. Clearly, this Ojibwe woman found a strong association between boarding school and forced sterilization, since both were practices implicated in this kind of state interference into Indian family life."[112]

As Child's recollections make clear, Indigenous peoples' lived experiences reflect interconnections between the federal boarding school system and other seemingly unrelated colonial endeavors, an argument that this chapter makes as well; the global history of women's forced confinement in Magdalene laundries, as the foregoing reveals, is also Indigenous history. Despite the legacy of this history for marginalized populations in the United States, however, the Reading home and similar facilities are generally not regarded as Magdalene laundries in the United States—except, perhaps, by the survivors themselves, their families, and their allies.[113]

What will justice look like? Survivors of these facilities, their kin, and their communities have strong ideas about the forms redress should take, and their perspectives must be heeded. Deidre Whiteman (Meskwaki, Dakota, Ojibwe, Hidatsa), the director of research and education at the National Native American Boarding School Healing Coalition, put it this way: "When we lead, we must lead in the interest of the survivors. . . . The survivors have said we need truth, justice, and healing" (fig. 3.6).[114] Thomas Biron similarly remarked, "The truth is not going to come from one of us, it is going to come from all of us."[115] As the Irish government continues to reckon with its history of forced confinement, the United States will have to as well. There are many online groups dedicated to connecting survivors of Magdalene laundries across the world with one another, and often these conversations highlight global interconnections; in one example, children born to unwed mothers in twentieth-century Irish laundries and mother and baby homes were illegally placed for adoption with American families.[116] As the US Department of the Interior undertakes listening sessions about the legacy of the federal Native American boarding school system, it is possible that similar stories of transinstitutionalization and forced child removal will come to light. Deb

3.6 US Department of Interior Secretary Deb Haaland (Laguna Pueblo) is honored during a blanket ceremony by staff from the National Native American Boarding School Healing Coalition, May 7, 2022. From left to right: Director of Healing Programs Sandy White Hawk (Sicangu Lakota), CEO Deborah Parker (Tulalip), Secretary Deb Haaland (Laguna Pueblo), Policy and Advocacy Director Theresa Shelton (Tulalip). Photo courtesy of the National Native American Boarding School Healing Coalition.

Haaland's Interior Department must continue to widen the scope of its boarding school investigation to examine settler institutions like the Good Shepherd home and compel the Catholic Church to release their records.[117] The entwined experiences of Indigenous and other confined women showcase the global reach of the Magdalene laundries; they also remind us that histories of institutionalization have not occurred in isolation—they have sustained one another.

The following chapter turns to the Canton Asylum for Insane Indians in Canton, South Dakota. As I demonstrate in this chapter, Indigenous people who refused to accept their assigned role in the prescribed social order were vulnerable to settler-ableist diagnoses of "abnormality." Drawing connections across institutions used to contain, reform, and punish Indigenous people in the Progressive Era, I examine experiences of forced confinement at Canton and situate the practices of this facility on a continuum of US policies aimed at the eradication of Indigenous people.

"CARE AND MAINTENANCE"

SETTLER ABLEISM AND LAND DISPOSSESSION AT THE
CANTON ASYLUM FOR INSANE INDIANS, 1902–1934

Care and maintenance. In the grammatical hierarchy of language used to refer to the Indian people confined at the Canton Asylum for Insane Indians in Canton, South Dakota, the phrase looms large. It appears in hundreds of official documents with alarming regularity—alarming given the staff's rampant abuse and neglect of those held against their will. "Enclosed please find list of patients at the Asylum . . . who have paid for their Care and Maintenance," reads one example.[1] From 1902 to 1934, when Canton ceased operation, approximately four hundred Indigenous women, men, and children from more than fifty tribal nations were forcibly confined to this institution, which was the first and only federal asylum intended exclusively for American Indian people. In an era that saw the proliferation of hospitals and reform facilities, US officials rationalized Canton's existence by contriving a need for a distinct space that would administer to destitute noncitizen tribal members.[2] Beyond the forced confinement of American Indian people for indefinite periods, however, Canton superintendent Oscar S. Gifford (1901–8) and his successor, Harry Hummer (1908–33), facilitated the expropriation of Indigenous land on a small-scale, case-by-case basis.[3] This fact underscores the specificity of Indigenous peoples' experiences of institutionalization under settler colonialism and complicates broader understandings about the relationship between disability and Indigeneity in the Progressive Era.

This chapter reads across the grain of archival materials relating to Indian women and men who experienced forced confinement at Canton. In so doing, it explores the relationship between Indigeneity and disability to show that disability is an important master category in the US settler-colonial project of land acquisition—one that is often overlooked in studies of Indigenous experiences of institutionalization. Existing literature about Canton describes conditions at the facility and is critical of power dynamics that conditioned the lives of the Indian people who endured and resisted abuse and neglect at the hands of employees there.[4] Existing work also discusses the effects of Indigenous confinement at the asylum and the legacy of this institution within Indigenous communities.

Susan Burch's book, *Committed*, places Native peoples' testimonies centrally in her examination of Canton's intergenerational effects, drawing on extensive work with tribes and descendants impacted by institutionalization; Pemina Yellow Bird (Hidatsa, Arikara, Mandan) refers to the destruction wrought by Canton staff as "horrors [that] cannot be erased."[5]

Building on this scholarship, I explore how Indigenous institutionalization at Canton furthered settler-colonial processes of land expropriation, which highlights the importance of social categories of difference, normalcy, dependence, and disability for analyses of settler colonialism. Disability scholars have demonstrated how race and disability are mutually entangled; as Nirmala Erevelles writes, race and disability "constitute one another through social, political, economic, and cultural practices that have kept seemingly different groups of people in strikingly similar marginalized positions."[6] Indigeneity, by comparison, has received less attention in disability studies scholarship and is often subsumed under the category of "race." Yet, this lack of attention to the specificity of Indigenous experience within disability studies scholarship elides important distinctions between race, ethnicity, and Indigeneity.[7] Canton records reflect that for Indigenous people—women and men who lived at the turn of the twentieth century, who were regarded as wards of the US government, and who were also often landholders—diagnoses of intellectual or physical disability presented a specific set of vulnerabilities in an era that saw the proliferation of institutions created, ostensibly, for their benefit. This chapter locates Canton on a historical continuum of settler practices and policies that sought to eliminate Indigenous people and further settler claims to Indigenous territories.

In considering Indigeneity in relation to Western biomedical diagnoses and Euro-American discourses about disability, this chapter explores the interrelationship between Canton and other settler institutions: boarding schools, jails, and county courts. In so doing, it documents the role diverse historical actors played in furthering the settler society's twin objectives of Indigenous erasure and land expropriation. As the first and only federal institution intended solely for the "care" of Indian people designated as "insane," Canton also had a unique role in maintaining the racial, class, and power hierarchies endemic to the settler order. Instances of Indigenous confinement reveal in finite detail how white racial power was transferred and traded among institutional spaces and the historical actors and social networks of which they were comprised.

These phenomena distinguish the characteristics of settler institutions from those of similar facilities and the frameworks used to analyze them, such as the "total institutions" that sociologist Erving Goffman has famously described.[8] Goffman explains, "A total institution may be defined as a place of residence and work where a large number of like-situated individuals, cut off from the wider society for an appreciable period of time, together lead an enclosed, formally administered round of life."[9] In some ways, Canton did resemble a "total institution," as historian Scott Riney has observed: "[Canton] in its all-encompassing character effectively isolated [Indigenous people] from the outside world, challenging their autonomy and their identities as both American Indians and human beings."[10] As Riney suggests here, Canton sequestered Indian women and men and attempted to efface their identities as Indigenous people—a process of extreme isolation and resocialization that Goffman argues is a characteristic hallmark of "total institutions."[11]

Yet, Canton records also reflect that Indian women and men forcibly confined to the institution often did not have their identities effaced; instead, they were constantly reminded of their status as Indian people. As one Canton employee remarked about a confined Lakota man named Peter G. B., on February 15, 1917, Peter "favors the Sioux patients and thinks they should do as they please; when excited, [he] calls the Sioux together, motions and talks to them, shakes his fists and immediately they begin doing something that will cause trouble."[12] Similar descriptions of Indigenous people held at Canton compel us to rethink the asylum and the role that it played in the broader, ongoing work of US settler colonialism in this era; these documents also require us to consider the relationship between Canton and other contemporaneous institutions created exclusively for the education, care, or employment of Indian people.

Canton was a settler institution: it pursued the objectives of settler colonialism by targeting Indigenous women and men for confinement by virtue of their Indigeneity. This practice was inextricable from the US settler-colonial project; to recall Patrick Wolfe's observations of settler colonialism's undergirding logic once more, "We cannot simply say that settler colonialism or genocide have been targeted at particular races, since a race cannot be taken as given. It is made in the targeting. Black people were racialized as slaves; slavery constituted their blackness. Correspondingly, Indigenous North Americans were not killed, driven away, romanticized, assimilated, fenced in, bred White, and otherwise eliminated as the original owners of the land *but as Indians*" (emphasis mine).[13] Building on Wolfe's insights, I explore how Indian women and men like Peter were confined to the facility *because* they were Indian and, once inside, remained there to be punished *as Indian people* as well.

The chapter begins with a historical overview of Canton and its founding. The following discussion examines anti-Indigenous sentiments in law, medicine, and culture that contributed to dominant Western pseudoscientific beliefs about Indigenous people and the prevalence, or lack thereof, of insanity in Indigenous communities. As I argue, these discourses helped shape the racial common sense and conditions of possibility necessary for the forced confinement of hundreds of Indigenous women, men, and children at Canton. Building on this discussion, I shift my analysis to close readings of archival materials to examine the ways in which boarding school superintendents, reservation agents, legal guardians, and disgruntled spouses leveraged extralegal processes of commitment to disappear Indian people to Canton. Drawing on Wolfe's definition of Indigenous elimination, this discussion details how Canton furthered a settler-colonial logic through forced confinement and reproductive suppression. This penultimate section also examines the institutional connections between Canton and boarding schools, which promoted the erasure of Indigenous lifeways and which were also responsible for the transfer of Indigenous people to the asylum. Finally, the remainder of the chapter engages the experiences of Robert Thompson (Quapaw), James H. (Sioux), and Emily Waite (Chickasaw) for what they reveal about land expropriation as a powerful motivating factor in the confinement of Indigenous people.[14]

Together, this analysis highlights the utility of Western biomedical diagnoses of "insanity" for the settler society and showcases the use of the facility as a contested space of Indigenous elimination, territorial dispossession, and settler empowerment. The details of Indigenous institutionalization at Canton highlight similarities between the asylum and other settler spaces of Indigenous education, labor, or "reform," and compel us to reconsider the interrelationship between the settler institutions that existed contemporaneously in this era.

A word on the nature and organization of this chapter is also in order. The history of the Canton Asylum is not a happy one; it is difficult to confront—especially for Indigenous survivors of settler facilities, their descendants, and community members impacted by institutionalization. Canton was a horrifying microcosm that encapsulated some of the worst atrocities the US government has ever committed against Indigenous peoples—a modernized version of the systematized violence and genocidal warfare the US military pursued against tribes across Turtle Island, which historians have amply documented. The archival materials that remain to detail the institutionalization of Indigenous women, men, and children at Canton were overwhelmingly authored by the US officials and citizens responsible for the commitment of Indigenous people to the facility. The historical record upon which this chapter is based is therefore a colonial one. As such, there is a fundamental historiographical one-sidedness to Canton materials, which contributes to the "systemic oppression of the truth," as former Truth and Reconciliation Commission coordinator Thomas Biron (Ojibwe) of the Native Justice Coalition described it.[15] This oppression of the truth, along with the attempted silencing of Indigenous voices in colonial records, has led survivors of settler institutions as well as their descendants to call for truth, healing, justice, and restitution. Yet, healing and justice in this instance are predicated on a transparency of the facts; our nations cannot heal or obtain justice without knowing what took place in facilities like the Canton Asylum. However, as Dian Million has observed, the "truth" is not self-evident, and witnessing is a "convoluted undertaking."[16]

In the language of my ancestors, the Choctaw language, the transitive verb _ạhlichi_ means to make true, to establish the truth, to fulfill a promise.[17] In what follows, I offer an imperfect attempt at radical truth-telling from my standpoint as a Choctaw community member and historian. In so doing, I document the facts of Canton's history of Indigenous human rights abuses while endeavoring also to fulfill my responsibility of being a good relative. In an effort to counter the paucity of Indigenous perspectives in the Canton archive, I have reproduced essays, letters of correspondence, and other writing by Indigenous women and men confined to Canton or their kin, interspersing their words throughout the chapter in italics. I have also included fully reproduced letters in the appendix. This is an intentional "intervention against dispossession," to borrow from historian Karen Roybal; Indigenous voices are interspersed throughout the following analysis in an affirmation of Indigenous self-determination and as a praxis of care, even when these passages bear what may appear to be only suggestive or tentative relation to the broader narrative in which they are embedded.[18] They are meant to be read and treated as interludes, and are themselves an archive of "felt analysis": moments and memories that disrupt, surprise, distort, and challenge the primacy of the settler institution in which they were produced or the colonial agents to which many of these pieces of writing were addressed.[19] Above all, they are meant to be read and understood as an assertion of Indigenous presence and as a form of Indigenous protest. We are meant to bear witness.

CANTON ASYLUM: A "PORK BARREL" PROJECT

The Canton Asylum for Insane Indians was founded in 1902 in Canton, South Dakota, as a result of legislation introduced by state Senator Richard Pettigrew. Hoping to prove his political acumen as a junior member of the Senate, the ambitious lawyer-turned-politician advocated for the construction of the facility as a way to attract attention to the state, which had been admitted to the Union in 1889. While the construction of Canton was formally a result of Pettigrew's bill, the inspiration for such a facility came from Peter Couchman, US Indian agent at the Cheyenne River Agency, who wrote in correspondence from May 1897 that he had been using the reservation guardhouse to hold the "demented Indians" under his jurisdiction.[20] As Canton historians Todd Leahy, Carla Joinson, and Diane Putney have also noted in their works, state hospitals refused to accept Indigenous and Black women and men into their facilities, citing overcrowding as a convenient way to disguise racial prejudice and the widespread conviction that the administration of Indian affairs was a federal, rather than state, issue.[21] Given the apparent need for an institution intended for the exclusive care of "insane" Indian people, Pettigrew's proposal thus appealed to philanthropically minded citizens and Indian Service officials alike, who saw the opportunity to extend their campaign of "uplift" into the purportedly abnormal psyches of Indian people.[22]

Despite garnering the vocal support of acting Commissioner of Indian Affairs Thomas Smith, however, Pettigrew's proposal was not universally accepted. Secretary of the Interior Cornelius Bliss was adamant that a new asylum would not, in fact, serve the interests of the Indian Service, especially when the Government Hospital for the Insane in Washington, DC—St. Elizabeths—already accepted Indian patients and had been designated for expansion.[23] But rather than abandoning his pet project, Pettigrew redoubled his efforts to win favor among his political peers and sent out surveys to Indian agents across the country in order to determine with hard data the extent to which Indian people reportedly suffered from mental illness. A letter dated June 10, 1897, sent from Pettigrew to the Indian agent of the Southern Ute Agency reads:

Dear Sir:

That I may act intelligently in connection with a proposition to create an asylum for insane Indians, I would like from you answers to the following questions:

How many insane Indians are there on the reservation under your charge?

Is insanity as common among Indians as among whites?

Have you any special course of treatment for mentally diseased Indians?

Truly Yours,

R. F. Pettigrew[24]

By September 1897, Pettigrew had received his answer: fifty-nine "insane" Indians resided across twenty-one Indian reservations, and according to US officials, of those fifty-nine, twenty-six required confinement. Though this small number seemed to contradict Pettigrew's insistence that Indian people required a psychiatric facility all their own, the survey results justified a separate institution for "insane" Indian people in the eyes of Congress, and appropriations were made for the construction of the asylum.[25]

⋮

I broke my way out from here on the night of monday Sept 31 1923, with the intentions of to be away from this Insane asylum. because I am not insane not in the least way to speak of. Why. I'd be satisfied here, but I don't even get fits, I would be contented here if I was in any way inclined to insanity but I am not. I know it. I am no more insane than all the people that think I am put together . . . for that simple reason I made my way out, with the intentions of striking a job somewhere, and start life over with a good, clean, decent life, have moonshine alone and behave; and then if I am insane why on earth don't I get treatment of some sort. I am here without any kind of medicine to speak of, whatsoever.

—Jerome C. (Sioux)[26]

Canton, like the off-reservation boarding schools that preceded and followed it, was founded during an ostensibly "benevolent" era in which the United States

4.1 Canton Asylum for Insane Indians, Canton, South Dakota, ca. 1901. N.d.

government shifted away from a formal campaign of violent warfare and toward a program of forcible assimilation and allotment, whereby tribal nations would be dispossessed of their landholdings and subordinated to US authority. As discussed in chapter 1, the process of allotment resulted in the expropriation of millions of acres of Indigenous lands; as Katherine Ellinghaus has observed, by the time Commissioner of Indian Affairs John Collier had implemented the Indian "New Deal," which repealed the allotment process, over ninety million acres of Indigenous lands had been lost.[27] Cutcha Risling Baldy (Hupa, Yurok, Karuk) asserts that violence was integral to the success of these and other postinvasion policies, as the settler society used force to establish the US nation-state, its Western epistemologies, and its settler-citizens as dominant.[28]

Situated along this historical continuum, Canton's 1902 founding marked a new frontier in the settler society's fight for total dominance over Indigenous nations (fig. 4.1). As a businessman and attorney at law, former mayor of Canton Oscar S. Gifford was an inappropriate choice for the director of any psychiatric facility. He had no medical training at all, a fact demonstrated by the twenty deaths that occurred at Canton while he was supervisor. But as a popular merchant and well-known politician, Gifford was nonetheless favored as superintendent of the new facility, and he occupied this position from 1901 to 1908, when he was removed after his gross incompetence and near-continuous absence from the institution were discovered. As Canton researcher Carla Joinson notes, while asylum superintendents elsewhere in the country were generally trained medical practitioners, "Canton Asylum was run like an Indian boarding school, and no one had thought to substitute a physician for a lay superintendent."[29] Todd Leahy similarly observes in his early study of the asylum that Canton's superintendents were not active participants in the fields of medicine or psychiatry, a fact that further demonstrates the extent to which Canton practiced bad medicine.[30]

Construction for the asylum began in 1900 under the aegis of architect John Charles on one hundred acres in Lincoln County, just two miles outside of Canton city limits.[31] As Diane Putney notes, the original structure consisted of a single building with four wings, in which the superintendent and his family, along with asylum employees, would reside in quarters apart from the Indigenous people confined there. Gifford assumed his position as superintendent in November 1901, before construction was complete; according to Putney, a year later, in 1902, Canton's staff (predominantly of Norwegian descent) had swelled to include assistant superintendent and physician Dr. John Turner, as well as a seamstress, matron, financial clerk, laundress, cook, night watchman, engineer, ward attendants, and two laborers.[32] Charles had laid plans to construct the building in a way that would withstand the harsh South Dakota winters, which facilitated a chilling and unintended practice: a 1933 investigation would reveal that asylum employees chained Indigenous women and men to the boilers and radiators found throughout the institution, rendering those held at Canton immobile for extended periods of time.

> *I am doing my best in every way not to step out of the way I hope I will get home soon as my time is up. I do my work the best way I know how. I am sending you one of my pictures*
>
> —*Susan W. (Menominee)*[33]

Gifford's control of the asylum did not last long. In 1908, Gifford and his assistant, Dr. Turner, were removed after shocking incidences of malpractice at Canton came to light. Shortly thereafter, Harry Hummer was installed as superintendent. Unlike Gifford, Hummer *was* a trained physician—educated at Georgetown University—but he too would be subject to numerous internal investigations and eventually removed on charges of neglect and malpractice. Over the course of

Gifford's superintendency and Hummer's tenure—a period that stretched in total thirty-one years—chaos reigned; but as Burch notes, the institution's architectural design and subsequent improvements conveyed a sense of *increasing* authority and orderliness to the general public. Burch writes, "A laundry was added in 1909 and enlarged in 1918; the superintendent's house was built in 1915; and a dairy barn followed in the next year. In 1917, the two-story Hospital Building was erected, its brick-and-concrete façade intended to 'harmonize in appearance' with the other structures on the campus."[34]

Canton's handsome exterior and well-kept grounds may have mimicked the serene and orderly environments of other psychiatric hospitals, but the institution's placid facade disguised truly hellish interior conditions. Hummer and his staff were at constant odds, and these dynamics were the subject of multiple Office of Indian Affairs investigations. In 1929, however, Hummer himself invited scrutiny into the facility. As Putney notes, Hummer hoped the Indian Office would force one of his attendants, Nurse Grace Fillius, to curb what he alleged to be her excessive drinking; in February of that year he wrote to the commissioner describing "the 'deplorable conditions' at his own institution and asserted that only a stranger and layman could provide an impartial and unbiased report."[35]

Shortly thereafter, Commissioner Charles H. Burke arranged for a full investigation, and appointed Dr. Samuel Silk, a psychiatrist at St. Elizabeths Hospital in Washington, DC, to the task. Silk visited Canton for six days in March 1929, and his findings were astonishing. According to his report of the institution's conditions, "patients" were kept confined to their beds, and meals were taken haphazardly on the floor. Women and men lay in their own excrement, chamber pots were found to be overflowing, and four men were found padlocked in their rooms.[36] The "operating room" was also inspected, and found to have no equipment whatsoever, aside from "a surgical table, a slop sink, and two wash bowls"; similarly, the windows of the "solarium," an open-air structure built for tubercular patients, were found to have wooden bars placed across them—in the event of a fire, no one would be able to escape.[37] As these conditions clearly illustrate, Canton was not a place of care, medical or otherwise; it was a place of chaos, social death, and disappearance, where Indian people were sent to languish, and where loss of life was routine. Of the hundreds of Indian people who suffered at the hands of Gifford and Hummer over the decades of this facility's operation, many perished at the asylum and were buried in unmarked graves in a small cemetery adjoining Canton's grounds. Putney estimates that an average of four people died at Canton annually, amounting to roughly 120 deaths between 1903 and 1934. Pemina Yellow Bird (Hidatsa, Arikara, Mandan) puts this figure even higher, at an average rate of ten "discharges" per year, nine of which she attributes solely to the deaths of Indian people.[38] As Yellow Bird writes of the atrocities perpetrated at Canton, "These horrors cannot be erased"—a powerful statement that captures the impact of the institution on subsequent generations of Indigenous people and their communities, as the effects of forced confinement traverse decades and span geographic space and reverberate into the present.

> *Trouble with a girl:—*
> *When the 1st time I came she gave me some shining smiles & peculiar looks, I know right there that there was some-thing in it, & it interested me, also, as it would with any other young man. At thereafter mealtimes she frequently shine her contagious smiles to me, of course I paid back with one or two of mine.*
>
> *—Jerome C. (Sioux)*[39]

SETTLER STRUCTURES OF DISENFRANCHISEMENT: LAW, MEDICINE, AND CULTURE

Indian people were generally considered "wards" of the US government at the turn of the twentieth century, having not been granted citizenship until 1924, when the Indian Citizenship Act was passed. In this and previous eras, anti-Indian discrimination pervaded American society and prevented Indian people from accessing equal protection under US law. With the installment of Cato Sells as Commissioner of Indian Affairs, these inequities played out before competency commissions that regularly assessed Indigenous peoples' "fitness" for citizenship and self-sufficiency using literacy, blood quantum, and adherence to Western ways of being as criteria.[40] Unsurprisingly, many Indian people failed these exams, and legal guardians were appointed to act, ostensibly, in the interest of those who had been declared incompetent.

As historian Anne Gregory has pointed out, those who failed to "conform to settler ideals"—such as her great-great-grandmother Emma Gregory, committed to Canton in 1905 at the behest of her younger brother, who acted as her trustee—were "especially vulnerable to being designated legally incompetent."[41] Gregory explains that after her great-great-grandmother parted ways with her husband in 1899, she needed to find a way to support herself. Emma Gregory thus went to live with her mother and sisters: "In addition to cross-generational childrearing and mutual aid—facets of Creek life that settler authorities targeted—Emma Gregory likely was not literate in written English and may have challenged other gendered and caste expectations."[42] Gregory further notes that the politics of land in this era "pitted family members against each other, promoting greed over interdependence and intergenerational collective care."[43]

Canton records reveal that multiple Indigenous women and men confined to the facility had similarly had legal guardians appointed to them by county courts, some of whom were family members. These records also document that many of those confined to Canton were in need of medical care or were perceived, often by the reservation agent, to be a burden on their communities. A general lack of protected rights for Indigenous people under US law thus exacerbated the probability of confinement at the facility, as Indian people were legally, politically, and physically vulnerable to individuals who sought to leverage Western legal structures to confine Indian women and men to the institution. That some of the Indian women and men sent to this facility were landholders—as Emma Gregory was—further illustrates the ways in which forced institutionalization furthered land expropriation.

For American Indians who lived in this era, racial prejudice and the lack of diagnostic criteria used by US officials who wished to assess the "sanity" of Indian people presented a specific set of vulnerabilities. These were distinct from those faced by white Americans, but entwined with the experiences of other populations of color in this era. As Rana Hogarth, Martin Summers, Deirdre Cooper Owens, and Wendy Gonaver have examined, anti-Black racism in Western medical practices contributed to high rates of morbidity and mortality and impeded Black Americans' ability to access medical treatment in the postbellum era.[44] Similarly, in an era of US federal Indian policies that aimed to "civilize" Indian people and incorporate them into the national polity by subjugating them to US authority, white Americans championed the notion that Western methods were superior to Indigenous ways of healing and traditional forms of labor and medicine, as discussed in greater detail in chapter 2. In an affirmation of this belief, reformers derogated the continuance of ancestral traditions as evidence of Indian peoples' stubborn heathenism and savagery, often likening these practices to forms of madness, illness, or uncleanliness.[45]

These anti-Indigenous attitudes reflect the mutual entanglement of ableism with settler colonialism, a phenomenon that further valorized white Americans' worldview and established white bodies and ways of being as normative.[46] As Native historians have pointed out, Indigenous cosmologies were complex and remain so today, with specific terms to denote individual or communal periods of illness, disease, or unwellness; many Indigenous languages do not have concepts that were comparable to the English concept of disability as so defined by the West, and tribes today and in the past emphasized the health and prosperity of the polity as a whole to assess collective well-being.[47]

$$\vdots$$

At the turn of the twentieth century, anti-Indigenous and settler-ableist attitudes pervaded the fabric of American society and frequently sutured Indigeneity to pathologized behavior. In one prominent example, in the late 1880s, politicians, reformers, and news publications circulated news of the Ghost Dance "hysteria" spreading across the plains, warning white Americans that the dances were preparations for a massive Indian uprising.[48] At boarding schools like Carlisle, student publications similarly warned against the destructive influence of Indigenous traditions, frequently using satire and parable as their weapons of choice. In 1887, an article authored by "Aunt Martha" entitled "Pawnee Medicine and an Indian Lodge" was printed in the *Indian Helper*, Carlisle's official school publication from 1885 to 1900.[49] Writing of the homes, ceremonies, and healers of the Pawnee—early adherents to Wovoka's Ghost Dance philosophy—"Aunt Martha" recounted a story she had once told to little boys and girls about the "queer doings" of this people. "There are men among the Indians who pretend to do wonderful things," Martha warned her audience of presumably Indian children. "They are called doctors and they make the other Indians think they have great power given them by Indian gods." "Is it true?" one little boy asked, bewildered. "No," Martha reassured him; "the Indian doctors are just as ignorant as the other Indians, but they have great influence in the tribe, and are more in the way of their real progress than anything else." This was evidenced, Martha continued, by the living conditions among the Pawnee. She explained,

> "I have seen such dirty things thrown in the ashes, and have noticed time and again men spit in the ashes near to where I thought the bread was baking. Then

the Indian women are not careful to wash their hands before they go at mixing the bread. So you see my dear children, I did not feel much hungry when they offered me that bread to eat. I have been told that it is generally good and sweet."

One child interjected,

"I should like to know about the *dance*."

"So should I."

"And I," said another, and before Auntie had time to say more, every tot in the room was swinging his or her hands and calling out "Dance! Dance! Yes, Dance! Auntie, tell us about the dance," but Auntie disappointed them by saying, "Not now, my dears, but next time you come to see me I will tell you all about the Pawnee Medicine dance."[50]

Suturing Pawnee ceremony to deception and filth, "Pawnee Medicine and an Indian Lodge," like other Carlisle parables, sought to inculcate within Indian youth a disdain toward their own people. As Aunt Martha (likely Marianna Burgess, Carlisle's printmaking instructor) pathologized Indigenous lifeways and derogated ancestral practices as "ignorance," she also reinforced white American ways of being as a norm to which Indian children and their communities should aspire. As this and other parables suggested, Indigenous lifeways were simply abnormal—deviant.

In the realm of American politics, Indigenous peoples' legal status as dependent wards of the US government similarly led many US officials to champion the notion that Indian people were incapable of transacting their own affairs, a marker of childlike dependence defined in opposition to the conditions of American individualism and adulthood.[51] As disability scholar Licia Carlson writes, justifications for institutionalizing disabled people in this era included four basic premises, which overlapped and intersected with ideas about Indigenous deficiency in important ways. These premises were that disability should be defined as an individual pathology in need of management; paternal authority should be exercised over disabled people unable to make decisions for themselves; disabled individuals warrant treatment in special facilities; and their lives are better managed by experts granted higher authority than the disabled individuals, own preferences and desires.[51] Similar guiding principles rationalized the institutionalization of Indigenous people at Canton, but with one critical distinction: by defining Indigenous people as disabled, "insane," or incompetent and institutionalizing them, US officials and white American citizens effectively disappeared Indian people and stood to gain Indigenous land and resources—a pattern that furthered settler aims of erasing and replacing Indigenous peoples and their polities.

In 1902, the year before the Canton Asylum opened, another article, entitled "A Protest Against the Abolition of the Indian Dance," appeared in Carlisle's *Red Man and Helper,* reflecting the endurance of this anti-Indigenous ethos in dominant discourse and boarding school vernacular alike. Originally authored by Dakota activist Gertrude Bonnin (Zitkala Ša) and entitled "The Indian Dance: A Protest against Its Abolition," the essay had been altered by Burgess in an ongoing dispute with Bonnin, who was a former Carlisle employee—just a few years earlier, in 1899, Pratt had dismissed Bonnin from the institution, where she had been employed as music instructor. As Kristen Brown writes of the protracted conflict, "On January 25, 1902, when the *Boston Evening Transcript* published her essay, [Bonnin] was already embroiled in a battle of words with Pratt and others. The bitter feud, rendered public spectacle by the press, had started two years earlier . . . when the *Atlantic Monthly* published her trilogy of narrative essays roundly condemning the compulsory education engine of the assimilation era."[52] Brown continues, noting that the boarding school press, including "Carlisle's *Red Man* and *The Indian Helper* used their publications as sites for rhetorical battle in the ongoing propaganda war defending assimilation's supposedly benevolent aims."[53] Bonnin's original piece—much like her work in the public sphere on behalf of Indian people—critiqued the classificatory schemes, taxonomies, and exclusions of "civilized" society. But the reprinted essay—taken out of context and heavily editorialized—used satire as a shaming mechanism to deter Indian enrollees from adherence to their lifeways: "I fail to see the necessity of checking the Indian dance," the piece stated. "If learned scientists advise an occasional relaxation of work or daily routine with such ardor that even the inmates of insane asylums are allowed to dance their dances then the same logic should hold good elsewhere. The law at least, should not be partial. If it is right for the insane and idiot to dance, the Indian (who is classed with them) should have the same privilege."[54]

Likening dancing Indians to those who might occupy the wards of the insane, the essay echoed a powerful idea that had taken hold in legal, political, medical, and cultural realms of American society: Indianness itself was an abnormal state of being, frequently construed in political circles as illness. In this instance, Indianness was a degree or two removed from insanity. A far cry from Bonnin's original intent in writing the piece, Burgess's manipulations of tone and context were, as Brown argues, "tantamount to semantic violence."[55]

In addition to more oblique references to Indigenous "insanity" such as those already examined, Carlisle's student publications also reported news of Canton's founding. In 1898, shortly before appropriations had been made for the construction of the asylum, the *Red Man* printed an article entitled "For Insane Indians" in which it was reported that "Col. D. M. Wisdom desires to be informed, for the information of the Indian Bureau, the names, addresses, age and sex of all insane persons in the Indian Territory, who are members of any of the Indian tribes, who would likely become inmates of an insane asylum."[56] The author's reference to Indian people "who would likely become inmates" rhetorically sidestepped the issue of formalized commitment procedures, while appearing to suggest that the only criteria required for confinement to Canton was public opinion that an individual was likely to wind up there anyway. Given the fact that Canton had no formalized commitment procedures and few checks and balances in terms of oversight, the article seemingly presaged what was to come.

The following year, the *Red Man* printed another piece about Canton, this time reporting news of the asylum's impending construction: "At its last session Congress appropriated $42,000 for the erection of an Indian Insane Asylum, and an additional $3,000 for the purchase of suitable grounds. . . . According to the best statistics obtainable, out of the total of 250,000 Indians in the United States, there are fifty-eight insane Indians, one doubtful, six idiotic and two partly idiotic."[57] This article went on to observe that the federal psychiatric institution, St. Elizabeths, was overcrowded and thus could not accept additional patients, while state hospitals were prejudiced in their views that the care of Indian people was a federal, rather than state, issue. Regardless of whether the "fifty-eight" Indigenous people enumerated in this piece legitimately required custodianship for mental health purposes, it is hard to imagine that this tiny number—0.02 percent of the US Indigenous population at the time—merited the construction of an asylum that would over the course of its existence regularly be at or over capacity.[58] Other Carlisle publications that appeared in this era detailed the appointment or "separation" of employees to Canton. Moreover, a 1906 issue of the *Arrow* illustrated how Carlisle furnished labor that greased the wheels of Canton's continued operations when it reported under "Industrial" notes that "A fine buggy has just been completed and shipped to Superintendent Gefford [*sic*] of the Asylum for Insane Indians at Canton, S.D."[59]

As these brief excerpts illustrate, Carlisle enrollees were kept abreast of developments in the asylum's objectives, construction, and founding, and even facilitated transportation for the asylum's first superintendent, Oscar Gifford. It is not difficult to imagine that the young Indigenous people who read about the asylum in their school's newspaper would experience a range of emotions about Canton's founding and perhaps worry about relatives or community members back home. In much the same way that Canton targeted Indigenous psyches as another battleground in the settler society's quest for ascendancy, these boarding school publications waged psychological warfare against enrollees, young and old.

By the turn of the twentieth century, the pathologization of Indigeneity was becoming a well-worn notion with great utility to US officials and other settler agents. In 1893, the year of the Columbian Exposition in Chicago and the United States' overthrow of the Hawaiian Kingdom and Queen Liliuokalani, American suffragist and superintendent of the Women's Christian Temperance Union Henrietta Briggs-Wall commissioned a four-by-six-foot portrait of educator and reformer Frances E. Willard. As the caption of the portrait, entitled "American Woman and Her Political Peers," suggested, "In many states women are classed, politically, with idiots, convicts, the insane, and Indians—not allowed to vote." The original was displayed at the Chicago World's Fair in 1893, as well as at the "Greater America" Exhibition of Omaha in 1896, and was later reproduced in numerous other mediums, including postcard format (fig. 4.2). While the image was meant to arouse shock and dismay on behalf of white American women who felt they were unfairly "classed" politically among the nation's disenfranchised, the painting also demonstrates how intimately entwined "Indianness" was with American cultural conceptions of criminality, insanity, effeminateness, and other forms of "degeneracy" in the American imaginary of this era.

In the world of Western medicine, psychiatrists similarly contemplated the nature of insanity—its causes, characteristics, and cures—drawing on contemporaneous theories that posited reason as the exclusive purview of mankind and European civilization as humanity's highest achievement. As the proceedings of the American Medico-Psychological Association reflect, the elite American and European men who dominated the Western medical profession had historically looked to women, nonwhite, and non-Western peoples who, in their estimation, had not achieved similar forms of intellectual, physical, or cultural "advancement" in order to determine whether insanity might be attributed to civilization gone awry. In the July 1847 edition of the *American Journal of Insanity*, for example, a Dr. Millingen pronounced that "Insanity is of rare occurrence in barbarous nations" and that "civilization appears to favor the development of madness." He explained,

(Copyright 1911 by Henrietta Briggs-Wall.)
AMERICAN WOMAN AND HER POLITICAL PEERS.
In many states women are classed, politically, with idiots, con-
victs, the insane, and Indians—**not allowed to vote.** Women do not,
however, escape taxation.
"Taxation without representation is tyranny."
"Resistance to tyranny is obedience to God."

4.2 "American Woman and Her Political Peers, 1893." Hutchinson, Kansas, Commis-
sioned by Henrietta Briggs-Wall, 1911. Caption reads: "American Woman and Her
Political Peers. In many states women are classed, politically, with idiots, convicts, the
insane, and Indians—not allowed to vote. Women do not, however, escape taxation.
'Taxation without representation is tyranny.' 'Resistance to tyranny is obedience to
God.'" Postcard. Manuscript Division, Library of Congress (116).

"The wants of the savage are circumscribed: he gives vent to the burst of his passions without control, and their violence subsides when they are gratified. In a more polished state of society, man dwells upon his injuries real or supposed, acts silently, and cherishes hopes of enjoyment, amongst which the sweets of revenge are not the least seductive."[60] Insanity, Millingen mused, was a lamentable, but perhaps unavoidable, byproduct of civilization.

Half a century later, British and American psychiatrists still clung to this self-congratulatory, if somewhat counterintuitive, notion. In 1904, Dr. Robert Jones authored an essay entitled "The Development of Insanity in Regard to Civilization," in which he stated:

> It appears that insanity increases as man departs from the savage and semi-civilized states and approaches the highest civilization. In primitive states of society and among uncivilized races, insanity is rare, the pure psychoses are unknown; the chief forms—apart from the low grades, idiocy and imbecility—being associated with the taking of drugs and corresponding to the insanities of civilization resulting from alcohol, ether, cocaine, morphine, etc., and which in the main are curable. . . . Highly civilized man thus lives in a more complicated environment, which calls for the higher forms of self-control and more prolonged and varied efforts than are customarily aroused by the simple emotions and elementary sensorial stimuli of a primitive life. In these efforts numbers of unfortunate ones will not succeed; they are incapable of elevation to this higher plane of civilization owing to mental, physical, and moral deficiencies.[61]

Jones continued, "Not having the qualities essential to success, they are left behind, evolution proceeding at the expense of the less fit—those, in fact, whom civilization itself in the struggle renders unfit for the standard it has itself fixed." He concluded, "It is thus seen that civilized society, in forcing the pace, practically manufactures its own unfit . . . its own paupers, its own lunatics, and its own criminals."[62] "Civilized" societies were so refined, so resplendent and decadent, that they drove themselves crazy with achievement. By comparison, Jones implied, non-Western peoples lacking in high incidences of insanity had simply failed to reach a comparable state of perfection.

> *Capital Punishment should have no place in a civilized country for these reasons It is not practical It defeats the very purpose for which it is prescribed. It is suposed to deter people from Murder. As a matter of fact it*

increases the tendency to Commit the Crime Manslaughter is more fre-
quent where Capital punishment is the law than in states where it is not
the law Capital punishment is presumed to impress offenders with the
sacredness of life. It work just the other way the psychological effect of it is
precisely the reverse. It provokes violence.

—Peter G. B. (Sioux)[63]

That same year, in 1904, Canton superintendent Oscar Gifford expressed similar views on insanity among Indian people that were published in a *Chicago Tribune* article entitled "Gain in Indian Insanity: Chief Cause Attributed to Forced Civilization." The article began, "At the close of the first year's existence of the National Hospital for Insane Indians the first data ever collected about Indian insanity indicate that forced civilization is responsible for much of it.... Supt. O. S. Gifford and Dr. J. F. Turner, assistant superintendent and physician of the hospital, agree that the chief cause of insanity among the Indians is despondency."[64] The reporter continued,

This is manifested in different ways, but most of these manifestations would have been improbable or impossible in the former wild life of the Indian.... That brooding should follow when the Indians cannot have the employment of hunting or making visits at a distance and are even prohibited from indulging in their native dances is natural.... There are now thirty-four insane Indians in the hospital, which is the only institution of its kind in the world, having been completed a year ago. Supt. Gifford has no doubt that all fifty rooms will be taken up within another year.[65]

As Gifford explained, "It is difficult to find Indians who are insane.... At first we could find not more than a half dozen in the entire United States. But we are beginning to hear from them now from the remotest districts." The reason for this dramatic increase, according to Gifford, was because Indigenous people were newly exposed to civilizing influences and tribes had "never made provision for their insane" or were inclined to abandon their kin: "It is a peculiar fact that Indians will desert unfortunates. Take, for example, the case of the great chief Red Cloud.... [He] is afflicted with a distressing ailment, but not one of his relatives save his wife will have a thing to do with him."[66]

"Gain in Indian Insanity" reflected a peculiar marriage between pseudoscientific racism and the ideology of Manifest Destiny, predicated on views of white superiority, Euro-American dominance, and Indigenous disappearance. As Burch similarly notes of Gifford's views in the article, "Native people were biologically tied to an inevitable path of erasure. Their mental incompetence would increase along the way, and white people would take care of their wards as a reflection of their benevolent superiority." She continues, "The growing institutionalized population, from Gifford's vantage point, was a positive indication, reflecting the great humanitarianism of white people taking care of the 'Indian problem' and the 'problem Indians.'"[67]

As US politicians, physicians, reformers, and everyday American citizens spun narratives about Indigenous people as intellectually, physically, and spiritually inferior to white Americans, these discourses positioned Indian people as irreconcilably different and targets for diagnoses of "insanity" and forced confinement alike.[68] Popular views about Indigenous deficiency additionally registered what historian Lorenzo Veracini describes as the "unresolved tension[s] between sameness and difference" inherent to settler-colonial dynamics.[69] These patterns lay bare the settler-colonial logic, or "settler grammar," to borrow from Mishuana Goeman (Tonawanda Band of Seneca), that undergirded notions about Indigeneity and insanity in this era, and which were similarly reflected in Canton superintendents' false promises of offering "care and maintenance" to the Indian people confined at the facility.[70] This settler grammar was not merely linguistic, although it was also that, but had material consequences. As Goeman reminds us, "Foundational to normative modes of settler colonialism are repetitive practices of everyday life that give settler place meaning and structure. Yet space is fluid, and it is only in the constant retelling and reformulating of colonial narratives that space becomes place as it is given structure and meaning."[71] In one example of the protocols of settler placemaking at Canton, Burch points out that Hummer and other US officials pathologized Indian peoples' nonstandard use of English in correspondence, citing this as evidence of insanity that necessitated ongoing confinement at the facility, often indefinitely.[72]

INDIGENOUS ELIMINATION: DISABILITY, EUGENICS, AND SETTLER COLONIALISM

Given the flimsy logic behind turn-of-the-century theories about race and insanity, it is no surprise that Indian people were committed to Canton for reasons that appeared to be entirely unrelated to soundness of mind. Unlike the general population, Indigenous people were more likely to be institutionalized by strangers than they were to be confined by close kin and relatives. As the following documents reflect, the motivations behind commitments were often inflected by white supremacist convictions about racial superiority, population control, and social degeneracy.

A 1918 report demonstrates that Indian Officials debated using Canton for the practice of negative eugenics—the process of selecting against traits viewed as undesirable in a human population—and openly discussed this possibility in correspondence to one another. In the spring of 1918, for example, Commissioner of Indian Affairs Cato Sells dispatched medical inspector R. E. Newberne to conduct an investigation of Canton, one of many over the institution's thirty years of operation. Hummer's conduct was generally the subject of these internal investigations, but asylum conditions were the topic of interest that year; as Newberne's report reflects, the facility was being considered for expansion, an improvement that he supported as an act of public service for the greater good.[73]

Under "Enlargement," he wrote, "I understand that Canton has a waiting list of 70 or more. This list does not include the feeble minded and many of the epileptics, who, for eugenic purposes as well as their personal comfort, should be incarcerated."[74] Vague, secondhand reports frequently characterized diagnoses of "feeblemindedness" in this era, and Newberne similarly drew on this layman's term to legitimize his recommendations.[75] "Regardless of what the general Indian policy of the future may be," Newberne's letter continued, "it would be humane and economical for the United States Government to make some provision for the mental derelicts of the Indian race before the problem is passed on to the states."[76] Echoing the prejudice expressed by employees of state hospitals across the nation, Newberne likewise felt that the "mental derelicts of the Indian race" were a problem to be dealt with in federal, rather than state, facilities. "Why not increase the capacity of Canton to 500?" he mused. "This will not be too large and the time is not far distant when the truth of this proposition will be evident."[77] Mass incarceration, he seemed to suggest, could also serve eugenicist ends.

We then accomplished some clothes washing & after that we had a lunch in the kitchen, I sat out on the porch with some friends

—Jerome C. (Sioux)[78]

As a federal institution, Canton was under the ultimate aegis of the Commissioner of Indian Affairs, who was—at least in theory—responsible for approving each new candidate for commitment to Canton after a physician's recommendation had been made and before an individual's transfer to the asylum. Indeed, letters of correspondence exchanged between Hummer, various Commissioners of Indian Affairs, and US officials scattered across the country document how individual cases of "insanity" were generally confirmed by agency superintendents, backed by the opinion of the resident physician, and occasionally affirmed by a short letter of approval from the commissioner. But these documents also demonstrate how, unlike the general population in the United States, Indian people were often committed to Canton at the behest of US officials and persons to whom they bore no immediate relation as family members.[79] Importantly, this fact demonstrates how the mere existence of the facility appealed to those who simply wanted to disappear "troublesome" Indian women or men, in much the same way that Carlisle's physician described that institution as a "Happy Dumping Ground for Incorrigibles."[80]

In one example of the ways in which US officials attempted to use Canton for explicitly carceral and eugenicist purposes, on March 11, 1918, agency physician H. C. Meek wrote to the superintendent of the Tongue River Agency John A. Buntin in regard to the potential confinement of a twenty-seven-year-old woman named Josephine S. As correspondence reflects, Meek felt that Josephine was destined for confinement—an opinion based, at least in part, on rumor and hearsay. He explained, "This woman is a hopeless imbecile, and shows a defective Physical development characterized bya [sic] marked lack of control over the muscles of locomotion." Meek went on, "She has had several children all born out of wedlock. These children are all dead with the exception of one and according to statements made to me they have all of them been defective either mentally or physically." He concluded this callous "medical" opinion by stating: "I suggest that an effort be made to isolate this woman in order to prevent the birth of any more defective children, as wellas [sic] to protect the morals of the community in which she lives. She is absolutely without moral responsibility and is, appearantly [sic], about to be confined again." "P.S.—," he scribbled at the bottom of the page, "This woman is also a deaf mute." For reasons that are unclear, Josephine was not committed to Canton that year. But Meek's correspondence demonstrates how US officials could leverage Western biomedical diagnoses to disappear unwanted Indian people. As historian Kelly Lytle Hernández observes of "human caging," incarceration is not incidental to settler colonialism; it is one of its pillars.[81] In this instance, the agency physician tasked with the medical care of those in his jurisdiction would have been responsible for confinement of an Indian woman and the separation of Indian children from their mother—part of a pattern of intentional familial destruction disguised as moral imperative.

Other documents illustrate how US officials used Canton as an explicitly carceral space in which Indian women's sexuality could be controlled and reproduction suppressed.[82] Documents relating to a Sisseton-Wahpeton woman, Nellie K., show that Hummer authorized the confinement and prevented the release of disabled Indian women or others with perceived disabilities as defined by agency physicians like Meek and legitimated this practice as an act of public service and civic duty.

On June 30, 1919, Hummer wrote the Commissioner of Indian Affairs regarding Nellie, an eighteen-year-old woman who had been diagnosed with epilepsy and committed to Canton from the Pipestone Indian School in Montana. He began, "We are dealing here with a constitutional psychopath, who occasionally manifests hysterical symptoms, who is a pathological liar and who has a very decided weakness toward the male sex, probably nymphomania."[83] Debating whether Nellie's conduct merited continued confinement at Canton, Hummer went on, "The question is, what is to be done with her. If we decide to hold her, it would seem equivalent to a life sentence. If we decide to permit her to leave, we should expect to hear disconcerting news at almost any time."[84] After two years at Canton, Nellie was released into the custody of her sister; other Indian women Hummer similarly described as sexually "unbridled" were generally confined indefinitely.

During her confinement, Nellie was able to assist another Indigenous woman, Elizabeth Faribault (Sisseton-Wahpeton), in writing letters back home to her husband, using her knowledge of the English language and years of previous schooling to aid in her friend's efforts. Remarkably, Nellie mounted one of the most powerful forms of resistance at her disposal when she ran away from Canton and remained uncaptured for two days, until she was located in Rock Valley, Iowa, twenty miles to the east of the asylum.[85] As demonstrated by these incredible acts of courage, Indigenous people like Nellie and Elizabeth seized on opportunities to exercise resistance to institutionalization in the face of overwhelming odds.

I am in good health & would be able to work for myself.

—Emma A. (Chippewa)[86]

In another instance of long-term confinement, Agnes C. (Menominee) spent seventeen years at Canton, committed to the facility in November 1917 at the age of twenty-six. As her institutional file indicates, Agnes attempted to secure her own release from the asylum on numerous occasions by corresponding with the Commissioner of Indian Affairs and keeping him informed of her "good health."[87]

> *Dear Sir*
>
> *I must take the pleasure of writting you a few lines to you just to let you know how I am getting along in a very good, Health and fine. I hopeing you are the same I am doing fine ever day I was just in Dr Hummer Office Saturday noon talking to him about if I could soon I was feeling so good when Dr. told me that to the to wrote to Commissercon asking him if I could please go home my folks and my little children whant to now to if I can go home.*
>
> *—Agnes C—. (Menominee)*[88]

As communications from Hummer to Sells indicate, Hummer construed Agnes's many letters to the commissioner as evidence of her ongoing insanity. On October 21, 1919, Hummer wrote:

> Sir:—
>
> I have the honor to enclose herewith a letter written to you by Agnes [C—.], patient. This woman is feeble-minded, as you will readily detect from reading her letter, and wishes to be discharged and allowed to go to her home at the Keshena Agency. Several days ago she received a letter from her husband asking her why she did not come home, as he thought she had been here long enough. It would not prove a surprise to me, if it developed that the husband was not mentally alert. It would be highly improper in my opinion to discharge this woman, though she will never be bright, as she experiences great difficulty in getting along under the best of conditions and I am sure that with this husband and several children to look after, she would be immeasurebly [*sic*] worse off than she is here.[89]

Hummer drew on the notion of heritable feeblemindedness—the same rationale that would serve as the basis of the Supreme Court's 1927 landmark ruling, in *Buck v. Bell*, that states could perform involuntary sterilization procedures on those deemed "unfit"—to characterize Agnes's family's collective determination as evidence of mental instability shared between relatives.[90]

Other details contained in Hummer's letter reveal how "white managerialism," discussed in chapter 2, also figured strongly at the asylum. After describing a fight between Agnes and another person confined at Canton, Hummer continued his letter, "Agnes has had several fights during her residence here, but ordinarily gets along fairly well. She helps with the dish-washing in the hospital building, but this is under supervision." As was the case at Carlisle and other boarding schools in this era, those confined to Canton provided much of the labor and upkeep that kept the institution running; in the Canton context, however, "hoe handle medicine" took on very literal and material connotations, as Indian women like Agnes were assigned work intended to "improve" their ostensible ailments. Concluding his letter, Hummer wrote, "Another potent argument against her discharge is that she is well within the child-bearing age and any offspring must be defective."[91] His final sentence was seemingly an afterthought, but a potent one that captured American anxieties about Indigenous people and dominant discourses about the correlation between feeblemindedness, femininity, and social degeneracy. Far from being evidence of "feeble-mindedness," Agnes's letters document the ferocity with which she fought for her own freedom.

As historian Brianna Theobald has observed of the tensions between the assimilationist imperatives of the era and eugenicists' campaigns, "Eugenicists' emphasis on heredity seems contrary to the prevailing assimilation agenda, but ideas about biology and culture had long coexisted uneasily in Indian affairs." Theobald continues, "The question is not so much whether Native people were explicitly targeted in eugenic campaigns but how colonization created the conditions that allowed Native women and men to be caught up in these processes."[92] Although South Dakota had passed a compulsory sterilization law in 1917, Hummer did not have the means to perform surgical sterilization—a fact which further illustrates how the facility, "run like a Indian boarding school," was not equipped with the accoutrements befitting a medical facility of the era.[93] Nonetheless, as Yellow Bird has pointed out, the long-term confinement of Indigenous women during childbearing years offered an alternative that similarly suppressed sexual reproduction.[94] As these records reflect, Hummer used his power and station as the superintendent of an "insane asylum" to suppress Indigenous reproduction, drawing on dominant ideologies of Indigenous deficiency to rationalize his actions.[95]

Like many other Indian women at Canton deemed threatening by virtue of their Indigeneity, Hummer confined Agnes for the purpose of preventing the birth of Indian children, a decision that was reinforced and perhaps dictated by Assistant Commissioner of Indian Affairs E. B. Meritt. As Meritt explained in response to one of Agnes's letters, "You are advised that the Office does not believe it to be to your best interest to permit you to return to your home at this time. Dr. Hummer has been directed to keep you at Canton *indefinitely*" (emphasis mine).[96] In a classic study of the ways in which diagnoses of "feeblemindedness" were used at the turn of the century to control women's sexuality, legal historian Paul Lombardo explains that "worries about hereditary feeblemindedness fed into concerns about sexual misconduct. . . . Fears of deteriorating sexual morality and shifting social expectations for women accompanying America's increasing urbanization and mobile immigrant populations were only exacerbated by the new emphasis on the danger of feebleminded women."[97]

As records relating to Agnes and others reveal, Indigenous women were especially and uniquely targeted for indefinite confinement at the asylum in order to prevent the birth of Indigenous children—which points to the ways in which many of the struggles at Canton were, in fact, struggles over the right to exist as an Indigenous person. By the same token, these records demonstrate how US officials viewed Indigenous ways of relating as powerful and threatening assertions of Indigenous sovereignty in the face of colonial incursion.

Documents relating to Edith S. (Chippewa) demonstrate similar struggles for survival and show how confinement at Canton extended the Office of Indian Affairs' policy of removing Indigenous children to boarding schools and away from their kin and communities. On November 17, 1924, twenty-nine-year-old Edith was committed to Canton on the recommendation of Mrs. Spinney, the field matron at the Lac du Flambeau Agency. A handwritten letter from Edith's friend, a Mr. B. Fitzgerald, indicates that Spinney had secured Edith's removal from the agency without court sanction—a fact that Assistant Commissioner Meritt both acknowledged and dismissed. As he explained to Mr. Fitzgerald,

Acknowledgement is hereby made of the receipt of your letter of November 16, 1924, asking whether Mrs. Spinney, field matron at Lac du Flambeau, has a right to send people to the insane asylum without examination. . . . The records of this Office show that Mrs. S—was committed, not because she was insane, but because she was feeble minded, and that the commitment was made upon the recommendation of Superintendent C. H. Gensler.[98]

Evidently unbothered by the illegality of Edith's commitment, Meritt sidestepped the issue by suggesting that "feeblemindedness" and "insanity," while perhaps medically distinct, were synonymous from the standpoint of the Indian Office and its application of federal authority over Indian people. Drawing on the opinion of the agency physician, Meritt continued,

> Mr. Gensler uses the following language:
>
> We have a feeble minded woman here aged about 29 years who is having a baby every year. We must get rid of her as she is a nuisance and a menace to society. She was married at one time but is now divorced. The man was forced to marry her. She has babies just the same whether married or not.[99]

As Meritt's letter reveals, Spinney and Gensler worked together to "get rid" of Edith—to incarcerate an Indian woman they defined as a "menace to society," using their unquestioned power as US officials to confine her to the asylum. In so doing, they mobilized the rhetoric of sexual moralism popularized by reform organizations such as the Women's Christian Temperance Union and American Purity Alliance.[100] Yet, Gensler also duplicated the rationale expounded by eugenicists who promoted the sterilization and isolation of society's "defectives" as a way to prevent the transmission of undesirable traits.

Lombardo notes that the rise of "feeblemindedness" as a public malaise marked a shift in the role of medical practitioners and social reformers alike, from philanthropic officials to guardians of the established social order in which white, native-born Americans occupied the upper echelon. "Progressivism," Lombardo writes of this era of contradictions, "had many faces."[101] As Meritt was a public official tasked with the supposed "uplift" of Indian communities, his correspondence likewise suggests that Indian Office officials legitimated the institutionalization of "degenerate" Indian people with diagnoses of "feeblemindedness," recasting those commitments—however wrongful—as necessary to the protection of an American society in various stages of degradation. Drawing on paternalistic discourses of "protection" mobilized by Indian Service employees and social reformers, Meritt concluded in his remarks to Fitzgerald, "After you have read this letter you will understand why [Edith] was committed to the asylum. The Office believes that if you are a true friend of this woman you will be glad that she is now in a place where she will be protected."[102] It was Fitzgerald's duty as friend and patriot, Meritt implied, to condone Edith's confinement at the Canton facility. Like Agnes,

Edith would experience long-term incarceration at the asylum. She was released when Canton closed in 1934, a decade after her initial commitment.

These long-term confinements, typically initiated by non-Indigenous people, reflect the eliminatory logic behind Hummer's desire to keep Indigenous women at Canton indefinitely as an alternative to forced sterilization—a practice Northern Cheyenne Reservation chief tribal judge Marie Sanchez has referred to as a "modern" form of genocide.[103] So extreme were Hummer's actions that Dr. Samuel Silk, tasked in 1933 with investigating Hummer's malpractice, would later report to Commissioner John Collier that he "was especially impressed with the relatively large number of patients who were free from any mental symptoms, and whose behavior in the institution over a period of years did not show anything strikingly abnormal to justify their detention there." He continued,

> I pointed out such patients to Dr. Hummer and he agreed with me that they did not show any evidence of active mental disease and could take care of themselves in any community, especially on an Indian reservation, but assumed the position that these people were below normal—mentally deficient—and they should only be discharged after they were sterilized, and as he did not have any means of doing this, there was nothing left but to keep them there.[104]

As the experiences of Agnes, Nellie, and Edith reflect, Hummer and other US officials used Western biomedical diagnoses of "feeblemindedness" in attempts to destroy the futurity of Indigenous nations. Yellow Bird similarly observes, "Obviously, nobody went to Canton to get well. Incarceration at Canton meant no medical care of any kind and what's more, incarceration there was terminal: institutional policy declared these Native people to be 'defectives,' and as such, procreation must be prohibited and they must be sterilized before they could be discharged."[105] As Burch notes of the legacy of this institution, "Many descendants [of those confined at Canton] have shared the reality of living with unanswered and unanswerable questions, and, even so, they have continued seeking."[106]

In one example of this quest for answers, in a private conversation, Anne Gregory detailed the lengths to which she has gone to access the facts of her ancestor's experience at Canton. She expressed that in the mid-2000s, research into Canton had been all-consuming; as a solo act on tour in the Pacific Northwest in 2006, in between shows, she would head to the public library to conduct research about her great-great-grandmother, Emma. She explained, "At that point, the research floodgates just opened."[107] However, Anne also expressed that there are silences and erasures inherent to this work: "Other survivor stories fill in the gaps [about my grandmother's experiences]," she said.[108]

"THE INDIAN AS AN INDIAN WILL CEASE TO EXIST": BOARDING SCHOOL CONNECTIONS

By 1920, Hummer had tired of his limited sphere of influence over Indian people and began a campaign to purchase additional land that would enable him to increase Canton's holding capacity. In order to rationalize this expansion to Congress, he mailed surveys to Indian Service officials across the country to inquire into the number of "insane" living under each jurisdiction, as had been done years earlier at the institution's founding. In response to those queries, Ora Padgett, superintendent of the Pipestone Indian School, replied that he was currently unaware of any "Indians of unsound minds," but promised that "if at any time in the future it would be necessary to send any one to your institute who are mentally incompetent I will take the matter up with you by letter." As a seeming afterthought, he closed, "Do you ever take in children of school age, boys or girls, that are feeble minded?"[109]

Reservation agents, agency physicians, and field matrons frequently initiated the commitment of Indian people to Canton, but as Padgett's letter reflects, children and youth as much as adults were vulnerable to incarceration at Canton for a variety of ostensible psychiatric ailments, and their transfer could be made without parental knowledge or consent.[110] Many commitments, as Dr. Silk would observe in 1933, were as a result of "difficulty" with school officials. Given the anti-Indigenous sentiments frequently expressed in correspondence between boarding school superintendents and US officials, it is somewhat unsurprising that school authority figures were able to effectively convince their colleagues of an Indigenous person's insanity and rationalize their confinement at Canton.[111] These commitments illustrate how Hummer's relationships with school officials like Padgett could be mutually beneficial; this pattern also showcases the ways in which US officials worked together to confine "troublesome" Indian people to Canton.

In some cases, cooperation between officials increased their power and prestige as deputies of the settler order. Historian Cynthia Landrum notes in her monograph about the Flandreau and Pipestone institutes, for example, that Padgett shared the racist assumptions of Indian inferiority espoused by Estelle

Reel, Commissioner Charles Burke, and other US officials of this era; these sentiments shaped the disciplinary objectives of the boarding school system, the rhythm of Indian students' daily lives, and the nature of epigenetic trauma—as well as embodied knowledge of resistance—passed from one generation of Indian people to the next.[112]

In 1919, Padgett eliminated kindergarten and the seventh and eighth grades at Pipestone, a decision based on the students' purported lack of English-language proficiency—an ongoing source of bitterness for Padgett. As Landrum explains, Padgett stated in a 1923 report that "a number of older boys in the primary grades had 'stopped growing mentally.' . . . Padgett further described the boys as potentially subnormal individuals who should be assigned to an employer as a 'Robinson Crusoe where they can serve as his man Friday.'"[113] With such blatant anti-Indian racism espoused openly at Pipestone, Padgett's response to Hummer's inquiry suggests that the commitment of Indian children to Canton would be a way to eliminate the symbols of his own failures as superintendent. Contrary to the efforts of boarding school officials and against all odds, Indian students at Pipestone continued to speak their Indigenous languages, refusing powerlessness and choosing instead to resist the divestiture of their ancestral lifeways by strengthening their identities through the use of their linguistic worldviews. Yet, Padgett's use of this diagnosis captures how the disappearance of Indian children could be legitimized on medical grounds. It is unclear whether Padgett sent any "feebleminded" children to Canton in 1921, but two years earlier, Nellie K., discussed above, was transferred to the institution from Pipestone.

Other boarding school superintendents similarly corresponded with Hummer, and in some instances successfully confined Indian people to the asylum for reasons entirely unrelated to psychiatric need. As Dr. Silk stated in his 1933 report to Commissioner Sells, "Many patients, young males and females, who have been in Canton for many years, were sent to that institution because of some difficulty at a school or agency—a fight with a white man, or a fight with a husband or wife. . . . Some of them never had any schooling, can neither read nor write" (fig. 4.3).[114] As seen from this statement, conflicts between Indigenous people and white Americans resulted in confinement at Canton, reflecting the extreme social and legal disparities that Indian people navigated in this era. Silk did not name the superintendents responsible for the commitment of Indian people, but available records indicate that they were sent from, or had connections to, the following boarding institutions:

4.3 Statement by Peter G. B. (Sioux), written in Lakota, Canton, South Dakota, 1916. National Archives and Records Administration-Kansas City, RG 75, box 8, Records of the Bureau of Indian Affairs, Canton Asylum for Insane Indians.

Pima School, Arizona
Klamath School, Salem, Oregon
Ft. Washakie Shoshone School, Wyoming
Pipestone Indian School, Minnesota
Umatilla School, Oregon
Flathead Indian School, Montana
Rapid City School, South Dakota
Chilocco Indian Agricultural School, Oklahoma
Wittenburg Indian School, Wisconsin
Seneca Indian School, Wyandotte, Oklahoma
Hayward Indian School, Wisconsin
Carlisle Indian Industrial School, Pennsylvania[115]

In the context of the United States' forced removal of Indigenous children from their nations, this practice of transinstitutionalization—or the movement of an individual from one institutional context to another—underscores how settler agents were granted punitive authority over Indian people that they could exercise and transfer between facilities.[116] As Gilles Deleuze (following Foucault) has noted about disciplinary power, "discipline cannot be identified with any one institution or apparatus precisely because it is a type of power, a technology, that traverses every kind of apparatus or institution, linking them, prolonging them, and making them converge and function in a new way."[117] Similarly, these records illustrate how the relationship between Canton and boarding schools enabled US officials to reinforce one another's status as the disciplinary agents of Indian people, figured as national duty.

That Indian people were committed to Canton at the behest of boarding school superintendents, reservation superintendents, and other US officials is a notable departure from trends among other American populations at this time. Historian Gerald Grob observes that psychiatric institutionalization during the late nineteenth century was typically a private affair; immediate family members—rather than public officials—were often those who initiated the commitment proceedings of their kin, however reluctantly.[118] By comparison, lack of protections for Indigenous people as well as the absence of formal commitment procedures enabled local agents—boarding school superintendents, reservation officials, and officers of the law—to incarcerate Indian women and men at Canton for all manner of infractions, a fate that was widely protested by relatives in letters of correspondence.

Have you sent authority for Mary Man F release yet

—Charles F, husband to Mary (Winnebago)[119]

These actions appeared to be sanctioned by the US Department of the Interior: because Canton was under the direct aegis of the Commissioner of Indian Affairs, his approval was the sole obstacle that stood between an Indian person's freedom and long-term confinement. There was no reversal mechanism; the commissioner deferred to Hummer's medical opinion, which is one reason for the interminable sentences of confinement endured by many of those sent to Canton.[120] Moreover, unlike the general American population in which older adults increasingly made up the majority of institutional populations, Indian people held at the asylum were younger on average than those confined to almshouses or mental hospitals, the two predominant types of Progressive Era facilities in which infirm, disabled, or destitute Americans resided at the turn of the century. Grob notes, "No data is available for the age distribution of all of the mentally ill, but of the almshouse population as a whole 33 percent in 1880 and 40 percent a decade later were 60 years or older. In Massachusetts . . . more than 60 percent of the insane in almshouses in 1893 were 50 years or older—a statistic which indicates that almshouses provided care for a substantial number of aged insane persons."[121]

In contrast to Grob's estimates for the general population, clinical psychologist Anne Dilenschneider has found that many of the Indian people held at Canton from 1902 to 1934 were under the age of thirty, although age demographics at this facility are difficult to determine based on the available amount and quality of archival data.[122] Of the 182 people who passed away at this facility—over half of its overall population—Dilenschneider finds that the average age of death was just forty-two years old.[123]

COURT-ORDERED GUARDIANSHIP AND "LEGALIZED" LAND THEFT

As the corollary to forced confinement, Canton facilitated Indigenous territorial dispossession and enabled interested parties to profit off the land by leasing it or by extracting its natural resources. Indeed, Canton records reflect that the prospect of acquiring vast tracts of land and great wealth motivated white citizens and occasionally family members to initiate the commitment of an Indigenous person to the asylum, as Anne Gregory explains was the case with the commitment of her great-great-grandmother, Emma. In some cases, the US legal system facilitated these detainments. In 1907, for instance, the US court in Indian Territory appointed an unnamed legal guardian to an allotted Quapaw man named Robert Thompson who was committed to Canton for an unknown crime, where he would remain for the next sixteen years—a fact that illustrates how US officials used the asylum for explicitly carceral purposes in much the same way that Carlisle assumed a punitive function in the years before its 1918 closure.

According to one letter, 240 acres of Thompson's land had been leased out for agricultural, business, and mining purposes.[124] This letter also revealed that Thompson was a citizen of Oklahoma, as the state considered the Quapaws who resided at the Quapaw Indian Agency in 1921. However, this same letter also revealed that Thompson was simultaneously a ward of the US government, which means that he had been declared "incompetent" in a US court of law and therefore deemed incapable of fully assuming the self-sufficiency associated with the responsibilities of American citizenship before being sent to Canton.[125]

Other details about the circumstances of Thompson's confinement appear in a well-known 1924 report entitled "Oklahoma's Poor Rich Indians: An Orgy of Graft and Exploitation of the Five Civilized Tribes—Legalized Robbery." Coauthored by Dakota activist and scholar Gertrude Bonnin (Zitkala Ša), Charles H. Fabens, and Matthew K. Sniffen of the Indian Rights Association, the report revealed that the discovery of oil on Indian land and designations of "incompetency" often went hand in hand.[126] As Bonnin, Fabens, and Sniffen put it, "In many of the [Eastern Oklahoma] Counties the Indians are virtually at the mercy of groups that include the county judges, guardians, attorneys, bankers, merchants—not even overlooking the undertaker—all regarding the Indian estates as legitimate game."[127] Of Thompson, the coauthors made the following report: "Robert Thompson, an incompetent restricted Quapaw Indian, about fifty years old. He was sent to an Insane Asylum. When the present guardian took charge of this estate, a little over two years ago, $24,000 was receipted for. The Liberty Bonds and all securities have been disposed of, and the balance now on hand (November, 1913) amounted to $54.40."[128]

According to Canton records managed by Hummer, Thompson's oil-bearing allotment had been leased out for business purposes, garnering $28,758.41 ($505,946.20 in 2023) from mining royalties and $1,000.00 for agricultural lease rentals annually.[129] This huge income is a far cry from the $54.40 the 1924 report cited as the amount then at Thompson's disposal, and while this discrepancy may be an error in accounting, it is also possible that the disparity reflects Bonnin,

Fabens, and Sniffen's observation that guardians allotted their wards wholly inadequate monthly allowances, while siphoning off large sums for themselves.[130] In a similar case, the guardian of a young Choctaw girl named Ledcie Stechi withheld all of the income from her oil-bearing allotment appraised at $90,000.00 (over $1.5 million in 2023), aside from the $15.00 monthly allowance for the support of Ledcie and her grandmother.[131]

The settler structures of legal guardianship imposed on Indigenous people confined to settler institutions enabled US officials to be intimately involved in Indigenous financial and familial affairs. As discussed in chapter 1, Carlisle's superintendent frequently transacted business on behalf of Carlisle enrollees, and in some cases, Indigenous women and men leased, inherited, or sold their allotments. In those instances, it is difficult to tell from available records whether business dealings were desired and condoned by Carlisle enrollees or whether they were coerced into negotiating their affairs in this manner; perhaps both. At Canton, however, the misappropriation of Indigenous resources was more overt, coerced, and commonplace. In one example, on July 14, 1925, Hummer sent a letter to the superintendent of the Crow Creek Agency to inquire after the assets of Two Teeth, an elder Sioux man who had been sent to Canton in 1921 following the commitment of his wife two years earlier on the grounds of "senile dementia." As Hummer explained, he had been given "instructions" by "the House of Representative's subcommittee on appropriations and a representative of the Budget Committee" and thus was writing to determine whether Two Teeth was able to pay for his "maintenance" at Canton to the tune of $400.00 per annum.[132]

In reply, Wright wrote directly to the commissioner's office:

> Receipt is acknowledged of Office letter . . . requesting information as to whether or not Two Teeth, an inmate of the Canton Insane Asylum, is so financially situated so as to be able to pay for his maintenance at Canton at the rate of $400.00 per annum.
>
> In reply, I have to inform your Office that Two Teeth has to his credit in this office as Individual Indian money the sum of $622.48 which is available for the purpose mentioned above. He also has 160 acres of farm land, appraised at $3000.00, which can be sold and used for this purpose.[133]

In much the same way as the young Indigenous women who were sent to the House of the Good Shepherd in Reading, Pennsylvania, were expected to remit funds for their "upkeep," similar arrangements were made for those confined at the asylum. Indigenous institutionalization benefited the settler society; it resulted in tangible profits for individuals and for the state.

Historian Janet McDonnell estimates that forced fee patenting, as Wright suggested might be done with Two Teeth's land, resulted in the transfer of twenty-three million acres out of Indian hands from 1887 to 1934. The Indian Land Tenure Foundation puts the figure of expropriated land during this period even higher, at twenty-seven million acres of converted tracts. In all cases, it was virtually impossible for Indigenous people to defend themselves against the actions of those appointed or presumed to be their guardians, experiences that align with Tom Shakespeare's observation that social attitudes and institutions can constitute socially "disabling barriers."[134] For American Indian people who have historically struggled against the US government's abrogation of its treaty responsibilities, legislation designed to diminish tribal sovereignty, and, in many cases, lack of federal recognition of distinct Indigenous communities, the US legal system constitutes one such source of social incapacitation, or debility, especially in relation to forced confinement.[135]

> Also I want you write to Dr. Wm. A. White and fine out for me 8. dollar
> and ten cents Check sometimes I received that much check from Rose-
> bud so I sign and return but I never see no more so I would like to fine
> out that so I let you know. Very glad to shake you hand one of your Good
> Indian friend I am I say. Good by.
>
> —Peter G. B. (Sioux)[136]

Canton records are rife with similar examples of Indian people held against their will and denied access to any recourse, legal or otherwise. Backed by the county courts, US officials often initiated Indigenous confinement with impunity. Archival records document how the existence of the facility and the settler apparatus of which it was part contributed to the systematic disenfranchisement of Indian people: its existence encouraged the confinement of "insane" Indian people, and in some cases rewarded those who furthered the settler logic of Indigenous elimination. Tragically, Canton records also reflect that in some instances, exploitative family members attempted to take advantage of extralegal avenues of commitment and confine their kin to the facility, as Anne Gregory also described of her relative.[137]

In one example of an extralegal commitment—this time at the behest of a white spouse—James H. (Dakota) spent upward of seven years at Canton despite having been declared *sane* by the Insanity Commission of Boyd County, Nebraska, who had examined him at the request of his wife, Blanche. Evidently under the influence of alcohol at the time of his hearing, James was subsequently transferred to Canton while Blanche stayed behind on the Rosebud reservation with their seven children, who were between the ages of eight and twenty-one. During his confinement at Canton, James fled the institution twice; once in February 1918, and again in October 1919, with the assistance of his brother-in-law Christopher Anderson, in whose home he remained until 1920. According to a letter sent from Chief Medical Examiner Robert Newberne to the Commissioner of Indian Affairs, in January 1920, Newberne had been instructed to travel to Anderson's home to conduct an investigation into James's sanity, and included in the final report was a discussion of the circumstances that led to his institutionalization. As Newberne explained, "[James] began to drink at 21 years of age, and continued to use intoxicants with some degree of regularity . . . when they could be conveniently obtained, until the age of 44, when he promised his dying mother that he would drink no more—a promise which he kept for five years, [until] he plunged into the debauch that landed him into the insane asylum where he was detained for nearly six years."[138] Suturing James's perceived debauchery to his status as an Indian, Newberne went on to report that James was a "quarter-blood Cheyenne enrolled as a Sioux." After marrying a white woman, the couple had numerous children—one of which was described as "mentally deficient"; Newberne described another boy as "a hunchback." Under the heading of "Domestic Worries," Newberne continued:

> [James] grew old prematurely and his Indian blood, which was scarcely noticeable when he was a young man, came into evidence as the years went by. Today, the husband is an old man, gouty and rheumatic at 56, and the wife, although the mother of seven children, is a young woman, full of energy, ambition and visions for the future, at 39. It is she who vigorously opposed the release of her husband from the asylum throughout all the years of his incarceration. *It is she who demands and deserves the best of the bargain in the property settlement which she and her husband are trying to effect.* (Emphasis mine.)[139]

As seen from the details contained in Newberne's report, the surveillance of Indigenous people's bodies, habits, families, and biometric data was integral to processes of Indigenous pathologization, which in turn was used to rational-ize their forced confinement. Notably, in commenting on the couple's purported "domestic worries," Newberne echoed the contemporaneous and popular guiding logic of domestic "unrest" as a potential cause of Indigenous insanity.[140] Newberne's report similarly highlights how the "discovery" of "Indian blood" was leveraged as legal justification for James's commitment to Canton, and it was used as shorthand to imply latent criminality. Under "Reputation," for example, Newberne wrote, "James H— has a good reputation except for his drinking habits. His word and his credit are good, and his opinion is respected. No one regards him as insane. In the communities in which he is known he is classed as a white man—a good citizen. When his wife had him declared insane, the officials of Gregory County discovered for the first time that he could be classified as an Indian; hence he was sent to Canton instead of Yankton."[141]

By the same token, Newberne's report indexes a logic of white supremacy which, as Black feminist theorist bell hooks has argued, always already imbues cultural conceptions of whiteness with goodness.[142] Blanche's whiteness was an assumed status: it enhanced her credibility as an authority on her husband's "insanity." Her gender, along with her race, was also the basis on which Newberne viewed her as financially "deserving." By comparison, James's identification as Indian (despite having lived his entire adult life passing as, or being mistaken for, a white man) meant total—albeit temporary—divestiture of rights under the law. Documents relating to James's assessment of character exemplify the ways in which the commitment of Indian people to Canton disguised conflicts over land and could increase the likelihood of territorial theft. As white Americans initiated the act of commitment as an expression of supremacy, they drew on a collective fantasy of whiteness to assert their authority over Indian people as good, right, and natural.

The experiences of a Chickasaw woman named Emily Waite similarly highlight the complex dynamics behind Indigenous institutionalization at Canton. In 1906, Emily, who was twenty-seven years old at the time of her commitment, was sent to Canton at the behest of her sisters Irene Kerr and Sarah Lasater (née Waite) as a transfer from the State Sanitarium in Norman, Indian Territory.[143] As correspondence from the Indian agent at Muskogee to Commissioner of Indian Affairs Francis E. Leupp reveals, the circumstances around Waite's commitment were rather unusual. Sensing duplicitous motives, the newly appointed Indian agent Dana Kelsey wrote to Leupp in a letter dated October 21, 1905. Evidently, he was becoming impatient with Emily's relatives, who desired to have her transferred, but who refused the requisite protocol:

> During the early part of my term of office, the relatives of said Emily Waite addressed a letter to me saying that they had decided to place her in the Asylum at Canton, and asked that steps be taken immediately looking towards her removal. In accordance with the rules and regulations of this office, I called upon them to fill out certain papers, giving information in regard to her condition, and to have her adjudged insane by the United States Court. This they refused to do, saying that they could see no reason for adjudging a person as insane who had been recognized as of unsound mind for seven or eight years, and they have become very impatient about having her transferred at once.[144]

As a federal facility, Canton was ostensibly intended for noncitizen Indians who had no other means of caring for themselves—circumstances that would have been altogether unknown by Emily. In fact, the Waites were a prominent—and somewhat infamous—Chickasaw family: Fred Tecumseh Waite, Emily's brother, was a member of Billy the Kid's gang of outlaws before trading in his pistols for politics, and the Waite sisters were just as captivating (fig. 4.4).[145] Fred would serve as the attorney general of the Chickasaw nation before his death in 1895, and Emily and Sarah would go on to graduate with business degrees from Oberlin, the first coeducational college in the United States.[146] Emily's highly educated siblings also married quite well; in 1897, Sarah was wedded to a white man by the name of Milas Lasater, who would become one of the wealthiest men in their Chickasaw community of Paul's Valley.

Despite the Waite family's extensive resources, Emily was prevented from sharing in her family's comfortable lifestyle, and her siblings claimed that her mental decline was precipitous. As a lengthy letter authored by Emily's sister Irene and sent to the Indian agent suggests, the Waites mobilized a rhetoric of concern on behalf of their sister, who had embarked on elaborate travels after their father died and their eldest brother relocated the family to Ohio in 1891. As Emily's sister Irene explained, Emily did not care to finish her term of schooling at Oberlin like the rest of her siblings: "She at once laid in a handsome wardrobe and went on a visit to friends of the family in Gainesville, Texas, where she remained for some time leading a gay society life."[147] After traveling up and down the coast of California and eventually returning to Oberlin to earn her business

4.4 Fred Tecumseh Waite. Date unknown.

degree, Emily soon grew tired of life in Ohio and set sail for France. Irene continued, "[Emily] remained about four years in Paris, writing us at long intervals and seeming to be engaged in teaching young French children the English language." She elaborated, "All of her letters were filled with abuse of the American people whom she termed 'Foreigners,' saying the Indians were the only true Americans and the nobility of America."[148] Irene's letter went on for a page and a half more, detailing the many places Emily traveled and reporting that her sister had even laid claim to the Swedish throne.[149]

To twentieth-century Americans, this behavior would have certainly been regarded as outlandish; Emily's actions defied the cultural norms and racial common sense that dictated that Indian women accept their assigned place at the bottom of the social hierarchy. In much the same way that Ozetta and Emerald (discussed in chapter 2) were maligned for expressions of feminine independence and autonomy, it is also possible that Emily's sisters simply resented the fact that she marched to the beat of her own drum. Emily clearly rejected the gendered expectations that women limit their ambitions to better serve the needs of their husbands and families. In this light, it thus seems likely that the Waite sisters, although well-traveled and well-heeled themselves, were quite envious of Emily's gumption.

Significantly, buried in Irene's lengthy letter to Agent Kelsey is a note about Emily's earlier decision to separate her landholdings from those of her siblings. This detail, while seemingly incidental, likely explains the family's decision to commit Emily first to the Norman Sanitarium, and then to remove her even further to Canton, nearly seven hundred miles away from their home in Paul's Valley, Oklahoma. This decision was so unusual that her transfer from a local state facility to Canton even baffled the Indian agent and another US official, who exchanged letters that indicated they both thought the Waite siblings and Emily's legal guardian—a white man named John T. Hill, who approved the transfer—were in error.

In one letter, C. G. Moore, the probate clerk of Paul's Valley, queried Agent Kelsey, "Is it possible that some private Sanitarium could be selected that would not be to [sic] expensive, in which ward would receive better treatment, that is, more individual care and attention[?]" He explained, "This ward has an allotment, a good one, that is rented out on a share crop basis, and produces about $500. annually; the Judge feels that this ward is entitled to the best that her estate will afford, and desires that you state your ideas concerning same. From your

experience do you know of a better place [than Canton], that her estate will justify the sending her to[?]"[150]

Evidently, at least a few US officials knew that Emily came from a family of
means and could thus afford a private facility if she was to be institutionalized.
The officials' remarks similarly acknowledge that the general public was becoming increasingly aware of the terrible conditions at Canton, which had been the
subject of newspaper reports and local gossip. Despite the dubious circumstances
around her commitment, however, her transfer was approved, and in 1906, Emily
was sent from Oklahoma to South Dakota. Several years later, when Emily's first
legally appointed guardian, John T. Hill, died in 1913, her sister Sarah's husband,
Milas Lasater, assumed her legal guardianship, thereby also assuming authority
over her land and income.[151]

Oklahoma historian Angie Debo's extensive work on corruption in Indian Territory in this era provides crucial insight into what was likely happening behind
closed doors in the Waite family. As Debo remarks of the consequences of rampant Indian-white intermarriage within the southeastern tribes, "The Chickasaws
had been recklessly generous to their intermarried citizens, and as a result these
white men monopolized the best agricultural lands in the Nation. In 1890 the Indians attempted to protect themselves by enacting a law providing that intermarried
citizenship should confer no property or political rights, but the white men held
meetings and defiantly resolved that if any attempt were made to dispossess them
they would 'exterminate every member of this council from the chief down.'"[152]

Given these realities, it takes no great leap of the imagination to surmise that
the Waite's vast landholdings, Lasater's political ambitions, and the prospect of
acquiring great power likely contributed to the bizarre conditions of Emily's
confinement, even in the absence of a smoking gun. Despite these unknowns,
however, some remarkable facts are clear. In 1906, an advertisement for the Paul's
Valley First National Bank appeared in the Thursday, September 13, edition of the
Pauls Valley Democrat, a newspaper that Milas Lasater founded in 1898. Included
among a list of the board of directors was John T. Hill, Emily's first guardian,
while Milas Lasater served as vice president of "The People's Bank."[153]

There was at least one concrete business connection between the two men
who authorized Emily's removal from her community and incarceration hundreds of miles away; indeed, Milas's business acumen would serve him well—he
would go on to enjoy a long career in politics and banking, earning widespread ad-
miration for his philanthropy and the substantial role he played in the drafting of

the Chickasaw Constitution.[154] One other detail rings out across historical time and space: Milas and Sarah Lasater would gain control over the entire Waite estate, including Emily's separated landholdings, and after Oklahoma was admitted to statehood, donate the land for the development of a state-run epileptic hospital.[155] Emily would live out her remaining years at the Canton facility, where she would die in 1929. Heart failure was listed as her cause of death.[156] Although Emily came from a family of means, was a landholder, and was highly educated, these relative privileges did not offset her brother-in-law's power and authority as her legal guardian or her vulnerability within a society that defined and regarded her as dependent, as incompetent, and—above all else—as an Indian woman. Under the skewed logic of settler colonialism, as Emily's experiences attest, acts of violence toward Indian people were legitimized as acts of care.[157]

:

The Canton Asylum, its employees, and its settler paradigms of insanity, competence, and wardship facilitated Indigenous confinement, resource extraction, and land theft on a small-scale, case-by-case basis. Records relating to Indian people forcibly confined to this facility reflect a disregard for Indigenous life, disguised by false promises of "care and maintenance" in institutional correspondence. Deconstructing the double entendre of racialized discourse reveals the quotidian violence embedded in the coded rhetoric and practices of white supremacy, and we see the powerful effects of these discursive strategies play out in settler institutions like this South Dakota institution. Dozens of Indigenous women and men were disappeared to Canton, often indefinitely—an explicit form of Indigenous elimination authorized by the US officials responsible for the incarceration of Indian people in this space of chaos, social death, and homicide. Yet, Canton facilitated more than Indigenous disappearance; it also eased the transfer of Indigenous territory to white ownership as Indian people were removed physically, spiritually, and legally from the land and its protection. In this context, medical violence toward Indigenous people was always already settler-colonial violence.

In consulting with community members and leaders about histories of Indigenous institutionalization, common threads emerge around calls for truth and transparency so that our communities can begin the process of healing. As Anne Gregory explained of the impact of institutionalization on her family, "Having the federal government kidnap your family member is unbelievably difficult. But I am not alone in this."[158] Canton is part of a larger story: the use of this institution by boarding school superintendents, legal guardians, and other interested parties for the purpose of Indigenous disappearance underscores punitive connections between boarding schools and other American institutions that existed, ostensibly, for the "benefit" of Indian people. As the foot soldiers of this settler project, Canton superintendent Harry Hummer and his cadre of institutional employees abused, neglected, and disappeared Indigenous women, men, and children until 1934 when the facility was closed and those held there were returned home to their nations or transferred to St. Elizabeths in Washington, DC.[159]

Canton's history did not end with its forced closure. Today, tribal nations continue to feel the effects of this institution and continue on a path toward healing and justice. As Burch has documented in her work with the descendants of those institutionalized at Canton, remembrance has taken many forms. From 1987 to 2007, Lakota activist Harold Iron Shield facilitated ceremonies at Canton to honor communities impacted by institutionalization at the facility. Creative works such as quilt-making, geospatial mapping, praying, and drumming as well as genealogical research and archival investigation constitute other sources of reclamation as descendants and their tribes bear witness to the harms wrought by the facility and work to recover from this past.[160] "As is often the case with social movement efforts," Burch reflects, "organizing remains a work in progress. Still, observances honoring the hundreds of people involuntarily committed to Canton and the thousands more impacted by institutionalization have provided focal points to fortify community relations that have been frayed or broken."[161] As an act of Native self-determination in the face of collective trauma, storytelling is important, as stressed by Indigenous rights activist Pemina Yellow Bird: "We must then tell our stories of loss of violation, of what happened to us, and we must at long last grieve those things; we must determine how the past informs us, is part of who we are, and how it walks with us every day of our lives as Native people."[162] In honor of the Indigenous relatives impacted by the unconscionable practices of this settler institution, I offer these words as an act of bearing witness in the spirit of solidarity, _ahlichi_, and radical care.

> *I hope you won't notice the writing and spelling if you want to know more let me know and I will tell you more later on.*
>
> —*Lucy G. (Flathead)*[162]

You don't need magic to be a warrior, but the Creator's medicine certainly helps.
—UNCLE BROWNIE, *Reservation Dogs* (2022)

Bad Medicine reads across the grain of the colonial archive to offer a new perspective on Indigenous experiences of institutionalization at the turn of the twentieth century. Centering a diverse array of records related to Indigenous people who traversed the Carlisle Indian School, Canton Asylum for Insane Indians, Ford Motor Company Factory, the House of the Good Shepherd, and other Progressive Era facilities, this book examines understudied sites of Indigenous presence and shows how these institutions furthered the aims of US settler colonialism. Juxtaposing punitive patterns at ostensibly distinct institutions reveals a commonality: white officials and US citizens who oversaw Indigenous people in facilities like boarding schools, asylums, and reform institutions used punishment to assert themselves as the disciplinary agents and racial superordinates of Indian people under their aegis. *Bad Medicine* offers a new paradigm of historical inquiry to expose the interconnected nature of settler facilities and to illustrate how institutionalization was inherent, rather than incidental, to US settler colonialism in this era.

This work takes as its point of departure the Carlisle Indian Industrial School in Carlisle, Pennsylvania—the United States' most infamous federally funded off-reservation Indian boarding school. In so doing, it renews attention to the adult enrollees—Indian women and men eighteen years of age and older—who traversed Carlisle's grounds, but who are not often the subject of sustained scholarly engagement. As *Bad Medicine* illustrates, Indian women and men entered Carlisle for many reasons and, once at the institution, found ingenious ways to negotiate the complex, oftentimes infantilizing dynamics of the "school" in which they found themselves. They used all the resources at their disposal to secure labor opportunities, obtain additional years of schooling, pursue advanced training in nursing or other vocations, and assist their families—monetarily or otherwise—on or off the reservation. The length and character of adults' "terms" of enrollment depended on individual factors specific to their personal circumstances—including their age, their reason for seeking entrance, and their prior education, as well as whether they had relatives at Carlisle, and whether they were perceived (by Carlisle officials) as deserving affiliation with the institution. As revealed by the rich archival materials examined in this book, adults who enrolled at Carlisle of their own accord did not view themselves as children or consider themselves to be in particular need of oversight. The disjuncture between the way Indian women and men viewed themselves and the ways in which the institutional regime insisted on adherence to inapplicable school rules contributed to shifting power dynamics as older enrollees fought to exert control over their lives.

Like many of their younger counterparts, adult enrollees were adept at negotiating, resisting, and selectively accommodating Carlisle officials' expectations and the institution's disciplinary regime. But unlike school officials' treatment of Indigenous children and youth of prior eras, adults—especially Indian men—were regarded as potentially threatening to Carlisle's institutional order and the hierarchies of racial power that sustained dynamics at the school and beyond its gates. In response to this influx of older enrollees—which, according to institutional ledgers reached its apex in 1912—Carlisle authorities devised new means of controlling the institution's transformed population. As chapter 1 illustrated, these punitive measures involved a diverse array of historical actors: Carlisle officials, private citizens, and public servants such as rail station operators and law enforcement officers helped consolidate a network that ensnared Indian people in concentric circles of surveillance, discipline, punishment, and various forms of institutional confinement.

Chapter 2 further explored the complexities of these dynamics through the lens of Indigenous experiences of wage work in the private sector. Adult Indian women and men often expressed an interest in enrolling at Carlisle to secure work in the Outing system or in one of the vocational training programs offered through the institution, especially after 1915. Indian men sought entrance to the automotive industry by way of Carlisle's training "partnership" with the Ford Motor Company in Detroit. By comparison, Indian women were constrained by the gendered expectations of the era, which prevented many from securing work outside the home. Overwhelmingly, Carlisle girls and women performed domestic service in white households, as this kind of labor was one of the only options available to them while "under the Outing." A few young women, however, successfully entered nursing programs, and their experiences highlighted the difficulties encountered while furthering their training. Ozetta and Emerald's experiences of punishment and pathologization at the General Hospital in Lancaster, Pennsylvania, underscored how disciplinary power could be transferred between and among institutions and institutional authority figures. Although many nurse training programs around the country refused to accept nonwhite women in this era, archival records demonstrate that hospital officials made an exception for the Indian women at Carlisle—an exception likely negotiated by Carlisle's superintendents Moses Friedman and Oscar Lipps, and one that could have reflected good intentions or, perhaps, a philanthropic investment in Indigenous "uplift." Although training and labor experiences at Carlisle were riven with racial, gendered, and class inequalities, the opportunity to participate in nurse training programs illustrates how enrollment at Carlisle could offer tangible benefits for the young women who traversed the institutional threshold.

Archival records reflect that the women and men enrolled in the training partnerships at the General Hospital and Ford Motor Company regarded these opportunities as some of the best that Carlisle offered. But although these programs granted enrollees a greater degree of independence, they also exposed Indian enrollees to discrimination, exploitation, and anti-Indigenous sentiment. Records relating to Indian men at Ford reflect subtle and overt forms of prejudice; stereotypes about Indian women as promiscuous informed the women's experiences on the ward at the nursing hospital. Carlisle officials often maintained that enrollees who entered into these labor arrangements benefited from "competing" with non-Indigenous laborers; but archival records also reflect how structures of presumed guardianship at Carlisle and beyond enabled employment supervisors at Ford and the General Hospital to assume disciplinary authority over Indian women and men. In so doing, these authority figures reinforced and enhanced their own professional status—a process of deputization that expands our understanding of the quotidian and material benefits that settler institutions offered to white Americans in this era.

The turn of the twentieth century also saw the proliferation of dominant discourses that characterized Indigeneity and traditional Indigenous lifeways as deviant, abnormal, and pathological. As chapter 2 also illustrated, the use of medicalized discourse in wage labor scenarios reveals instances of Indigenous pathologization in the American workforce. In other instances, pathologizing language was used to rationalize the confinement of young Indian women deemed threatening to Carlisle's institutional order. As chapter 3 argued, young Indian women's forced confinement at the House of the Good Shepherd in Reading,

Pennsylvania, highlights a history of institutionalization that has global reverberations; as has been widely documented, Irish women experienced confinement in Good Shepherd Homes—Magdalene laundries—from the eighteenth century all the way until 1996, when the last facility on Seán McDermott Street in Dublin was closed. The arrangement between Carlisle and the Good Shepherd Home, a Catholic institution, is somewhat peculiar; the Reading facility was seemingly misaligned with Carlisle's institutional ethos, which was rooted in the mores of Protestantism. Yet, as the oral transcripts of interviews with Irish survivors examined in chapter 3 reflect, a similar pattern of transinstitutionalization played out in the Irish context as well. These parallels offer insight into the interrelationship between punitive and carceral institutions in the United States, as well as their global reach.

If institutions such as Carlisle, the Ford factory, or the Good Shepherd home failed to elicit the "improvement" of Indian people's comportment, psychiatric diagnoses of "insanity" could be of enormous social utility to retrenching the settler order. As chapter 4 examined, the Canton Asylum for Insane Indians facilitated more than Indigenous confinement; it also furthered the essential work of settler colonialism as it eased the transfer of Indigenous land to white ownership. Records relating to the Indian people forcibly confined to this facility reflect a "caring" disregard for Indigenous life, disguised by false promises of "care and maintenance" in institutional correspondence. The Canton facility, its employees, and the legal structures that defined Indian people as always already deficient, abnormal, or childlike facilitated Indigenous land theft on a small-scale, case-by-case basis. In this context, medical violence was always already settler-colonial violence.

The Carlisle Indian School graduated very few of its "students," and the Canton Asylum neglected more Indigenous lives than it preserved, but these facts did not prevent officials from celebrating the "success" of either institution during their heyday. The stories of Indigenous struggle uncovered in the colonial archive suggest that these institutions were successful not because they "assimilated" Indian people, but because they produced and fortified structures of power that benefited the settler society. Drawing connections between and among settler institutions, *Bad Medicine* locates the punitive practices of these facilities on a continuum of US policies aimed at the attempted eradication of Indigenous populations. In so doing, the book offers a new way of understanding interconnections between settler institutions used to contain, reform, educate, or punish Indian people at the turn of the twentieth century. Analyzing institutions alongside one another paints another picture of interconnected settler structures of white racial empowerment that Indian people negotiated with varying degrees of success.

Taking stock of current affairs in Indian country today and in the United States more broadly, it is obvious that this history of institutionalization continues to produce consequences for Indigenous communities. Statistics fail to capture the nature and complexity of the challenges Native people continue to face, but they do provide a fragmented snapshot of significant inequities. The Indian Health Service reports that in 2010, American Indians and Alaska Natives experienced lower health status overall as compared with the general American population; Native people were victims of homicide at a rate that is more than double that of Americans (11.4 per 100,000 versus 5.1 per 100,000); and Native people's life spans were 5.5 years shorter than the general population (73 years versus 78.5 years).[1] Following the global COVID-19 pandemic, the US National Center for Health Statistics found that American Indian and Alaska Native (AIAN) life expectancy rates decreased most significantly for AIAN males, by 2.3 years (63.8 to 61.5)—the most of any racial group—followed by AIAN women, whose life expectancy decreased by 1.5 years (70.7 to 69.2).[2] Many of these disparities can be attributed to discrimination, disproportionate poverty, and lower educational attainment, all of which have been linked to the ravages of federal policies aimed at the eradication of Native peoples and our lifeways.

Institutionalization, confinement, and incarceration as examined in this book also continue to explicitly impact Indigenous people's freedom of mobility. According to a 2015 report issued by the Lakota People's Law Project, Native Americans are the population most likely to be killed by law enforcement officers in the United States. Native men are jailed four times more frequently than white men; Native women experience incarceration at a rate of six times that of their white counterparts; and Native people as a whole experience incarceration at the state and federal levels at a rate of 38 percent above the per capita national average for the general American population.[3] These figures are not limited to Native women and men eighteen years of age and older. Indigenous youth also experience incarceration in juvenile detention facilities at a staggering rate, representing 70 percent of those incarcerated by the federal Bureau of Prisons despite making up only 1 percent of the youth population in the United States.[4]

Even beyond incarceration in a single facility, today, as in the past, patterns of transinstitutionalization—the movement from one institution to another, often involuntarily—continue to be very visible in the lives of Indigenous people.

According to the Lakota People's Law Project, in 2015, the state of South Dakota received more than $79,000 of federal monies per year for each Indigenous youth placed in a foster home or in the juvenile custodial system, thereby underscoring how monetary reward continues to accompany the erosion of tribal sovereignty in the United States.[5] The well-being of Indigenous children continues to be undermined in the courts as well, with legal challenges such as *Haaland v. Brackeen* (2022), which sought to overturn the Indian Child Welfare Act (ICWA)—a law passed in 1978 that sought to limit the placement of Native American children into white foster homes—on the basis of unconstitutionality. On November 9, 2022, an unprecedently conservative US Supreme Court heard the case, which was brought by three non-Native couples and the state of Texas; somewhat miraculously, the Supreme Court upheld ICWA in June 2023.

The phenomena examined in this book highlight powerful historical continuities between past and present patterns of racialized violence that continue to impact tribal nations in quotidian, yet profound, ways. Even just a cursory overview of recent news headlines and current events reveals connections between the racialized struggles of the past and the ways in which they play out today: the resurgence of Klan visibility in ostensibly "legitimate" political forums; white Americans who relentlessly call the police on Black and brown people for simply existing, as was the case at a family barbecue at Lake Merritt in Oakland, California, in 2018; killings at the hands of law enforcement and mass public arrests . . . the list goes on. Seeking to put a stop to this kind of racialized violence, in San Francisco in July 2019, at a San Francisco Board of Supervisors meeting, a board member introduced the Caution Against Racially Exploitative Non-Emergencies (CAREN) Act as a possible deterrent. As *Bad Medicine* illustrates in historical relief, white supremacy is legislated and institutionalized, condoned and often mandated by the very establishments that proclaim to protect and ensure "freedom and justice for all." Moreover, racialized struggles do not only play out at the institutional level; they are furthered at the hands of anonymous, ordinary civilians.

In one stark example, in July 2019, the US Department of Homeland Security announced that it would be bringing its "Citizen's Academy" to Chicago, where it would teach civilians about "defensive tactics, firearms familiarization, and targeted arrests" during the six-week course. This caused significant outcry from immigrant rights groups such as the Illinois Coalition of Immigrant and Refugee Rights as well as the American Civil Liberties Union (ACLU) and National Immigrant Justice Center, and eventually ICE announced that the course would be postponed until September 2021. Critics of the "Citizen's Academy" pointed out that ICE already had similar courses on offer, and that this was just one more in a series of PR stunts to improve the agency's public image. Despite officials' claims that the course was intended only to be a way to help dispel misconceptions about the work of ICE agents, opponents asserted that the course would incite violence, encourage racial profiling, and inevitably lead to "increased fear in immigrant communities."[6] As Chicago congressman Mike Quigley said of the academy during a 2020 interview, "The United States is not a police state where ordinary men and women are deputized to carry out immigration enforcement based on discriminatory racial profiling practices." He continued, "The so-called 'Citizens Academy' program would do nothing less than train Americans to suspect their friends or neighbors of being dangerous criminals, regardless of their actual immigration status."[7]

Many might be disinclined to agree with Quigley. He is right in his assertion that this offering would stoke racial fears and lead to racial profiling; but he is wrong in his statement that the Citizens Academy would provide Americans, especially white Americans, with *new* tools and techniques with which to police and surveil their neighbors and those who live and work in their vicinity. He is wrong in his assessment that the United States is *not* a place where "ordinary men and women are deputized to carry out" racially discriminatory activities, because ordinary American men and women have historically served this function on behalf of the settler state.

Once more, hindsight reveals significant historical continuities: in the 1830s, during the period of Indian removal west of the Mississippi, President Andrew Jackson's rhetoric mobilized extralegal vigilante groups to help dispel the Choctaws, Cherokees, and other so-called Civilized Tribes from our ancestral homelands in the southeastern region. Similarly, Fugitive Slave Acts, like that of 1850, which is sometimes referred to as the "Bloodhound Bill," authorized enslavers to sic dogs on Black women and men running toward freedom. This act required that escaped women and men be returned to their enslavers and *mandated* white American citizens' compliance. The enforcement of racist curfews; the existence of sundown towns; the establishment of racialized enclaves, ghettos, and reservations; and the policing of those borders all share the same genealogy of state-sanctioned white supremacy and racialized violence. As this book also illustrates, quotidian acts of citizen-policing have historically been more insidious, more violent, and often more effective than official state mechanisms of racialized terror. *Bad Medicine* argues that our present moment has a history; it informs contemporary experiences of race, racism, and inequality more than the general public may realize.

The settler state, alive and well today, draws upon this time-honored custom of civilian deputization in the drafting of legislation that not only involves vigilantism, but relies on it. In 2021, Texas passed one of the nation's most stringent anti-abortion laws, which calls on civilians, rather than state authority figures, to uphold it by encouraging citizens to file suits against private citizens suspected of having assisted someone in terminating a pregnancy in Texas. As *New York Times* writer Frank Bruni remarked in a 2022 opinion piece titled "There's a New Surveillance State: It's Your Neighbor," "Just about anyone who knows or suspects that a Texan has aided someone in getting an abortion can file a civil lawsuit against that person and, if the suit succeeds, expect at least a $10,000 reward. A person can collect that reward multiple times by identifying abettors of additional abortions. . . . This is scary and wrong."[8]

These and similar practices underscore both how much and how little has changed in the promotion and maintenance of white supremacy, gendered surveillance, and racialized forms of oppression in the United States in the past two centuries, as discriminatory attitudes manifest in seemingly new ways and are transmitted, reinforced, and renewed by unprecedented legislation and technological capabilities. Such policies and practices continue to etch away at the quality of daily existence for Indigenous people and others in the United States, compounding threats to communal well-being and further contributing to inequitable health, economic, and educational outcomes. Moreover, legislation designed to deny the existence of institutionalized racism in the United States—or prohibitions against teaching of the history of slavery in the Americas—serves only to produce future generations who will continue to believe that anti-Indigenous, anti-Black, and anti-Asian racism, as well as xenophobia rooted in white American nationalism, are things of the past, if they happened at all.[9] This ahistoricism will ensure that the political leaders of tomorrow will have a limited understanding of US history and will continue to enact legislation that continues to profoundly harm Indigenous sovereignty, women, communities of color, disabled persons, and other marginalized groups deemed expendable by the state.

Despite ongoing challenges to Indigenous self-determination, however, tribal nations are fighting harder than ever for healing for our communities. Recent headlines from Indian country have included news of historic firsts, as we reckon with the legacy of settler colonialism and fortify our nations for the future. But these efforts are never straightforward and have often involved a great deal of re-traumatization for tribal members who must relive past events. In one example, on May 27, 2021, the Tk'emlúps te Secwépemc First Nation announced that the remains of 215 Indigenous children had been found buried at the Kamloops Indian Residential School in British Columbia, Canada. As Chief Rosanne Casimir explained of the horrific development, "It was an unthinkable loss that was spoken about but never documented."[10] From 1890 to the late 1970s, Kamloops operated one of Canada's Indigenous residential schools in a system that, much like that of the United States, forcibly removed Indigenous children from their home communities and divested them of their ancestral lifeways. Kamloops was the largest facility in Canada's residential school network, housing over 500 First Nations youth at its peak. In the aftermath of Canada's establishment of a Truth and Reconciliation Commission and the commission's findings in 2015 that over 4,100 Indigenous children passed away at residential facilities, the "discovery" of the Kamloops youth affirms what Indigenous communities have known all along: boarding schools were places of chaos but also resilience, of death and of life. These facilities were characterized by contradictions, tensions, and, oftentimes, overwhelming challenges that many Indigenous enrollees navigated with skill and determination. Others, however, succumbed to these alien environments that sought their destruction; they are the root of many Indigenous tribes' shared experiences of US settler colonialism and of historical trauma that often impacts multiple generations.

Soon after the revelation at the Kamloops Residential School, in June 2021, US Secretary of the Interior Deb Haaland (Laguna Pueblo) announced that the US Department of the Interior (DOI) would launch its own Federal Indian Boarding School Initiative to investigate Native American residential institutions in the United States, an effort which remains ongoing. According to the initial report issued in May 2022 by Bryan Newland, the assistant secretary of the US Department of the Interior, the federal boarding school system in the United States was comprised of 408 federally supported schools in operation from 1819 to 1969 across thirty-seven states or territories. Research conducted by the National Native American Boarding School Healing Coalition (NABSHC) reflects that this figure of operational institutions is perhaps even higher; Director of Education and Research Deidre Whiteman (Meskwaki, Dakota, Ojibwe, Hidatsa) noted in one of our consultations that NABSHC's research reflects that the federal boarding school system in the United States was comprised of approximately 521 facilities—including 108 not funded by the federal government. The DOI report further estimates that attendance and enrollment at each of these institutions ranged from one individual to more than one thousand between the years 1820 and 1932, which illustrates something of the scope, impact, and longevity of this system. Notably, the DOI report indicated that although the Interior Department had identified more than 1,000 additional "Federal and non-Federal institutions, including Indian day schools, sanitariums, asylums, orphanages, and stand-alone dormitories that may have involved the education of American Indian, Alaska Native, and Native Hawaiian people," these institutions fell outside the scope of the Federal Indian Boarding School Initiative and were therefore not included in the investigation at the time of this writing.[11]

Given these conflicting figures and the limited nature of the current federal investigation, it is clear that the extent, complexity, and impact of this settler institutional network is only now beginning to be identified, much less understood. In an acknowledgment of these lacunae, as of 2023, legislation for a Truth and Healing Commission on Indian Boarding School Policies Act, introduced by Senator Elizabeth Warren, is again before the US Senate.[12] It remains to be seen whether the Truth and Healing Commission will be implemented. Among other key provisions, such a commission would assist in the collection of public testimony from boarding school survivors, locate church and government records pertaining to individuals who spent time at a boarding institution, make the findings of the commission publicly available, and produce recommendations for justice and healing for tribes.[13] But beyond this federal effort, it is also evident that additional community-engaged research into this history is urgently needed. Many local, regional, and national Native-led organizations, such as the Intertribal Friendship House in the San Francisco Bay Area, the National Native American Boarding School Healing Coalition, and the Native Justice Coalition, are already involved—and have been, in some cases, for decades—in critical work to provide survivors of boarding schools and their descendants and communities with healing and spiritual wellness services.

My discussions with Indigenous community members and organizational leaders about this history has often highlighted a pervasive sense of frustration with the limited amount of culturally appropriate information that communities have about the institutions that impacted their lives. As Whiteman put it, "The complete erasure of history is unbelievable. . . . This is why we [the National Native American Boarding School Healing Coalition] do the work that we do, and why it's important to get the information out there." Whiteman also expressed that in her

E.1 Deidre Whiteman (Meskwaki, Dakota, Ojibwe, Hidatsa), Director of Research and Education for the National Native American Boarding School Healing Coalition, speaks at the Wisdom Steps Annual Conference in Cloquet, Minnesota, 2022. Photo courtesy of the National Native American Boarding School Healing Coalition.

work with Indigenous communities impacted by boarding schools, tribal members express the importance of having accurate information about the number of individuals sent away to school with the question "How many students?" For this reason and many more, Whiteman and others in leadership positions believe that a commission would be of utmost importance for furthering truth, justice, and healing initiatives by and for Indigenous peoples. Not only would a commission begin to acknowledge and help paint a better and more accurate picture of the impact of the US federal Indian boarding school system, but it would assist tribes in accessing the critical mental health and spiritual resources that community members have identified as essential to healing from this past (fig. E.1).[14]

This dearth of consistent, documented information about boarding schools and other institutions of the settler state are reflective of the United States' investment in historical amnesia. As such, it is also important for non-Native organizations and individuals to tell reflecting truthful, accurate, and community-informed histories about Indigenous peoples on Turtle Island and the legacy of settler colonialism. Rose Miron, director of the Newberry Library's D'Arcy Mc-Nickle Center for American Indian and Indigenous Studies in Chicago, expresses that a commitment to "making visible Native history that is often overlooked and erased" is central to the ethos of the center's many community-led and public history projects. "Native people are experts in their own histories," Miron said during a phone call, and "changing attitudes [to the contrary] is essential for institutions that want to be in a listening position."[15]

Megan Baker, Choctaw historian, scholar, and former research associate to the Choctaw Nation of Oklahoma's Historic Preservation Department, is one such Native expert. As Baker noted in a private conversation, much of her work involves "finding ways to make Choctaw knowledge more legible" to the general public. However, the work of historic preservation—of preserving the past, and of preserving community knowledge for future generations—is anything but linear and often yields surprises. She recently assisted in the curation of *Bok Abaiya: Practiced Hands and the Arts of Choctaw Basketry*, a basketry exhibition on display from July 2023 to March 2024 at the Choctaw Nation of Oklahoma's Cultural Center in Calera, Oklahoma, and recalled some of the complexities inherent to communal memory. For this display, Baker and exhibit curator Claire Green Young created an object plaque noting one basket's stylistic origination outside of the tribe—a basket created by an elder and traditional weaver, whose granddaughter had insisted that the technique used in her relative's basket was of Choctaw provenance. To the exhibit team, the style was definitively of non-Choctaw origin, but for the granddaughter, the basket was thoroughly Choctaw, as family tradition dictated that her grandmother had learned basket weaving from Choctaw weavers. After reconciling all of the details about the basket—the weaver, time period, and technique—it was determined that it was a product of intercultural transmission; the Choctaw elder likely learned new techniques from non-Choctaw weavers through a government program while sharing her knowledge of Choctaw weaving in exchange and then later learned more from other Choctaw weavers about how to make Choctaw-style baskets, possibly in the same program. As Baker explained of complex issues of cultural memory, "I knew there was more to the story; [the basket] exists outside of this event in a larger social milieu."[16] For my tribe and many others, the ability to tell our own stories in accordance with our tribal histories is paramount. Our pathways toward healing are similarly specific, rooted in the particularities of place and ceremony and generational knowledge. But our experiences are also interwoven with those of other peoples, tribes, and communities—much like the Choctaw rivercane basket in Baker's story.

E.2 Willie Jack (played by Paulina Alexis) seeks guidance from the ancestors. Still from *Reservation Dogs*, season 2, episode 9, "Offerings," air date September 21, 2022.

. . . .

Recent events have illustrated the ongoing impact of settler invasion and of policies designed to erase and replace Indigenous peoples, but the past decade has also seen some incredible triumphs in Indian Country. The unshakeable determination of land protectors at the Standing Rock Sioux reservation, as well as allies from all over Turtle Island, successfully stalled the construction of the Dakota Access Pipeline in 2020; the ongoing presence of protectors at Mauna Kea have halted the construction of a thirty-meter telescope; and the #LandBack movement and efforts of Indigenous-led nonprofit organizations such as the Sogorea Te' Land Trust secured the return of a sacred Shellmound site from the City of Berkeley to Lisjan Ohlone stewardship in July 2024. In June 2022, the lieutenant governor of the Zuni Pueblo Tribe in New Mexico similarly announced that Bears Ears would be comanaged by his tribe and the US Bureau of Land Management, another unprecedented success and historic first. Indigenous self-determination has played out across the silver screen in recent years as well, in a flourish of Indigenous-produced film, television, and other media told from an Indigenous perspective, for Indigenous audiences. This new renaissance has included a host of films and television shows such as Peacock's *Rutherford Falls* (2021–22) and FX's *Reservation Dogs* (2021–2023). "*Rez Dogs*" is beloved in particular in Native communities, because of the complexity and ordinariness of its storylines, as exemplified by the scene featured in season 2, episode 9, when Willie Jack (played by Paulina Alexis) seeks guidance from the ancestors during a visit with her friend Daniel's mother Hokti (played by Lily Gladstone), who is incarcerated (fig. E.2). As *Reservation Dogs* cocreator Sterlin Harjo remarked in an NPR interview about how the show's storytelling goes beyond the television screen, "My dad, one day, said to me, 'This show has given people, Native people, a reason to hold their heads up a little higher.'" Harjo continued, "Every year at Halloween, there's people that dress up in these fake, dime-store Indian clothing. And they are 'Indian' for Halloween. And we've all seen that growing up. We've all seen it. And my kids are going to have to see it. But all of a sudden, after Season 1, people, kids started dressing up as the Reservation Dogs. So many pictures flooded in on social media of them dressed as the Reservation Dogs."[17]

The effects of centuries of colonial excursion will not be easily reversed, as our tribal nations continue to negotiate affronts to our political and cultural autonomy, and challenges to our inherent sovereignty. But, if the stories explored in this book illuminate anything, my hope is that it is that our histories are still being written. Our medicine will carry us forward.

appendix

1. Letter from Justin R. H. to Carlisle superintendent Oscar H. Lipps, December 3, 1914. Justin's letter to Carlisle Superintendent Lipps reflects a dispute over a debt, but it is unclear from his file what the context is. What is clear, however, is that Justin feels he is liable to starve if Lipps fails to release some of his savings from the bank in Carlisle. This letter reflects in stark relief the complexities and contradictions of the settler institution's relationship with Indigenous people under its jurisdiction. "Justin H—. (R—. H—.) Student File," RG 75, series 1327, box 2, folder 82, NARA, CISDRC.

Dec 3rd 1914

Trenton N.J.
Mr. O. H. Lipps
Carlisle Indian School
Carlisle Pa.

Sir

I am, very, very, very, very, sorry, sorry, sorry, sorry, about that. I always think about to help me, but you are not a man enough to help me for anythings. you wanted me to sign these check but I am not going to sign it. if you got no money you may have that, what I got left in bank there, with these check. I am going to x send these check back to you without no sign.

I will pay Mr. Boyer after starving from death, nobody feed me without no money you know that very well, if you x go on to any houses or store to get something to eat, you wouldin get some to eat would you? without no money, no man can get anything to eat without no—money I tell you that.

O, right my Friend, I see now, you wanted me starving to death I told some of people a round here their asked me about—why is it, I Borrowed 3.00 by Suit I had, and put in there to Mr. Pawn Broker. [illegible] 11 East front Street Trenton N.J.

But I can et the Suit back now. I thought you are kind enough to send me money so I Borrowed money on my Suit. I am shame myself to do like that but I can help it, I dont wanted starving to death I got no money to pay my way to go back there to.

I am sorry about you Mr. Lipps. I all ready say it.

If you wanted to answer these letter, you may answer, you dont want it that is alright to it don't make any Different to me.

I am going to write to the party to Washington D.C. I think they let have the money to pay for all what I owe, that a shame & shame. Mr. Friedman he never treated me like that. he always help me & keep me from starving. I always aske him about my money he let have it all time.

I am going to Borrowed money and tell them what I Borrow for, for starving.

from Justin H—.

501 Calhoun Street
Trenton N. J.

2. Letter from Otto T. (Chippewa) to Carlisle superintendent Oscar H. Lipps, January 8, 1917. Otto's letter reveals his ambitions in Detroit and details his frustration and disappointment with the Ford apprenticeship course. Otto's language similarly illustrates the limits of his patience in dealing with Ford supervisor Griswold, and reveals the discrimination he and the other Indian workers faced while working at Ford. "Otto T—. Student File," RG 75, series 1327, box 113, folder 4674, NARA, CISDRC.

43 LaBelle Avenue,
Highland Park, Michigan, Jan. 8, 1917.
Supt. Oscar H. Lipps,
Carlisle, Penna.

Dear Sir:

Your letter of the recent date, in response to my telegram recently delivered to you, is received. You cannot understand the cause of any release from the students' course until Mr. Griswold explains it to you because I never stated in the telegram. I will try to explain to you from my own experience, and there is no doubt that some of the things he will state in his report will be beyond the actual reason.

I was called up to the office of Mr. Griswold on the 5th of January. He then commenced to ask me why I don't attend the students' meeting held every day up at the

Educational Dept. I told him that I dare not say that I have gone to every meeting, but I told him I have attended some of the meetings, and was there day before that day. I told some of the reasons why I can't go every meeting. He commenced to say some of the things that I didn't feel like hearing which is as follows:

"There are five hundred men behind you, looking for a chance to get in the factory as students; waiting for you to gettout [*sic*] if you don't follow the rules of the students' course."

"Don't you know that it is the only reason why you are working for the Ford Motor Company is simply because you are a student, there is nothing else."

"The only thing we can do for you is to hold your time card, or else ship you back to Carlisle!'

I told this young man that if there five hundred men waiting for me to get out, there is no doubt that nine out of ten of these men are more hard up for jobs and will be better qualified to hold any position for the Company than I would be if I finish the course. Why not let those five hundred men get in and leave me get out of the way?

#2

I am making arrangements to attend one the Auto schools in the city. I am in the heart of automobile industry and will not get out until I learn the different makes of cars.

A student finishing the course in the Ford factory does not know but about automobile. Think of the many different kinds of cars. A man willing to run a garage business want to be able to handle any car that comes to his shop besides Ford car. To do this a man must have training in the place where they teach the automobiles in the proper way. My next step is this. The only thing I will ask from the school is to send all my money, and let us see what I can do in the automobile world.

I have already paid the tuition for my business course and will attend the school all day from now on. I hope to finish soon.

Trusting that my departure from the boys will not cause you annoyance, I am,

OT—.

3. Letter from Ozetta B. (Potawatomi) to Carlisle superintendent Oscar H. Lipps, June 29, 1916. Ozetta's letter illustrates her ongoing determination to become a nurse as well as the many responsibilities that Indigenous people often confronted while enrolled at Carlisle and shortly after leaving. Her letter similarly illustrates how affiliation with Carlisle might have some benefits for Indian people who sought to leverage superintendents' connections. "Ozetta B—. Student File," RG 75, series 1327, box 106, folder 4506, NARA, CISDRC.

Sharon, Okla.

June 29, 1916

My Dear Mr. Lipps:

As my sister

is improving rapidly I would like very much to be able to take the Civil Service examination while I am here.

I expect to go to New Mexico on a visit to my father in August some time.

And would like to start work in September, if such Can be the arrangements.

I will be ready to take them about the middle of July or any time the arrangements can be made. I will take them at Wood-ward, Okla.

I will be greatly indebted to you for any service you can give in helping me secure a position soon.

Very Respectfully Yours,

Ozetta M. B—.
Sharon,
Okla.

4. Letter from Agnes W. to Carlisle superintendent Oscar H. Lipps, August 1914. Agnes's powerful letter to Superintendent Lipps while confined at the Good Shepherd home in Reading, Pennsylvania, reflects a bargaining phrase that other young women at Reading similarly used: "I have made up my mind to be a good girl." Her request for her sweater reflects a desire for a comforting personal item. It is unclear who Pete and the little children are. "Agnes W—. Student File," RG 75, series 1327, box 103, folder 4439, NARA, CISDRC.

Convent of Good Shepherd
Reading, Pa.,

Aug. 1914

Supt. O. H. Lipps
Indian School
Carlisle Pa,

Dear Sir:

I am going to write a few lines this after-noon to let you know that I am well and contented here, but I certainly do get lonesome for the girls sometimes.

How is little Pete and the rest of the children?

I am going to take piano lessons from the mothers so I am asking you to please send me my money. and a nother thing I'd like to ask you is. When Evelyn B——. comes in from the country this month would or will you please send me my sweater she took out with her when she went out to the country

Well, Mr. Lipps I have made up my mind to be a good girl I am very sorry for what I've done in the past

Mr. Lipps will you please tell the girls I send them my best regards and wishes

I hope you will come and see us some time but I know you are always busy and can't get off

I will now close my letter by Thanking you very much for the things you sent us.

I am very truly

Agnes W——.

5. Letter from Christine S. to Carlisle superintendent Moses Friedman, April 21, 1914. Christine sent this letter regarding the release of her granddaughter Hannah K. (Onondaga) from the Sleighton Farm Reform School. "Hannah K——. Student File," RG 75, series 1327, box 92, folder 4123, NARA, CISDRC.

Syracuse N.Y.
April 21, 1914

Dear Sir:-

I would like to have my grand-daughter back home. It seems to me as if they have stolen my child when they sent her to the Reform school without informing me.

I am in poor health and I certainly will be glad if I can see her face again before I die.

I think it would have been better if they have notified me before sending her there.

Trusting in God you will kindly look over this matter and write to me if my girl can come home.

Respectfully

Mrs. Christine S——.
Syracuse
New York

R. F. D. #5

6. Essay on Capital Punishment written by Peter Thompson G. B. (Sioux), no date. This essay was authored by Peter while confined at the Canton Asylum for Insane Indians in Canton, South Dakota, and provides insight into the thoughts, experiences, and convictions of the Indian people held at this settler institution. "Peter G—. B—. File," RG 75, Department of the Interior, Office of Indian Affairs, Canton Asylum for Insane Indians, Individual Patient Files, 1910–1916, box 8, Case File 152, NARA-KC.

Capital Punishment should have no place in a civilized Country For these reasons It is not practical. It defeats the very purpose for which it is prescribed. It is supposed [*sic*] to deter people from Murder. As a matter of fact it increases the tendency to commit the crime Manslaughter is more frequent where capital punishment is the law than in states where it is not the law Capital punishment is presumed to impress offenders with the sacredness of life. It work just the other way The psychological effect of it is practically the reverse. It provokes violence. The opposition to Capital punishment is asserted to be purely sentimental. It is not. It is severely practical based on facts history and science. It is Capital punishment itself that is pure sentiment The vicious morbid and dangerous sentiment of vengeance. The death penalty is not Justice It is revenger retaliation. Crime is not stopped by retaliation but by intelligent restriction and change of environment Capital punishment is and [*sic*] anachronism. It belongs to the former times when men were ignorant and hence cruel. It is a practice that fitted well with a time when it was believed that men could be made righteous by threatening them with burning eternally in literal hell fire. The level of personal morals is higher and human life safer now. When the world does not believe such hideous doctrine and murder will be less common where we quit murdering men legally Capital punishment is irreparable. If it is found to be a mistake in any case if the victim is shown to be not guilty the error cannot be rectified. The processes of human justice are too faulty to be considered absolutely certain Capital punishment debauches the state It brutalizes those who must execute it and the public who read of it Its influence is to lower the General esteem of human life. The state does not give life it has right to take it away Liberty and the pursuit of happiness are due to the state and those it has the right to restrict; God alone gives life God alone has the rights to take it When we inflict the death penalty upon a Criminal we do not know what we are doing to him Perhaps we are doing him a favor nobody knows what death means The aim of the State should never be to hurt but to cure to cure both the Criminal and the tendency of others to initiate his Criminal Murder is an act of horror and morbidity Horror cannot be cured by horror nor morbidity by morbidity Sanity Justice and humanity are the curative Agencies Crime is abnormal the death penalty is abnormal one abnormality Cannot cure another Capital punishment therefore is Contrary to Common sense Contrary to psychology Contrary to reason Contrary to humanity Contrary to the spirit of Civilization and Contrary to the teaching of Christ It is a rotten offensive ignorant stupid and harmful practice a hold over from barbarism and ought to be abolished in every intelligent state

7. Letter from Agnes C. (Menominee) to Commissioner of Indian Affairs, Charles H. Burke, April 30, 1927. The reproduced letter below was one of many that Agnes wrote on her behalf to Canton Superintendent Harry Hummer, as well as various Commissioners of Indian Affairs. RG 75, CCF 1907–39, Canton Asylum, box 14, NARA-DC.

April 30 1927

Indian Insane Asylum
Canton So. Dak.
The Commissioner of the
Indian affairs
Washington DC

My Dear Commissioner

I feel as though I ought to see My Mother as long as I am in a good health and getting along nicely and able to work: I should think I would be returned to home now if it isnt necessary for me to go home

I would please Kindly ask you to give me a permission to Make a visit to My Mother at least; Will you please make the arrangement for me to Doctor Hummer;

I haven't seen my Mother for ten years now and I would like to see her as she is old now she isn't in a good condition Well you please kindly take this matter up and notify me so I can write to my Agent at home and he will look after Me. this will be all

Your Turly [sic]

Agnes. [C—].

notes

INTRODUCTION

1.   "Pablo H—. Student File," RG 75, series 1327, box 111, folder 4625, NARA, CISDRC.
2.   "Pablo H—. Student File."
3.   "Pablo H—. Student File."
4.   Deleuze, *Foucault*, 26.
5.   See Carlisle Quarterly School Reports, 1912, 1913, 1914, 1915, 1916, 1917, 1918, RG 75, series 745, NARA, CISDRC.
6.   White, "Who Gets to Tell the Stories?" Days of remembrance, symposia, and other gatherings have been held to honor Carlisle enrollees and bring together descendants, families, and tribes impacted by Carlisle's legacy, as White discusses in this essay.
7.   Carlisle's founding, history, operation, and legacy is the subject of a robust body of academic scholarship as well as novels and films; I have drawn upon the wisdom of boarding school historians and community members in this work. For information about Carlisle's founding and history, see Lomawaima and Ostler, "Reconsidering Richard Henry Pratt"; and Pratt, *Battlefield and Classroom*. For enrollee experiences at Carlisle, see especially Bell, "Telling Stories out of School"; and Fear-Segal and Rose, *Carlisle Indian Industrial School*.
8.   Carlisle was located in Cumberland County, Pennsylvania, and in 1980, the Cumberland County Historical Society (CCHS) received a grant to conduct oral interviews of former Carlisle students and local townspeople for posterity. These testimonies are invaluable, and Garvie's is included in this collection. See Carlisle Indian School History, Oral Histories, James Garvie, December 3, 1980, CCHS.
9.   Carlisle Indian School History, Oral Histories, James Garvie, December 3, 1980, CCHS.
10. Robertson, "Age of Consent Law."
11. Gorman, "Maiden Tribute"; and Robertson, "Age of Consent Law."
12. Filter, *Child Labor in America*, 33.
13. Juvonen et al., *Focus on the Wonder Years*, 11.
14. Robertson, "Age of Consent Law." For more on the history of childhood in the West, see Aries, *Centuries of Childhood*; Brockliss, "Introduction"; Heywood, *History of Childhood*; and Fass, *Routledge History of Childhood*.
15. Lake, *Progressive New World*, 6.

16. Ellinghaus, *Blood Will Tell*, 82.

17. Lajimodiere, "Healing Journey."

18. The Indian Reorganization Act of 1934, known also as the Indian "New Deal," was touted by commissioner of Indian Affairs John Collier as a radical departure from previous policies, designed to put a stop to allotment and restore tribal nations to self-government. The act fell short of its stated objectives and many tribes expressed strong opposition to the "New Deal" and voted against it. For more information, see Ellinghaus, *Blood Will Tell*, especially chapter 4, "The Same Old Deal: The 1934 Indian Reorganization Act."

19. Hoxie, *Final Promise*, 196–203. Frederick Hoxie points out that between 1905 and 1910, enrollment at off-reservation boarding schools declined by more than 10 percent, while attendance at day schools increased by more than 47 percent. He also notes that "under Reel the Indian school system continued to expand, but its curriculum and objectives changed. Although the number of students attending nonreservation boarding schools grew by more than one-third, admission was limited to graduates of other schools" (196–97).

20. For a nuanced discussion of Pratt's educational philosophy and relationship with Carlisle enrollees, see Lomawaima and Ostler, "Reconsidering Richard Henry Pratt." See also Prucha, *Americanizing the American Indians*.

21. For more information about Estelle Reel's impact on Indian education, see Lomawaima, "Estelle Reel, Superintendent of Indian Schools."

22. *Annual Report of the Commissioner of Indian Affairs*, 1905, 3.

23. See "Color or Race, Nativity, and Parentage of Occupied Persons," 343.

24. Few Indian people graduated from Carlisle. According to Fear-Segal and Rose, fewer than 750 individuals, or approximately 7.2 percent of over 10,500 enrollees, left with diploma in hand. See Fear-Segal and Rose, *Carlisle Indian Industrial School*, 2.

25. Lomawaima and McCarty, "To Remain an Indian," 45–46.

26. Lomawaima and McCarty, "To Remain an Indian," 45–46.

27. See, for example, Risling Baldy's *We Are Dancing for You*; Gilbert's study about the role of athleticism for the Hopi in *Hopi Runners*; and Bonnin's discussion of gender roles and kinship responsibilities in "The School Days of an Indian Girl," in Bonnin, *American Indian Stories*.

28. See "Walter A——. Student File," RG 75, series 1327, box 91, folder 4105, NARA, CISDRC.

29. Lomawaima's text *They Called It Prairie Light* is an early, groundbreaking study of the remembrances and recollections of students at Chilocco in 1930s Oklahoma, and it treats gendered distinctions in students' experiences with great care and precision. Child's early work *Boarding School Seasons* has been similarly foundational to the subfield of Native American boarding school studies. Analyzing letters of correspondence in finite detail, Child's work grapples with the legacies of Haskell and Flandreau from the perspective of Indigenous students and their families; the result is a powerful portrait of the ways in which Indigenous families and nations grappled with the changes to their lifeways wrought by the boarding school era. While Lomawaima's and Child's

texts are foundational examples of community-centered scholarship that helped to define the contours and direction of boarding school studies, and which inform this book as well, Adam's *Education for Extinction* offers a capacious overview of the development and implementation of OIA policy as related to Indigenous students and boarding schools across the United States. The Sherman Institute (previously known as Perris Indian School) in Riverside, California, also occupies a prominent place in boarding school scholarship and is the focus of much of Trafzer's work. Newer work extends these analyses, often by focusing on a single institution, or several boarding schools in comparative relief. For example, see Klotz, *Writing Their Bodies*; Whalen, *Native Students at Work*; Vučković, *Voices from Haskell*.

30. See, for example, Lomawaima, Child, and Archuleta's *Away from Home*, which resulted from a permanent exhibit at the Heard Museum in Phoenix, Arizona, entitled *Remembering Our Indian School Days: The Boarding School Experience*.

31. Wolfe, "Settler Colonialism and the Elimination of the Native," 387–88.

32. Benjamin, *Illuminations*, 256–57.

33. Lowe, *Intimacies of Four Continents*, 84.

34. Chapter 2, "Hoe Handle Medicine," discusses the concept of settler ableism in greater depth, which refers to the coarticulation of settler colonialism with dominant, limited, and non-Indigenous understandings of disability that often center and reinforce the primacy of able-bodiedness as a prerequisite for normative personhood. See chapter 2 of this book for more on this topic. In addition, see Whitt, Voyles, and Burch, "Settler Ableism." See also Cowing, "Settler States of Ability."

35. For more on Indigenous mobility, see Miller, *Indians on the Move*.

36. Smith, *Ireland's Magdalen Laundries*.

37. Recent monograph-length publications about Canton's history and legacy include Joinson's *Vanished in Hiawatha*, as well as Burch's excellent community-centered study, *Committed*.

CHAPTER 1. "AN ORDINARY CASE OF DISCIPLINE"

An earlier version of chapter 1 appeared in the *Western Historical Quarterly*. See Whitt, "'An Ordinary Case of Discipline.'"

1. I use first names and last initials only due to the nature of topics discussed and out of respect for the descendants of the Indigenous people included in this work.

2. "Justin H——. (R——. H——.) Student File," RG 75, series 1327, box 2, folder 82, NARA, CISDRC.

3. "Secretary Haaland Announces Federal Indian Boarding School Initiative."

4. According to the quarterly reports for years 1912–1918, all adults (women and men) eighteen and older constituted the following percentages of Carlisle's population: 56 percent in 1912; 58 percent in 1913; 57 percent in 1914; 56 percent in 1915; 57 percent in 1916; 50 percent in 1917; 55 percent in 1918. See Carlisle Quarterly School Reports, years 1912, 1913, 1914, 1915, 1916, 1917, 1918, NARA, CISDRC.

5. *Annual Report of the Commissioner of Indian Affairs*, 1905, 2.

6. Adams, *Education for Extinction*, 18.

7. The Carlisle Indian School Digital Resource Center organizes archival materials along similar axes of student experience; for more information, see Dickinson College's CISDRC.

8. Hernández, *City of Inmates*, 8.

9. A carceral logic attends processes of institutionalization. See Ben-Moshe, *Decarcerating Disability*, 3.

10. See Wolfe, "Settler Colonialism and the Elimination of the Native." For the full discussion on "total institutions," see Goffman, *Asylums*, 388.

11. Under the United States government's policy of "assimilation," Indian children were forced to attend boarding institutions like Carlisle and undergo a process of deculturization designed specifically for Indigenous youth. See, for instance Bell, "Telling Stories out of School"; Child, *Boarding School Seasons*; Jacobs, *White Mother to a Dark Race*; Landrum, *Dakota Sioux Experience*; Lomawaima, *They Called It Prairie Light*; Riney, *Rapid City Indian School*; Trafzer, Keller, and Sisquoc, *Boarding School Blues*; Trennert, *Phoenix Indian School*.

12. For more on shifting age demographics at Haskell and Sherman, respectively, see Vučković, *Voices from Haskell*; and Whalen, *Native Students at Work*.

13. For more information about gendered experiences, see Child, *Boarding School Seasons*, especially chapters 6, "Working for the School," and 7, "Runaway Boys, Resistant Girls"; Ellinghaus, "Assimilation by Marriage"; Lomawaima, "Domesticity in the Federal Indian Schools."

14. Fear-Segal, *White Man's Club*, 9.

15. Fear-Segal writes in the prologue to *White Man's Club*, "At Fort Marion, adult Indian prisoners, not children, walked to class past mounted cannon and piles of old cannon balls. Their jailer, Captain Richard Henry Pratt, had made himself their self-appointed teacher. By turning prisoners into pupils, Pratt was determined to demonstrate to white Americans that savage fighters could readily be tamed and civilized" (1).

16. Historian C. Kalani Beyer remarks that General Samuel Chapman Armstrong, founder of the Hampton Institute, "opposed classical higher education for blacks and Native Americans, preferring that nonwhite students be educated in rudimentary subjects and the ethics of work. . . . Armstrong was helping to accommodate the white power brokers by providing an education that prepared nonwhites to be trained for secondary roles in American society." Beyer, "Connection of Samuel Chapman Armstrong," 33.

   By comparison, Fear-Segal, in "Nineteenth-Century Indian Education," asserts that Richard Henry Pratt adhered to universalism, a belief in a fundamental human capacity that Armstrong rejected in favor of racial types. Fear-Segal writes, "For Pratt, the concept of racial 'types' was anathema. At Carlisle, he insisted on a set of principles rooted in a fundamentally different attitude of the Indian. As a young army officer, commanding both black soldiers and Indian scouts, he quickly decided that the apparent differences between the races were the product of environmental factors not innate variance" (329). "The situations of Indians and immigrants were comparable," she continues: "both needed to be absorbed into American society to achieve full participation. . . . Where Pratt was a universalist, Armstrong was an evolutionist" (329–30). These differing views would soon cause Pratt to seek approval for a facility of his own. See Fear-Segal, "Nineteenth-Century Indian Education."

17. In the autobiographical *Battlefield and Classroom*, Pratt reflected on Carlisle's founding and his proposal, brought before Congress, to site his new Indian boarding school at the military barracks in Carlisle, Pennsylvania. Writing of the ease with which he secured both congressional support and that of the War Department for his plan, Pratt explained, "I counted this one of the most eventful days of my life. . . . I was elated to find that things could be so easily and quickly attended to if you only had best help and directions. . . . I went to Carlisle, found the barracks neglected and much out of repair, hunted up a builder, and we itemized the condition of all the buildings and estimated the cost of temporary repairs, and I returned to Washington and made my report. Secretary McCrary showed me that General Hancock had approved, saying, 'I know of no better place to undertake such an experiment,' and General Sherman had 'Approved, provided both boys and girls are educated in said school,'" Pratt, *Battlefield and Classroom*, 217–18.

18. As historian Margaret Jacobs has discussed, the US model was also influential in Australia from 1910 to the 1970s, as officials stole Aboriginal youth from their families and subjected them to forms of cultural genocide similar to that pursued in the US context. Writing of globalized forms of Indigenous child abuse under pernicious forms of settler colonialism, Jacobs observes in *White Mother to a Dark Race*, "Schools, missions, and homes resembled prison camps. . . . Lame Deer recalls that 'in those days the Indian schools were like jails and run along military lines, with roll calls four times a day. We had to stand at attention, or march in step'" (218). Zitkála Šá, a well-known Dakota activist, scholar, and former Carlisle instructor, similarly described her own contemporaneous experiences with the "iron routine" of boarding school life. Mvskoke historian K. Tsianina Lomawaima has documented complex, gendered forms of labor at the Chilocco Indian School in mid-1930s Oklahoma. In addition to indoctrinating Indian children and youth into a "civilized" way of being defined by Protestant values, Christian mores, and a belief in the superiority of the English language, boarding institution officials used corporal punishment, isolation in carceral facilities, and prolonged separation from kin and community to beat Indian children and youth into spiritual, intellectual, and physical submission. See Margaret D. Jacobs's chapter (9) "The Removal of Indigenous Children in the United States and Australia, 1880–1940," in *Boarding School Blues*. Lomawaima's *They Called It Prairie Light* extensively documents

Indian women's experiences with domestic instruction and labor at Chilocco. This work is based on oral testimonies and thus offers firsthand accounts of Indigenous labor and vocational instruction in this era. Zitkála Šá, also known as Gertrude Bonnin (Dakota), published *American Indian Stories* in 1921, just a few years before Congress passed the Indian Citizenship Act (1924). This collection of stories includes one entitled "Iron Routine," in which Bonnin reflects on her time as a pupil at boarding school. She writes, "It was next to impossible to leave the iron routine after the civilizing machine had once begun its day's buzzing; and it was inbred in me to suffer in silence rather than to appeal to the ears of one whose open eyes could not see my pain, I have many times trudged in the day's harness heavy-footed, like a dumb sick brute." *American Indian Stories*, 41.

19. *Annual Report of the Commissioner of Indian Affairs*, 1905, 3.

20. *Annual Report of the Commissioner of Indian Affairs*, 1905, 3.

21. *Annual Report of the Commissioner of Indian Affairs*, 1905, 3.

22. Lake, *Progressive New World*, 6.

23. *Benevolent Institutions 1910*, 11.

24. *Benevolent Institutions 1904*, 14.

25. *Benevolent Institutions 1910*, 18.

26. From 1878, when the General Allotment Act was passed, to 1934, when Commissioner John Collier halted this policy, over ninety million acres of Indigenous lands had been expropriated. See Ellinghaus, *Blood Will Tell*, 82.

27. Typically, each head of household was allotted between 40 and 160 acres of land to live upon and farm. Land designated as "surplus" by surveyors was thrown open to white settlement, which resulted in massive loss of territory for tribal nations. For more on the effects of general allotment in Indian Territory, see Debo, *And Still the Waters Run*; and Ellinghaus, *Blood Will Tell*, especially chapter 1, "Fraud: The Allotment of the Anishinaabeg."

28. See Clara Sue Kidwell's entry on "Allotment" in the Oklahoma History Society's online encyclopedia. For a legal reference, see Kappler, *Indian Affairs, Laws and Treaties*.

29. By 1906, with the ratification of the Burke Act, Congress granted the Secretary of the Interior the power to forcibly remove allotments from trust status and issue patents before the standard twenty-five-year trust period had expired. This process, known as forced fee patenting, had immediate consequences: millions of acres passed out of Indigenous possession, as avaricious white Americans saw the opportunity to procure desirable tracts of land at a cost well below their actual value. In her seminal work, "Competency Commissions," historian Janet McDonnell estimates that forced-fee patenting alone resulted in the transfer of twenty-three million acres out of Indian hands from 1887 to 1934; the Indian Land Tenure Foundation puts the figure of expropriated land during this period even higher, at twenty-seven million acres of converted tracts.

30. Ellinghaus, *Blood Will Tell*, 82. For pre-Allotment Era history, see also Case, *Relentless Business of Treaties*.

31. Chilcote, *Unrecognized in California.*
32. See Whitt, "Care and Maintenance"; and Burch, *Committed.*
33. Esch, *Color Line and the Assembly Line.*
34. "Return of Richmond M—. and Discontinuance of Enrollment of Pupils from New York State," RG 75, CCF Entry 121, #32211-1908-Carlisle-826, NARA, CISDRC, 24.
35. Governmental appropriations were delegated to schools like Carlisle based on the number of enrolled pupils: in short, "the more children, the more money." See *Annual Report of the Commissioner of Indian Affairs,* 1908, 17.
36. "Return of Richmond M—.," 17.
37. I borrow the phrase "settler grammar" from Mishuana Goeman. See also Calderon (Tigua), "Uncovering Settler Grammars in Curriculum."
38. Lomawaima and McCarty, *"To Remain an Indian,"* 45–46.
39. See "Industrial Training Reenrollment Guidelines," NARA, CISDRC.
40. White (Mohawk) writes of the diversity of Carlisle enrollees' experiences and how family traditions can enrich our understanding of the institution's legacy. See White, "Who Gets to Tell the Stories?"
41. See CISDRC, Behavior/Disciplinary Information.
42. Hernández, *City of Inmates,* 28.
43. Wolfe, "Settler Colonialism and the Elimination of the Native," 3.
44. Following Buffington, Hernández, *City of Inmates,* 29.
45. "Justin H—. (R—. H—.) Student File," NARA, CISDRC.
46. These details are a classic example of what Foucault describes as a "field of documentation," or a corpus of knowledge that facilitated, in this instance, the exercise of settler power. Foucault, *Discipline and Punish,* 186–87.
47. "Justin H—. (R—. H—.) Student File."
48. "Howard S—. Student File," RG 75, series 1327, box 72, folder 3555, NARA, CISDRC.
49. "Justin H—. (R—. H—.) Student File."
50. "Justin H—. (R—. H—.) Student File," 90.
51. "Justin H—. (R—. H—.) Student File," 90.
52. "Justin H—. (R—. H—.) Student File," 85.
53. "Justin H—. (R—. H—.) Student File."
54. Carlisle's administration of Indian peoples' monies was contiguous with the OIA's treatment of Indian people on the reservation. According to the Meriam Report, if they "wanted something they would go to the government agent, as a child would go to his parents, and ask for it." Meriam, *The Problem of Indian Administration,* 8. Similarly, Carlisle authorities controlled enrollees' funds because they believed them to be irresponsible and profligate.
55. "Justin H—. (R—. H—.) Student File," 87.
56. "Justin H—. (R—. H—.) Student File."
57. Government residential institutions received per capita payments for enrollees.
58. "Justin H—. (R—. H—.) Student File."

59. Dickey's remark about the "laws of guardianship" highlights how the juridical apparatus undercut Indigenous self-determination. County courts appointed legal guardians to Indian people declared incompetent, and these arrangements resulted in loss of land, rights, and resources. US officials also assumed formal guardianship over Indian people presumed to be their legal wards, as Dickey's comment implies of Lipps and Justin. For more information on competency commissions and legal guardianship, see McDonnell, "Competency Commissions."

60. The historical record is ambiguous; it appears that Meritt is insinuating that Lipps might want to blame Justin for distributing liquor to three Carlisle enrollees who were under the age of twenty-one, and who had been detained pending investigation of this federal crime. See "Justin H——. (R——. H——.) Student File." See also Deverell and Hyde, *Shaped by the West*, vol. 2, chapter 10, "The 1920s: Prohibition and the West," 161–77; and Lappas, *In League against King Alcohol.*

61. Nyong'o, *Amalgamation Waltz.*

62. Hartman, *Scenes of Subjection*, 174.

63. Nichols, "Colonialism of Incarceration."

64. "George F——. Student File," RG 75, series 1327, box 30, folder 1412, NARA, CISDRC.

65. "George F——. Student File."

66. "George F——. Student File."

67. "George F——. Student File."

68. "George F——. Student File," 37.

69. *Rules for the Indian School Service*, 7.

70. Foucault, *Discipline and Punish*, 214.

71. Witgen, "Seeing Red," 600.

72. "Gertrude B——. Student File," RG 75, series 1327, box 96, folder 4242, NARA, CISDRC, 16.

73. "George F——. Student File."

74. "George F——. Student File."

75. Carlisle officials enumerated 310 Indian men in the quarterly enrollment report for December 1912, and adults eighteen years of age and older made up 55 percent of the institutional population that year. See Carlisle Quarterly Student Report (Dec. 31, 1912), RG 75, series 745, Carlisle Quarterly School Reports, NARA, CISDRC.

76. "Inspection Report of James McLaughlin for November 1910," RG 75, CCF Entry 121, #95269-1-1910-Carlisle-150, NARA, CISDRC, 109.

77. Child, *Boarding School Seasons.*

78. Carlisle enrollees, regardless of age, were prevented from going home to visit and from communicating with their families. See Child's chapter on "homesickness" in *Boarding School Seasons*; as well as Stephen Colmant et al., "Constructing Meaning to the Indian Boarding School Experience."

79. Friedman, "Carlisle Plan Makes for Independent Citizenship."

80. "Sending 'Florida Boys' at Hampton on Outings," RG 75, M234, roll 482, frames 507–510, NARA, CISDRC.

81. Friedman, "Carlisle Plan Makes for Independent Citizenship."

82. "Stopping Carousals of Carlisle Students."

83. "Return of Three Runaway Students from Chicago," RG 75, CCF Entry 121, #86543-1907 -Carlisle-821, NARA, CISDRC.

84. "Arrest of Robert D——. and Jesse G——.," RG 75, CCF Entry 121, #53263-1910-Carlisle-824, NARA, CISDRC, 1.

85. "Fees Paid to Carlisle Police," RG 75, CCF Entry 121, #38426-1914-Carlisle-821, NARA, CISDRC, 4.

86. At the time of this writing, I have not been able to determine whether white citizens were subjected to similar arrest fees; the fine appears to have been an extralegal, informal arrangement between the Carlisle Indian School and the Carlisle Police Department.

87. "Pay for Returning Runaway Pupils," RG 75, CCF Entry 121, #119496–1915-Carlisle-821, NARA, CISDRC.

88. Foucault, *Discipline and Punish*, 214.

89. Foucault, *Discipline and Punish*, 201.

90. Fear-Segal, *White Man's Club*.

91. See, for example, Laura Dominguez's discussion about the role of zoning ordinances in the preservation of white American racial fantasies in Los Angeles. Dominguez, "Courtyard Sisters."

92. Foucault, *Discipline and Punish*, 214.

93. "Adolph M——. Student File," RG 75, series 1327, box 91, folder 4098, NARA, CISDRC, 9.

94. "Adolph M——. Student File," 9.

95. Stoler, *Carnal Knowledge and Imperial Power*, 43.

96. "Simon S——. Student File," RG 75, series 1327, box 98, folder 4282, NARA, CISDRC, 29.

97. "Max F——. Student File," RG 75, series 1327, box 5, folder 202, NARA, CISDRC.

98. Indian women and men eighteen and older made their own application to Carlisle; they were not appropriately "school-aged" and thus could not legally be held at the institution by force.

99. Hartman writes, "Certainly Prigg v. Pennsylvania, the Fugitive Slave Law, the power of police exercised by any and every white person over slaves and free blacks, the interference of the state in disposals of slave property . . . and the modeling of racial relations in the image of master-slave relations attest to the public character of [slavery]." Hartman, *Scenes of Subjection*, 174.

100. This observation is influenced by Hernández's engagement with Wolfe. See Hernández, *City of Inmates*, 8.

101. Hernández, *City of Inmates*, 8.

102. Hernández, *City of Inmates*, 9.

103. "Walter S——. Student File," RG 75, series 1327, box 129, folder 5108, NARA, CISDRC, 13.

104. "Walter S——. Student File," 17.

105. "Walter S——. Student File," 17.

106. "Edward J——. Student File," RG 75, series 1327, box 91, folder 4115, NARA, CISDRC, 11.

107. "Winnie D. R——. Student File," RG 75, series 1327, box 129, folder 5120, NARA, CISDRC, 50.

108. Jacobs, "Working on the Domestic Frontier," 166.

109. Beth Piatote (Nez Perce) argues that the end of the so-called Indian Wars in the 1880s did not mark the end of Indigenous struggle and settler violence. "Indian economies, lands, kinship systems, languages, cultural practices, and family relations—in short, all that constituted the Indian home—became the primary site of struggle. The battle, although not the stakes, moved from the indigenous homeland, what I call the tribal-national domestic, to the familial space of the Indian home, or the intimate domestic. In the assimilation era, the tools of conquest were not so much armed commanders as administrative circulars. The cavalry man was supplanted—or, rather, supplemented—by the field matron, the Hotchkiss by the transit, and the prison by the school." Piatote, *Domestic Subjects*, 2–3.

110. For information about the increased public role that white women played in US Indian affairs, see especially Jacobs, *White Mother to a Dark Race*, chapter 3, "The Great White Mother."

111. Bauer, *Tender Violence*, 5–6.

112. Simonsen, *Making Home Work*, 3.

113. *Eadle Keatah Toh.*

114. Bell also details the abysmal compensation that Outing pupils could expect to receive: 50 cents to $2 a week for girls, and $5 to $15 a month for boys. Bell, "Telling Stories out of School," 171.

115. I borrow this phrase from Brunhouse, *Apprenticeship for Civilization*.

116. Foucault, *Discipline and Punish*, 186–87.

117. Adkins, *Gossip, Epistemology, and Power*.

118. "Inspection Report of J. H. Dortch for May 1915," RG 75, CCF Entry 121, #31080-1917-Carlisle-150, NARA, CISDRC, 19.

119. "Inspection Report of J. H. Dortch for May 1915," 19.

120. "Inspection Report of J. H. Dortch for May 1915," 22.

121. "Lucinda R——. Student File," RG 75, series 1327, box 8, folder 364, NARA, CISDRC, 25.

122. Alexander H. Holcombe, U.S. Presbyterian Church records, 1701–1970, Ancestry.com. Accessed January 15, 2021. https://www.ancestry.com/search/collections/61048/.

123. "Lucinda R——. Student File," 27.

124. "Lucinda R——. Student File," 29.

125. "Lucinda R——. Student File," 30.

126. "Lucinda R——. Student File," 31.

127. "Lucinda R——. Student File," 35–37.

128. Katrin Horn writes, "Gossip lends itself to [a] dual use of containment (keeping women in their place) and exposure (revealing secrets homes are supposed to keep) due to its dual connection to domesticity and semipublic knowledge of uncertain truth value." Horn, "Dangerous Domesticity," 25.

129. "Lucinda R—. Student File," 38. Nelly signed this letter "Outing manager," including the initials NRD in the bottom left-hand corner. The Outing manager was likely
Nelly Denny (neé Robertson), a Sisseton Wahpeton Sioux woman who was a former Carlisle enrollee and married Wallace Denny (Oneida), who served as Carlisle's
disciplinarian.

130. Lucinda's institutional history fits a familiar pattern: it ends where her enrollment at
Carlisle ends. At the time of this writing, I have found no other reference to Lucinda
or her child in census records or other repositories likely to contain data about the rest
of her life. These archival silences, as I and other historians have pointed out, complicate a fuller recovery of Indigenous histories, lives, and experiences.

131. See Keliiaa, *Refusing Settler Domesticity*; Million, *Therapeutic Nations*; Smith, *Conquest*
and "Boarding School Abuses"; Burrage, Momper, and Gone, "Beyond Trauma"; and
Deer, *Beginning and End of Rape*.

132. Adkins writes, "Weaponized gossip . . . is often a marker of underlying and unjust
social structures, rather than merely a self-contained problem to be addressed directly," and she asserts that "most gossip is premised on trust and intimacy." Adkins,
Gossip, Epistemology, and Power, 181, 182. She goes on to say that "compromised trust
and intimacy facilitate gossip- and rumor-spreading . . . compromised social trust and
community insularity . . . typically emerge in communities with sharp and stark divides of power (social, economic, racial, gender), or communities in which power is
being renegotiated, challenged, or undermined" (182–83). Fine and Turner suggest
that in circumstances in which more information is demanded than is known, rumor
proliferates. Fine and Turner, *Whispers*, 54.

133. "Lucinda R—. Student File," 27.

134. Moreton-Robinson has theorized the "white possessive logic" of settler states. See
Moreton-Robinson, *White Possessive*. Federal paternalism and legal guardianship undercut Indigenous self-determination in numerous ways. Like other Carlisle enrollees, Lucinda was presumed to be under the complete oversight of Carlisle officials.
She lacked legal personhood: she was not a US citizen; she had not been declared
"competent," the status of which was typically tied to owning one's allotment outright, having demonstrated competency before a commission, or having graduated
from a federal boarding school; and until she turned eighteen, her enrollment at Carlisle was considered compulsory. For more information on federal Indian policy, US
law, and the "assimilation era," see Gross, *What Blood Won't Tell*, especially chapter 4,
"Citizenship for the 'Little Races,'" and chapter 5, "Black Indian Identity in the Allotment Era"; and Ellinghaus, *Blood Will Tell*.

135. Horn, "Dangerous Domesticity," 24.

136. "Lucinda R—. Student File," 45.

137. Stoler writes, "The very categories 'colonizer' and 'colonized' were secured through
forms of sexual control that defined the domestic arrangements of Europeans and the
cultural investments by which they identified themselves." Stoler, *Carnal Knowledge*,

42. The sexual overtones embedded in Holcombe's description of Eva as "filthy" reveal anxiety about miscegenation. As Stoler elaborates, "Racial degeneracy was thought to have social causes and political consequences, both tied to the domestic arrangements in which Europeans lived. . . . Through sexual contact with native women, European men 'contracted' disease as well as debased sentiments, immoral proclivities, and extreme susceptibility to uncivilized states" (68).

138. Writing of the cultural dictates by which colonial communities arranged themselves, Stoler explains, "Europeans . . . constructed communities built on asymmetries of race, class, and gender. . . . European women . . . experienced the cleavages of racial dominance and internal social distinctions very differently than men precisely because of their ambiguous positions, as both subordinates in colonial hierarchies and as agents of empire in their own right." Stoler, *Carnal Knowledge*, 41. She continues, "Treating the sexual and conjugal tensions of colonial life as more than a political trope. . . . [I examine] how gender-specific sexual sanctions and prohibitions not only demarcated positions of power but also prescribed the personal and public boundaries of race" (42).

139. "Lucinda R—. Student File."

140. In her seminal article, Barbara Welter writes, "The attributes of True Womanhood, by which a woman judged herself and was judged by her husband, her neighbors and society could be divided into four cardinal virtues—piety, purity, submissiveness and domesticity. Put them all together and they spelled mother, daughter, sister, wife— woman." Welter, "Cult of True Womanhood," 152. For discussions about race and "true womanhood," see also Cummins, *Herstories on Screen*, especially chapter 2, "Debunking the Cult of True Womanhood/Motherhood on the Frontier"; Kaiser, "Black Madonna"; and Segrest, "Rebirths of a U.S. Nation."

141. Tompkins, *Racial Indigestion*.

142. In *Groundless*, historian Gregory Dowd examines how gossip, hoaxes, legends, and rumors were important discursive technologies for both American Indian people and colonists. Dowd argues that "flying reports"—as rumor was called on the early American frontier—have served as the basis of received wisdom on a surprising array of topics, and demonstrates how the veracity of master historical narratives is perhaps less interesting than the manner in which they were created. For another important discussion of discursive forms of resistance, see James C. Scott's work, *Domination and the Arts of Resistance*, especially chapter 6, "Voice under Domination."

143. In 1915, for example, Carlisle Superintendent John Francis Jr. wrote to the father of a seventeen-year-old Potawatomi woman named Sarah D. to assure him that the Outing home in which she had been placed was excellent, and that there were no young men in the household. This assurance can be interpreted as both an acknowledgment of the risk that the presence of men posed to Indian women placed in the Outing system and Superintendent Francis's attempt to assuage Sarah's father's concern over his daughter's well-being and education, since she had not been attending school.

As Sarah's father, Francis, wrote Superintendent Francis, "We received a letter from [Sarah] saying that she was going out in the country to school again. She has been out [of] school for six month [*sic*]. And we do not approve [*sic*] of it. She ought to be at Carlisle in School. It seem to me you have no school there but have to send to Public school to learn something. . . . It may be alright but we don't feel that way." "Sarah D——. Student File," RG 75, series 1327, box 106, folder 4500, NARA, CISDRC, 20–23.

144. Guise, "Who Is Doctor Bauer?"

145. Paraphrased from White's observations in "Who Gets to Tell the Stories," 124.

146. Landownership and citizenship went hand in hand. See Ellinghaus, *Blood Will Tell*, especially chapter 2, "Chaos."

CHAPTER 2. "HOE HANDLE MEDICINE"

1. "Hoe Handle Medicine."

2. As historian Fear-Segal has pointed out, articles like "Hoe Handle Medicine" were likely authored by Carlisle's printmaking instructor, Marianna Burgess. For more information, see Fear-Segal, *White Man's Club*, especially chapter 8, "Man-on-the-Bandstand: Surveillance, Concealment, and Resistance." For another interesting discussion about the relationship between linguistic propaganda, labor, and artistic instruction at Carlisle, see Slivka, "Art, Craft, and Assimilation," 225–42. See also Emery, *Recovering Native American*.

3. See Glover, *United States Life Tables*. For a quick overview, see also Leon, "Life of American Workers in 1915."

4. Keller's monograph *Empty Beds* extensively documents contagious illnesses at the Sherman Institute in Riverside, California. Trafzer's recent text, *Fighting Invisible Enemies*, offers an overview of disease in Indian Country more generally, along with the ways in which tribal nations addressed these crises. McBride's dissertation "A Lethal Education" extensively documents morbidity and mortality rates at Carlisle and other off-reservation boarding schools, including Chemawa, Sherman, and Haskell.

5. I borrow the concept of the "safety zone" from Lomawaima and McCarty's discussion about shifts in federal Indian policy. See Lomawaima and McCarty, "To Remain an Indian."

6. As Traci Brynne Voyles, Susan Burch, and I have noted of settler ableism, "Applying an Indigenous studies lens to discussions about ableism highlights the settler structures that foreclose not only the possibility of normative personhood for Indigenous peoples—but of life at all. . . . Historical processes, shifts, and transformations, including the rise of manufacturing, expansion of Western biomedicine, and the proliferation of institutionalization, would not be possible without settler-citizens' systematic appropriation of Indigenous lands. Settler ableism is a structural precondition and consequence of the emergences of a range of social and environmental injustices with which [Indigenous] people continue to grapple." Whitt, Voyles, and Burch, "Settler

Ableism," 7–8. Here, I draw on these ideas in my discussion of the ideology of medicinal labor. See also Cowing, "Settler States of Ability."

7. For excellent resources on historical shifts in the treatment of illness in the United States from a public health standpoint, see Kraut, *Silent Travelers*; Tomes, *Gospel of Germs*; and Wald, *Contagious*.

8. These statistics are drawn from the Centers for Disease Control's report, "Achievements in Public Health."

9. Hinman, following J. A. Doull, "1889 to 1989," 378.

10. Haddad, "Medicine and the Culture of Commemoration."

11. Steere-Williams, "Germ Theory," 403.

12. For instance, see Lui, *Chinatown Trunk Mystery*; Patterson, "Germs and Jim Crow"; Shah, *Contagious Divides*; and Wald, *Contagious*.

13. *Contagious and Infectious Diseases among the Indians*, 1913.

14. Roberts, *Infectious Fear*, 4.

15. Roberts, *Infectious Fear*, 4.

16. Larkin-Gilmore, "On the Borders."

17. Larkin-Gilmore, "Hygienic Dispossession."

18. For instance, see Theobald, *Reproduction on the Reservation*; Trafzer, *Strong Hearts and Healing Hands*; and DeJong, *"If You Knew the Conditions."*

19. Jones, "Health Care Experiments," 756; Trafzer, *Fighting Invisible Enemies*.

20. See Keller, *Empty Beds*, 29; and Trafzer, *Fighting Invisible Enemies*, 21.

21. *Contagious and Infectious Diseases among the Indians*, 14.

22. *Contagious and Infectious Diseases among the Indians*, 12–13.

23. *Contagious and Infectious Diseases among the Indians*, 17.

24. *Contagious and Infectious Diseases among the Indians*, 79.

25. *Contagious and Infectious Diseases among the Indians*, 25.

26. Keller, *Empty Beds*, 117.

27. Keller, *Empty Beds*, 37.

28. McBride, "A Lethal Education," 345.

29. Adams, "'Very Serious and Perplexing Epidemic of Grippe.'"

30. *Contagious and Infectious Diseases among the Indians*, 82–83.

31. See Esch 2018, *Color Line and the Assembly Line*, especially chapter 5, 220. Medical historian Rana Hogarth documents a similar dynamic in her study of Black bodies, enslavement, and white supremacy in Jamaica in the early nineteenth century. Writing of white physicians' construction of Cachexia Africana (dirt eating) as a racialized disease, Hogarth explains that enslaved Africans' inability to labor during periods of illness figured prominently in physicians' identification of supposedly inferior Black bodies. "Rather than seeing the enslaved African body as one that was dispossessed from its homeland and weakened from abuse, forcible transport, and poor nutrition," she writes, "the image of the black body was one that was sturdy and ready to toil under brutal conditions. Failure to live up to this impossible ideal was immediately pathologized."

Hogarth, *Medicalizing Blackness*, 85. "This line of reasoning," Hogarth concludes, "validated the idea that black people's bodies had to be monitored and overseen by whites to reach their fullest potential and live up to the image of black people as ideal laborers that existed in the white imagination"—a dynamic she describes as "white managerialism" (85).

32. See "Iti Fabvssa" in *Biskinik*, September 1, 2018; "Iti Fabvssa" in *Biskinik*, April 1, 2019; and Thompson, *Choctaw Food*.

33. Littlefield and Knack, *Native Americans and Wage Labor*, 6.

34. Littlefield and Knack, *Native Americans and Wage Labor*, 11.

35. Littlefield and Knack, *Native Americans and Wage Labor*, 12.

36. Martha Knack examines wage labor economies among the Southern and Northern Paiutes, offering a fascinating discussion of the economic development of the Great Basin, and Indigenous women's and men's central roles in the creation of seasonal and short-term economies. See Knack, *Native Americans and Wage Labor*, especially "Nineteenth-Century Great Basin Indian Wage Labor."

37. Bauer, *We Were All like Migrant Workers Here*, 59.

38. Bauer, *We Were All like Migrant Works Here*, 58.

39. See Cahill, *Federal Fathers and Mothers*; Haskins, *Matrons and Maids*; and Jacobs, "Working on the Domestic Frontier."

40. Whalen, *Native Students at Work*.

41. Hernández, *City of Inmates*, 36–37.

42. In addition to the General Allotment Act, or Dawes Act, of 1887, subsequent legislature amended previous acts to expand the reach of allotment policies. One such piece of legislature was the Burke Act of 1906, also known as the Forced Fee Patenting Act, which authorized and, in some cases, mandated issuance of fee simple title to allotted individuals. Under this law, allotments held in trust by the US government were removed from trust status, oftentimes before the standard trust period of twenty-five years had concluded. In return, the Secretary of the Interior granted allottees US citizenship along with fee simple title, which rendered them vulnerable to land-hungry white settlers. For more on Indigenous resistance to settler encroachment, see O'Brien and Justice, *Allotment Stories*. For more on the consequences of forced fee patenting, see, for example, Tatro's entry on the Burke Act in the Oklahoma History Society's encyclopedia. For a legal reference, see Kappler, *Indian Affairs, Laws and Treaties*.

43. *Annual Report of the Commissioner of Indian Affairs*, 1907, 11.

44. Outing was a labor system developed by Carlisle founder Richard Henry Pratt that placed Indian students in the homes of white Americans to perform domestic and farm labor from 1879 to 1904. The Outing system underwent shifts in later years under the aegis of successive superintendents. Superintendent Oscar H. Lipps was responsible for developing the Ford Outing agreement, a radical departure from earlier iterations of the Outing, which mirrored shifting objectives in Office of Indian Affairs policy and racialist sentiments about American Indians' proper "place" in American society as menial or wage laborers.

45. "Ford 'Original Americans,'" 305.
46. Alice Littlefield has demonstrated that vocational training in federal boarding institutions was a process of proletarianization, as the schools prepared Indian people for employment in the wage-labor workforce. Following Littlefield, I draw on this phenomenon of proletarianization to examine American Indian participation in training "partnerships" in the private sector. See Littlefield and Knack, *Native Americans and Wage Labor*. For additional information about Native people and labor under various Outing programs at the turn of the twentieth century, also see work by William Bauer Jr., *We Were All like Migrant Workers Here*; Kevin Whalen, *Native Students at Work*; and Robert Trennert, *Phoenix Indian School*. Trennert has described how the Phoenix Indian School produced laborers for the citrus and agricultural industries in the Southwest.
47. "Blacksmithing Industrial Training Information," RG 75, CCF Entry 121, #55108-1917-Carlisle-920, NARA, CISDRC.
48. "Blacksmithing Industrial Training Information."
49. "George M——. Student File," RG 75, series 1327, box 116, folder 4747, NARA, CISDRC.
50. In correspondence with the Commissioner of Indian Affairs Cato Sells, Carlisle Superintendent Oscar Lipps noted that the Indian men from Carlisle would be enrolled in the "student corps" at Ford—an entity that appears to have been distinct from the Henry Ford English School in which non-English-speaking immigrants were also enrolled. See Oscar Lipps to Cato Sells, September 13, 1916, "Industrial Training Reenrollment Guidelines," RG 75, CCF Entry 121, #99699-1916-Carlisle-920, NARA, CISDRC.
51. Oscar Lipps corresponded with Commissioner of Indian Affairs Cato Sells about accepting Indian men at Carlisle who wanted to enroll primarily so that they could be placed in a position at Ford. In this correspondence, Lipps emphasized that the men were old enough to take care of themselves and benefit from such an arrangement. In one letter, Lipps explained that "in the majority of cases [the men] are over 21 years of age." He additionally explained to Sells, "I desire to be advised, therefore, whether or not the requirements that a definite course of work must have been completed before eligibility for enrolment at Carlisle can be established may be waived and whether or not a general authority may be granted to enroll students over 21 years of age and to retain those who are more than 24 years of age if it is shown that they are taking our preparatory course for work in automobile and other manufacturing establishments where special instruction is a part of the work that is given." In other words, Lipps wanted permission to transform Carlisle into a labor placement agency, and this formal permission was granted. See Lipps to Sells, September 13, 1916, "Industrial Training Reenrollment Guidelines."
52. Loizides, "'Making Men' at Ford," 76.
53. See Esch, *Color Line and the Assembly Line*.
54. See "Andrew B——. Student File," RG 75, series 1327, box 144, folder 5605, NARA, CISDRC; "Henry Ford Trade School Information Brochure, 1931–1941"; and Gaft, "History of the Henry Ford Trade School, 1916–1952."

55. Loizides, "'Making Men' at Ford." Ford employed Frederick Taylor's ideology of Scientific Management, along with the notion that different types of people were better suited to different types of work. In the space of the Ford factory, this meant that racial discrimination was pervasive, as white Americans and European immigrants were assigned more coveted jobs than were the Black employees in Detroit. From documents relating to Carlisle men at the Ford factory, we can extrapolate that they were similarly assigned jobs on the basis of apparent capacity, which broke along racial lines. Loizides writes of the ways in which Taylorism facilitated racial discrimination, "The idea that there were different types of men, and that each type was best suited to particular occupations comprised a justification, or at least a rationalization, for the racial stratification of work, which was dominant at that time. This was not specific to the Ford Motor Company, but was part of a more general racial stratification of work. Many employers of the time, justified job segregation and inequality (giving Blacks the worst jobs) by calling it a measure for preventing racial tension. This was the case at the Ford Motor Company as well" (133). For more about racial dynamics at Ford plants around the world, see, especially, Esch, *Color Line and the Assembly Line*. See also Taylor, *Shop Management*.
56. Loizides, "'Making Men' at Ford," 133.
57. Esch, *Color Line and the Assembly Line*, 1. In a similar vein, Stephen Meyer discusses immigrant experiences at Ford in "Adapting the Immigrant to the Line."
58. Mays, *City of Dispossessions*.
59. This came with strings attached; as Ford historian Elizabeth Esch explains in *Color Line and the Assembly*, "The five-dollar wage signified the most dramatic commitment on the part of the company to controlling production through controlling the lives of workers" (36). For more information about racial hierarchies and Ford, see Esch, *Color Line and the Assembly Line*. Similarly, historian Kyle T. Mays writes that Ford's five-dollar day helped spur the Great African American migration from Southern states north, and he asserts that anti-Black racism in Detroit contributed to housing insecurity. See Mays, *City of Dispossessions*, 64.
60. As quoted in Loizides, "'Making Men' at Ford," 134.
61. Hoxie, *Final Promise*, 206.
62. Meyer, "Adapting the Immigrant," 68.
63. "Grover M——. Student File," RG 75, series 1327, box 117, folder 4770, NARA, CISDRC. This arrangement would be inverted by 1917, when the men would work day shifts and attend night courses, as discussed. See "Blacksmithing Industrial Training Information."
64. Brandt, *No Magic Bullet*, 7–8.
65. "Grover M——. Student File."
66. "Grover M——. Student File."
67. Grant and Osborn, *Passing of the Great Race*.
68. "Grover M——. Student File."

69. "Real Ownership," 472.
70. "Doing Nicely Thank You!," 466.
71. "Grover M——. Student File."
72. "Grover M——. Student File."
73. "George M——. Student File," 59.
74. "Andrew B——. Student File," 44.
75. "Industrial Training Reenrollment Guidelines."
76. "Industrial Training Reenrollment Guidelines."
77. "Industrial Training Reenrollment Guidelines."
78. "Pablo H——. Student File," RG 75, series 1327, box 111, folder 4625, NARA, CISDRC, 98–99.
79. According to Frederick Hoxie, under Cato Sells, the increasing specialization of off-reservation boarding schools continued. Carlisle was to train Indian men in automotive mechanics; it appears that this program was facilitated, at least in part, by Charles Dagenett's Employment Bureau. Hoxie, *Final Promise*, 201–204.
80. "David B——. Student File," NARA, CISDRC, RG 75, series 1327, box 114, folder 4705, 57–58.
81. Miller, "Willing Workers," 51.
82. See also Fixico, *Urban Indian*; and Deloria, *Indians in Unexpected Places*. Kevin Whalen also documents the experiences of Native students who were enrolled at Sherman and participated in Outing in Los Angeles in *Native Students at Work*.
83. "Otto T——. Student File," RG 75, series 1327, box 113, folder 4674, NARA, CISDRC.
84. "Otto T——. Student File."
85. "Otto T——. Student File."
86. Elizabeth Esch writes in reference to the impact of Ford's standardization process upon productivity: "Even as production at Ford was rapidly becoming deskilled and the company was furthering the idea that 'intellectual activity should be separated from manual work,' employees were not stripped overnight of the knowledge they possessed or their interest in self-defense. . . . Between 1909 and 1913 the productivity of workers at Highland Park increased by 60 percent, an impressive figure but one limited by problems managing both skilled and unskilled workers." Esch, *Color Line and the Assembly Line*, 36–37.
87. "Otto T——. Student File," 11.
88. "Otto T——. Student File," 11.
89. "Otto T——. Student File," 5.
90. Based on available archival documents, it is unclear why Otto was transferred to Chicago and who authorized this decision. As a letter from Griswold to Lipps reflects, Otto was a good worker: "We are arranging to transfer Mr. Otto T——., Carlisle Man and student of this Company from the Home Office to the Chicago Branch, effective January 25th, 1917. Mr. T——. has about completed his Students Course here and should be in a position to do good mechanical work in the Assembly Plant at Chi-

cago." According to other letters of correspondence, another Carlisle man by the name of Charles B. accompanied Otto to Chicago. "Otto T—. Student File," 40.

91. He would go on to fight in WWI and become active in Minnesota politics. See Otto T—. "WWI Draft Card"; and *1964 Press Photo Otto T—. Minnesota Convention Rep.*

92. "Joe Gilman Student File," RG 75, series 1327, box 98, folder 4290, NARA, CISDRC, 24.

93. "Joe Gilman Student File," 24.

94. In fact, as Loizides points out, Ford company materials promoted the purchase of a home and automobile among its employees because it was believed to be an indicator of thrift, one of the prerequisites for participation in the company profit-sharing plan. However, Loizides also points out that housing discrimination was pervasive in Detroit. Ford's promotion of the purchase of a home, and discrimination against boarding, resulted in inequitable housing opportunities and residential segregation for Black workers. Based on the correspondence about Gilman's finances, it also appears that Indian men had greater difficulty accessing the resources required to establish themselves in single-family residences as compared with white workers. See Loizides, "'Making Men' at Ford," 128–30.

95. See Theobald, *Reproduction on the Reservation.*

96. Clifford Trafzer, *Strong Hearts and Healing Hands,* describes the role that Western medicine played in furthering US colonialism among tribal nations: "The [OIA's] introduction of biomedical medicine to Indians obviously included elements of medical colonialism. Indian service field nurses participated within a well-established colonial system, intended to make Native people part of the dominant society" (87). For more on this, see Trafzer, *Strong Hearts and Healing Hands,* especially chapter 3, "Developing Field Nursing."

97. "Nurse Training Program at German Hospital, New York," RG 75, CCF Entry 121, #44034-1917-Carlisle-810, NARA, CISDRC.

98. For more on nurse training programs in the United States, see Reverby, *Ordered to Care.*

99. "Ozetta B—. Student File," RG 75, series 1327, box 106, folder 4506, NARA, CISDRC, 6.

100. For more information about Indian homes and forms of domesticity as sites of colonial conflict in this era, see Cahill, *Federal Fathers and Mothers;* Haskins, *Matrons and Maids;* Jacobs, *White Mother to a Dark Race;* Lomawaima, *They Called It Prairie Light;* Piatote, *Domestic Subjects;* and Wexler, *Tender Violence.*

101. Lomawaima, "Domesticity in the Federal Indian Schools."

102. Lomawaima, "Domesticity in the Federal Indian Schools," 228.

103. Lomawaima, "Domesticity in the Federal Indian Schools," 228.

104. Risling Baldy, "Mini-Kiwhe:N," 3.

105. "Ozetta B—. Student File," 6.

106. Wexler, *Tender Violence,* 31–34.

107. Photography was used as a tool of colonialism at Carlisle and other major boarding institutions, such as Hampton. For more on this, see Laura Wexler's discussion of

Francis Benjamin Johnson's *Hampton Album*, in *Tender Violence*; also see Klotz, *Writing Their Bodies*.

108. Million, *Therapeutic Nations*, 6–7.

109. Million, *Therapeutic Nations*, 6–7.

110. I thank my friend and colleague Alán Pelaez Lopez for this insight, given in a private conversation.

111. "Ozetta B—. Student File."

112. "Ozetta B—. Student File."

113. Indeed, one of Ozetta's relatives referred to "Big Aunt Ozetta" as "feisty" in private correspondence.

114. "Emerald B—. Student File," RG 75, series 1327, box 105, folder 4482, NARA, CISDRC, 8.

115. "Emerald B—. Student File," 8.

116. Jacobs, in "Diverted Mothering," writes of Indigenous women's participation in the San Francisco Bay Area Outing Program, "Despite . . . indignities, many women stuck with the work—at least temporarily—and still sought out such jobs. Many were drawn to the social opportunities the Bay Area afforded, particularly with other Indian youth. . . . Young Indian women valued this social life so much that many of them avoided or sought to leave positions if they interfered with their leisure pursuits."

117. "Emerald B—. Student File."

118. "Emerald B—. Student File."

119. American historian Claude Fischer writes of the rise of the automobile and changing mores in American culture, especially with regards to race and gender dynamics. Specifically, he writes of the impact that Ford's most famous car model had on public life in the United States: "Henry Ford's Model T really brought rural Americans into public spaces in the 1910s and '20s. . . . Rural women in particular eagerly took to driving and praised the automobile for letting them escape the house. Celebrity home economist Christine Fredrick declared in 1912 that 'the car has wrought my emancipation, my freedom. I am no longer a country-bound farmer's wife. . . . The auto . . . brings me into frequent touch with the entertainment and life of my neighboring small towns—with joys of bargains, library, and soda-water'" (171). See chapter 5, "Public Spaces," for the complete discussion, in Fischer, *Made in America*. See also Deloria's chapter on "Technology" for a rich discussion of Geronimo and his prized Cadillac in *Indians in Unexpected Places*.

120. "Emerald B—. Student File."

121. "Emerald B—. Student File."

122. "Emerald B—. Student File."

123. "Emerald B—. Student File," 7.

124. As illustrated by correspondence about Emerald and her expulsion from nurse training, Carlisle authorities viewed personal enjoyment—or "having a good time," in Lipps's words—as antithetical to serious study and the racial "uplift" of Indian people. "Having a good time" also carried subtle overtones of sexual impropriety.

An earlier version of chapter 3 appeared in Whitt, "'Wash Away Your Sins,'" in the *American Indian Culture and Research Journal*.

1. "Landmark Comes Down."
2. Child, "Boarding School as Metaphor," 49.
3. Smith, *Ireland's Magdalen Laundries*.
4. See *Federal Indian Boarding School Initiative Investigative Report*.
5. See Reiter and Blair, "Punishing Mental Illness," 177–96. For a discussion of transincarceration, which is a related concept, also see Ben-Moshe, *Decarcerating Disability*. For a discussion of transinstitutionalization through the Canton Asylum for Insane Indians, see also Susan Burch, *Committed*.
6. Take, for example, the recollections of Sam Kenoi (Apache), who was a former Carlisle enrollee. In the 1930s, Morris Opler interviewed Kenoi, and his remembrances have been preserved for posterity. As Sam explains, coerced movement was a familiar part of his experience "at Carlisle": "So in '98 I went to Carlisle. I got there in August . . . They began shipping some of the students out into the country to work . . . This bunch of fifty that I was with went through Harrisburg, then Reading, then to Philadelphia. From here half of us were going towards Bristol and Trenton, New Jersey. They we got to Tallytown [*sic*], Pennsylvania. Four of us boys got out there." "Sam Kenoi's Autobiography Part II," Cornell University, courtesy of Paul Conrad, 338.
7. As Ruggles remarks of the Protestant Magdalen Society of Philadelphia, other institutions were the greatest source (31.9 percent) of referral for "inmates" confined between 1903 and 1907. Ruggles, "Fallen Women," 10.
8. The Protestant Magdalen Society Asylum was founded in Philadelphia in 1800; the first Catholic "asylum" was founded by the Good Shepherd Sisters in Louisville in 1842.
9. Phillips, "Education for Girls," 92; Jones and Record, "Magdalene Laundries," 171.
10. For example, see Conway, *In the Footprints of the Good Shepherd*; Fitzgerald, *Habits of Compassion*; Ruggles, "Fallen Women"; and Teeters, "Early Days of the Magdalen Society."
11. Phillips, "Education," 32.
12. Jones and Record, "Magdalene Laundries."
13. Jones and Record, "Magdalene Laundries," 174.
14. Phillips writes in "Education," "The majority of the Good Shepherd schools supplemented their income by doing commercial laundry and sewing embroidered clothing. Rural facilities had gardens and small animal farms for provision of food. The girls . . . provided the manual labor as part of the re-education process . . . the labor supported the facility without formal wages for the workers" (21).
15. Smith, *Ireland's Magdalen Laundries*, 24.
16. Finnegan, *Do Penance or Perish*, 51; Smith, *Ireland's Magdalen Laundries*, 28.

17. Smith, *Ireland's Magdalen Laundries*, 25.
18. See McGettrick et al., *Ireland and the Magdalene Laundries*; O'Donnell and O'Sullivan, *Coercive Confinement in Ireland*; and Coen, O'Donnell, and O'Rourke, *Dublin Magdalene Laundry*.
19. Smith, *Ireland's Magdalen Laundries*, 2.
20. Smith, *Ireland's Magdalen Laundries*, 25.
21. Smith, *Ireland's Magdalen Laundries*, 25.
22. Smith, *Ireland's Magdalen Laundries*, 25.
23. McGettrick et al., *Ireland and the Magdalene Laundries*, 28.
24. McGettrick et al., *Ireland and the Magdalene Laundries*, 30.
25. McGettrick et al., *Ireland and the Magdalene Laundries*.
26. The Justice for Magdalenes (JFM) campaign sought a memorial for women who were exhumed from a mass grave in the early 1990s, a redress and compensation scheme for those impacted, and a formal apology from the Irish state for the role it played in the forced confinement of women and children in laundries across the country. According to the JFM's official website and statement on the JFM Political Campaign from 2009–2013, "The driving force behind JFM's establishment was [Irish journalist] Mary Raferty's exposure in August 2003 that the nuns of the Sisters of our Lady Charity of Refuge had received exhumation licenses from the Department of the Environment for 155 bodies in 1993, without producing death certificates for 80 women or the full names of 46 women," all of whom were disinterred from a grave at the High Park Magdalene Laundry in Drumcondra. Justice for Magdalenes Research Archive and website, jfmresearch.com.
27. McGettrick and colleagues point out that in the years following Kenny's apology, the state and subsequent investigations began changing the narrative back to one of victim blaming. McGettrick et al., *Ireland and the Magdalene Laundries*, 17.
28. K. O'Donnell, S. Pembroke, and C. McGettrick, "Oral History of Martha," 2013, Magdalene Institutions: Recording an Oral and Archival History, Government of Ireland Collaborative Research Project, Irish Research Council, DRI, 1–98, 94.
29. K. O'Donnell, S. Pembroke, and C. McGettrick, "Oral History of Bernadette and Francis Murphy," 2013, Magdalene Institutions: Recording an Oral and Archival History, Government of Ireland Collaborative Research Project, Irish Research Council, DRI, 1–170, 118.
30. The redress and compensation scheme followed on the heels of several government-sponsored investigations and reports. In February 2013, the Irish Interdepartmental Committee issued a report (the MacAleese report) about the legacy and impact of the Magdalene laundries as well as the extent of State involvement. Later that month, Taoiseach Kenny announced that the president of the Law Reform Commission, Justice John Quirke, would issue recommendations for the redress and compensation of survivors. In June 2013, Taoiseach Kenny adopted all of Justice Quirke's recommendations, which included state-sponsored assistance for Magdalene survivors to meet one

another, health insurance, and housing provisions. See *Magdalene Restorative Justice Ex-Gratia Scheme*. See also *Magdalene Commission Report*.

31. McGarry, "Nuns Who Ran Magdalene Laundries."

32. Phillips, "Education for Girls in the House of the Good Shepherd," 7.

33. As discussed in chapter 1, in 1904, 4,207 facilities, including private orphanages, hospitals, and sanitariums, housed a total population of 2,040,372 "inmates," or 329 persons per 100,000. By 1910, that number had leapt to 3,360,184, or 587.1 per 100,000, while the number of private facilities had increased the same year by 1,201, to 5,408. See *Benevolent Institutions 1904*; *Benevolent Institutions 1910*.

34. Rothman, *Discovery of the Asylum*.

35. See Freedman, *Their Sisters' Keepers*; and Kunzel, *Criminal Intimacy*. For other critical carceral studies works, see also Gilmore, *Golden Gulag*; and Davis, *Are Prisons Obsolete?*

36. Fitzgerald, *Habits of Compassion*, 194–95.

37. "Lillian C——. Student File," RG 75, series 1327, box 119, folder 4814, NARA, CISDRC, 10.

38. This designation allowed Carlisle administrators to continue carrying enrollees on the rolls (and continue to receive governmental appropriations for that individual's support, as Lipps states), while avoiding bad publicity or scrutiny from the commissioner of Indian Affairs. Similarly, this practice enabled Carlisle officials to continue to exert control over older Indigenous women and men by maintaining pseudo-guardianship over them, as those enumerated in Carlisle ledgers were presumably, if not legally, under the jurisdiction of the Carlisle Superintendent. Adults who had surpassed twenty-one, the age of majority, could not legally be held at Carlisle—but as demonstrated by the experiences of adults over the age of twenty-one described across the chapters of this book, illegal detention nonetheless occurred. For additional information on the ways in which federal funding for off-reservation boarding schools was secured, see Adams, *Education for Extinction*, 71.

39. There are very few extant first-hand accounts of life in US Magdalene laundries. Minnie Morrison's account is unique and therefore invaluable; although it is difficult to say whether her extreme experiences of abuse are representative, Nancymarie Phillips's extensive research on Good Shepherd homes illustrates the systematic nature of Good Shepherd homes' intervention into the lives of "fallen women," as well as the continuity of educational, social, and reformative objectives across Good Shepherd locations in the United States. As Phillips explains, "The Good Shepherd Sisters began as a social service congregation and not a teaching order. However, they added the provision of education to girls in their care because of changing social needs. . . . Specific educational and developmental activities based on . . . Christian womanly behavior established according to the foundress Mother Mary of Saint Euphrasia's guidelines became the cornerstone of the approach used by the teaching staff. These practices were consistently applied in all houses of the Good Shepherd throughout the world, with minor modifications only where cultural or ethnic influences required

special attention. The consistency of the Sisters' responses to the situation involved with each penitent's re-education was the key to the long-term success of the House of the Good Shepherd over all. During Mother Mary of Saint Euphrasia's lifetime, there were at least fifteen other lay Catholic groups taking charge of criminal women and girls that were not largely supported by the Bishops of the time. They differed from the Good Shepherd Sisters because they lacked a sense of order and purposeful organization." Phillips, "Education for Girls," 7–8.

40. Morrison, "Life Story," 12–13.
41. Morrison, "Life Story," 10–11.
42. Morrison, "Life Story," 10–11.
43. Morrison, "Life Story," 16–17.
44. While in the hospital, Minnie recounts that Catholic Sisters forced her to put in writing that she agreed never to sue the institution for damages, and she was made to sign an attestation that she had injured her hand in the mangle due to her own "carelessness." Morrison, "Life Story," 20.
45. Phillips, "Education for Girls," 22.
46. Phillips, "Education for Girls," 18, 192.
47. Phillips, "Education for Girls," 92.
48. Kunzel, *Fallen Women*, 25.
49. Phillips, "Education for Girls," 35.
50. For example, see Cahill, *Federal Fathers and Mothers*; Haskins, *Matrons and Maids*; and Piatote, *Domestic Subjects*.
51. Piatote, *Domestic Subjects*.
52. Harrison, "Usefulness of Saving Babies."
53. Sells, "Save the Indian Babies," 28.
54. Sells, "Save the Indian Babies," 28. As Brianna Theobald has noted of Sells's campaign, "Reservation-level surveys led . . . Cato Sells, to the oft-repeated conclusion that 'approximately three-fifths of the Indian infants die before the age of 5 years.'" Theobald, *Reproduction on the Reservation*, 48. Theobald continues, "Sell's figure demands some skepticism given the inadequacy of available data. . . . Nonetheless, the gravity of the situation on reservations ravaged by malnutrition, illness, decreased mobility, and the suppression of cultural practices is indisputable, and it is at least as plausible that infant deaths were underreported in some locations because of dispersed settlement and continued mobility" (49). Inasmuch as infant mortality was a significant problem on many Indigenous reservations, however, the campaign also exemplified the ways in which settler colonialism was furthered through the realm of the intimate, a phenomenon that Ann Laura Stoler, Laura Wexler, Lisa Lowe, and other cultural historians have observed in other colonial contexts. For a discussion of intimate colonialism, see Stoler, *Carnal Knowledge*; Wexler, *Tender Violence*; and Lowe, *Intimacies*.
55. Historian Alexandra Minna Stern has observed that Indiana's "Better Babies" campaign targeted poor, white Americans living in rural areas. Although Sells's "Save the

Babies" campaign was a specific iteration of eugenicist thought aimed, ostensibly, at improving the health and longevity of Indigenous lives, it occurred alongside and within a broader project of US nation-building that drew upon the ideological linkage between white women's suffrage and the betterment of the white race in this era. Stern explains, "Progressive maternalists . . . assert[ed] that the biological and social experience of motherhood endowed women with a heightened sense of moral duty that was beneficial to both family and nation. . . . This logic was employed by suffragettes who asserted that New Zealand's low infant mortality rate was a direct result of more than 20 years of female enfranchisement. One leaflet issued by the National Woman Suffrage Publishing Company, for instance, portrayed a toddler looking warily at a door that was barely ajar and swarming with deadly microbes. The accompanying caption read: 'I wish my mother had a vote—to keep the germs away.'" Stern, "Making Better Babies," 18.

56. "Lucinda R—. Student File," RG 75, series 1327, box 8, folder 364, NARA, CISDRC.
57. "Lucinda R—. Student File."
58. "Agnes W—. Student File," RG 75, series 1327, box 103, folder 4439, NARA, CISDRC. Agnes's enrollment card reflects that she was sent to the Good Shepherd home on July 31, 1914, the same day she was cleared by the physician, who reported that she and Carrie were "not entirely well. Carrie has a valvular lesion of the heart, while Agnes has a chronic inflammation of the larynx which has resisted treatment in the past" (49).
59. The archival record is ambiguous as to whether Lipps sent Myrtle to Reading. Even after Myrtle's father had vociferously protested her transfer, Carlisle's physician performed an examination on Myrtle along with Agnes, Carrie, and Gertrude, and cleared all of the women for removal to the Good Shepherd home.
60. Miller, "Spider's Web."
61. Jones and Record, "Magdalene Laundries."
62. The Reading home in Pennsylvania was explicitly for "erring women and unprotected children." See Benevolent Institutions 1910, 246.
63. Wolfe, "Settler Colonialism and the Elimination of the Native."
64. Hernández, City of Inmates, 1.
65. Institutionalization is attended by carceral logics. See Ben-Moshe, Decarcerating Disability, 3.
66. "Lillian C—. Student File."
67. Kevin Whalen has documented similar tactics at the Sherman Institute in Southern California. He writes, for instance, "Once on the job, discontented domestic workers wielded a number of different strategies in order to improve conditions or, if need be, get sent home. A common form of resistance involved feigning incomprehension of instructions." Writing of one young Indigenous woman who refused to perform simple household tasks, Whalen continues, "[Sherman's superintendent] Conser's propensity for switching laborers, combined with the simplicity of the tasks

requested, raise the possibility that this student feigned the inability to sweep dust or scrub dirty diapers as a means of escape." Whalen, *Native Students at Work*, 48.

68. See Child, *Boarding School Seasons*; and Lomawaima, "Domesticity in the Federal Indian Schools."

69. "Lillian C——. Student File," 16.

70. "Lillian C——. Student File," 12.

71. "Lillian C——. Student File," 12.

72. "Lillian C——. Student File," 12.

73. "Carrie P——. A——. Student File," RG 75, series 1327, box 107, folder 4533, NARA, CISDRC, 15.

74. "Carrie P——. A——. Student File," 58.

75. "Gertrude B——. P——. Student File," RG 75, series 1327, box 47, folder 2327, NARA, CISDRC, 57.

76. "Gertrude B——. P——. Student File," 57.

77. "Gertrude B——. P——. Student File," 53.

78. "Gertrude B——. P——. Student File," 69.

79. "Agnes W——. Student File," 14.

80. "Agnes W——. Student File," 25.

81. "Agnes W——. Student File," 11.

82. Finley and Townsend, "'All He Had Told Them,'" 97.

83. Million, "Felt Theory."

84. See Smith, *Decolonizing Methodologies*, especially chapter 8, "Twenty-Five Indigenous Projects."

85. See Hartman, "Venus in Two Acts" and *Wayward Lives*; and Trouillot, *Silencing the Past*.

86. Ruggles, "Fallen Women," 76.

87. In her pathbreaking study, Luana Ross describes Indigenous women's historically disproportionate rates of incarceration: "From 1911 to 1943 Native women accounted for 7 percent of the total female prisoner population. Between 1944 and 1966, during a period of racialized assimilationist federal and state policy, the number of imprisoned Native women skyrocketed to a startling 25 percent, while Native Americans composed between 3 and 4 percent of the state's overall population. This high incarceration rate for Native women is also indicative of relaxed policy regarding the confinement of Natives to their respective reservations: without the pass system effectively jailing Natives on reservations, the incarceration rates increased in the state prison." Ross, *Inventing the Savage*, 85.

88. "John B——. P——. Student File," RG 75, series 1327, box 91, folder 4109, NARA, CISDRC, 7.

89. Carlisle utilized a "cadet system" of discipline in which enrollees achieved different ranks and were responsible for meting out discipline to one another; the "court martial" was one of the disciplinary procedures under this system.

90. "Grover A——. Student File," RG 75, series 1327, box 89, folder 4052, NARA, CISDRC, 4.

91. "Charles L——. Student File," RG 75, series 1327, box 97, folder 4278, NARA, CISDRC, 17.

92. "Charles L——. Student File," 43–44.

93. "Charles L——. Student File," 42.

94. "Hannah K——. Student File," RG 75, series 1327, box 92, folder 4123, NARA, CISDRC, 25.

95. "Hannah K——. Student File," 21.

96. Burch, *Committed*.

97. According to his institutional file, Miguel M——. (Mesa Grande) appears to have been sent to Canton from the Carlisle Indian School in 1899. See "Miguel M——. Student File," NARA, CISDRC.

98. "Hannah K——. Student File," 30.

99. Goeman, *Mark My Words*, 3.

100. Amelia H., for example, a twenty-year-old Tuscarora woman, was made to testify in a US court of law against George Kraft in 1913 after becoming pregnant. Other Indian women who were enrolled at Carlisle and who became pregnant were sent home and occasionally became similarly embroiled with the legal system. See "Amelia H——. Student File," RG 75, series 1327, box 16, folder 745, NARA, CISDRC.

101. K. O'Donnell, S. Pembroke, and C. McGettrick, "Oral History of Katherine R.," 2013, Magdalene Institutions: Recording an Oral and Archival History, Government of Ireland Collaborative Research Project, Irish Research Council, DRI, 1–104. IRC is a funding agency, and this project was supported by the IRC in part. I'm accessing the transcripts via the Digital Repository of Ireland's collections, or DRI for short.

102. I thank Brianna Theobald for this insight.

103. Private conversation between author and David Grignon, May 8, 2023. Cited with permission.

104. Lonetree, "Indigenous Child Removal," 9.

105. See "Federal Boarding School Initiative Investigation Report."

106. "Federal Boarding School Initiative Investigation Report," 48–49.

107. Private conversation between author and Thomas Biron, June 2, 2023. Cited with permission.

108. Jones and Record, "Magdalene Laundries," 167.

109. See Foucault's discussion of panopticism in *Discipline and Punish*, 214.

110. McGettrick et al. have pointed this out as well in *Ireland and the Magdalene Laundries*, 35.

111. McGettrick et al. write, "The new [Irish] Free State . . . utilize[ed] the largely inherited British colonial system of massive Victorian institutions funded by the State and managed by Catholic religious orders. . . . The mass institutionalization of the socially and economically vulnerable (particularly women and children) continued post-independence and was maintained by a system of capitation payments to the religious orders from the Irish State exchequer for most of the twentieth century." McGettrick et al., *Ireland and the Magdalene Laundries*, 25.

112. Child, "Boarding School as a Metaphor," 15.

113. Numerous support groups and online forums are dedicated to the survivors of US Magdalene laundries. Historians of American social reform have documented the rise of "charitable" institutions such as mother and baby homes under the Florence

Crittenton name, as well as other "philanthropic" enterprises that purported to offer supplication to women in need in the nineteenth and early twentieth centuries, but few studies have addressed the history of US Magdalene laundries. It is unclear whether the organizations examined in these works could also be classified or understood as Magdalene laundries, but it seems that this is a likely possibility. For example, see Kunzel, *Fallen Women*; Fitzgerald, *Habits of Compassion*.

114. Private conversation between author and Deidre Whiteman, May 31, 2023. Cited with permission.

115. Private conversation between author and Thomas Biron, June 2, 2023. Cited with permission.

116. See Sixsmith, "Catholic Church Sold My Son."

117. I have made several unsuccessful attempts to obtain records from the archivist at the House of the Good Shepherd in St. Louis. His silence intensifies my sense that this history is ongoing—and that it cannot fully be understood without considering global flows of people, ideologies, and power.

CHAPTER 4. "CARE AND MAINTENANCE"

An earlier version of chapter 4 appeared in a special edition of *Disability Studies Quarterly*. See Whitt, "'Care and Maintenance.'"

1. Harry Hummer to Commissioner of Indian Affairs, NARA-DC, June 30, 1919, and October 24, 1927.

2. The turn of the twentieth century ushered in dramatic shifts in the practice and administration of medicine in the United States. Simultaneously, Indian people across the United States were experiencing widespread epidemics of tuberculosis, trachoma, and other infectious diseases, exacerbated by the unhealthful conditions of off-reservation government boarding schools and years of federal neglect. In the first decade of the 1900s, the Office of Indian Affairs awakened to this epidemiological crisis and began a more systematic campaign of contagious disease treatment and prevention among Indian people, which included the establishment of hospitals near Indian lands. In the context of this changing medical landscape, Canton Asylum was founded. Nestled twenty miles southeast of Sioux Falls, South Dakota, Canton was sited near a half-dozen Indian reservations in the state of South Dakota alone, including the Cheyenne River Indian Reservation, Pine Ridge, Crow Creek, and Sisseton-Wahpeton. This location would prove to be especially convenient for Indian agents who sought to remove Indian people to the institution, largely on the grounds of being "troublesome." For more on Progressivism and settler colonialism in the United States, see Lake, *Progressive New World*. For information on the Office of Indian Affairs' implementation of Western medical practices and medical colonialism in Indian communities, see Theobald, *Reproduction on the Reservation*; and Trafzer, *Strong Hearts and Healing Hands*. For historical resources on the politics of South Dakota in this period, as well as the state's dealings with tribal nations, see Biolsi, *Power and Progress*.

3. As a businessman and attorney at law, ex-mayor of Canton Oscar S. Gifford was an inappropriate choice for the director of a psychiatric facility. He had no medical training at all, a fact demonstrated by the twenty deaths that occurred at Canton while he was supervisor. But as a popular merchant and well-known politician, Gifford was nonetheless favored as superintendent of the new facility, and he occupied this position from November 1901 until the summer of 1908, when he would be removed after his gross incompetence and near-continuous absence from the institution was discovered. Gifford's successor, Harry Hummer, was a trained physician—educated at University, no less—but he too would be subject to numerous internal investigations and eventually removed on similar charges of neglect and malpractice. For more on the backgrounds of Gifford and Hummer, see Joinson, *Vanished in Hiawatha*; and Putney, "Canton Asylum."

4. See, for example, Riney, "Power and Powerlessness."

5. Burch, *Committed*; Yellow Bird, "Wild Indians."

6. James and Wu, "Editors' Introduction"; Erevelles *Disability and Difference*; Patrick Wolfe, "Settler Colonialism and the Elimination of the Native."

7. See Davis, *Enforcing Normalcy*; and Garland-Thomson, *Extraordinary Bodies*. For nuanced discussions of disability's intersections with other axes of power, see also Kafer, *Feminist, Queer, Crip*.

8. Goffman, *Asylums*.

9. Goffman, *Asylums*, 1.

10. Riney, "Power and Powerlessness," 43.

11. As Riney argues of Canton's practice of isolating those confined to the facility, this deprivation of engagement with the outside world, with kin and community, resulted in what Erving Goffman has referred to as the curtailment or "mortification of the self." Goffman explains, "The inmate, then, finds certain roles are lost to him by virtue of the barrier that separates him from the outside world. The process of entrance typically brings other kinds of loss and mortification as well. We very generally find staff employing what are called admission procedures, such as taking a life history, searching, listing personal possessions . . . issuing institutional clothing . . . and assigning to quarters. . . . Many of these procedures depend upon attributes such as weight or fingerprints. . . . Action taken on the basis of such attributes necessarily ignores most of his previous bases of self identification." Goffman, *Asylums*, 15. Applying Goffman's theorizations to the Canton Asylum, Riney writes, "Distance combined with asylum policy to deter family visits. . . . Superintendent Hummer, in fact, discouraged [family visits], theorizing that the presence of relatives delayed or prevented recovery. Relatives often pleaded to have their family members released, but Hummer would not allow home paroles on even a trial basis. In this way, Canton Asylum went beyond maintaining strict control over inmates' lives to engage in a program Goffman identified as a 'curtailment of self.' In denying inmates roles outside the institution, such as that of family member, asylum officials deprived them of a source of individual autonomy." Riney, "Power and Powerlessness," 47.

12. "Peter G——. B——. File," RG 75, Department of the Interior, Office of Indian Affairs, Canton Asylum for Insane Indians, Individual Patient Files, 1910–1916, box 8, case file 152, NARA–KC.

13. Wolfe, "Settler Colonialism and the Elimination of the Native," 4.

14. Robert Thompson and Emily Waite are identified by their full names because they have been reproduced in full elsewhere.

15. Private conversation with Thomas Biron, June 2, 2023. Cited with permission.

16. Million, *Therapeutic Nations*, 3.

17. Choctaw speakers today might use the phrase *ạhli anoli* to indicate "telling the truth."

18. Roybal, *Archives of Dispossession*, 3.

19. I borrow this concept from the work of feminist theorist Dian Million and her seminal essay on the impact of Canadian First Nation women's narratives about residential schools, about which she writes, "These narratives were political acts in themselves. . . . I wish to discuss the conditions under which these women spoke at all. . . . In doing so, they transformed the debilitating force of an old social control, shame, into a social change agent in their generation. . . . A felt analysis is one that creates a complex for a more complex 'telling'" (54). Drawing on this definition, I have reproduced the writing of Indigenous people throughout the following pages as a countermeasure to Indigenous erasure. The existence of these materials is, as Million suggests, a political act, a testimony to the incredible strength and resourcefulness of their authors.

20. As quoted in Leahy, *They Called It Madness*, Bill S. 2042 (1897) for the construction of an insane asylum for Indians; referenced as an enclosure in a letter from R. F. Pettigrew to Secretary of the Interior, June 24, 1897, RG 48, box 227, NARA.

21. See, for instance, Carla Joinson's chapter "Where Will All the Insane Indians Go?" in *Vanished in Hiawatha*. Disability studies scholar Kim Nielsen also addresses Indigenous confinement at the Canton Asylum using a disability studies lens. See Nielsen, *Disability History*.

22. Pfister, *Individuality Incorporated*.

23. Leahy, *They Called It Madness*, 16.

24. R. F. Pettigrew, 1897, NARA–Denver, 26.

25. Leahy, *They Called It Madness*.

26. Statement of Jerome C. on running away from Canton, dated September 7, 2023, "Jerome C. File," RG 75, CCF 1907–39, Canton Asylum, box 16, NARA–DC.

27. Ellinghaus, *Blood Will Tell*, 82. For pre-Allotment Era history, see also Case, *Relentless Business of Treaties*.

28. Risling Baldy offers an important perspective on settler colonialism and heteropatriarchal violence in her discussion of Western menstrual taboos and menstrual practices among the Hoopa Valley Tribe of California. Here, I borrow from her observations about Western assumptions about Indigenous peoples, and how the settler society often responded violently to practices that were perceived as threatening to white hegemony. See Risling Baldy, "Mini-K'iwh'e:N."

29. Joinson, *Vanished in Hiawatha*, 80.

30. Leahy, *They Called It Madness*.

31. Putney, "Canton Asylum," 3.

32. Putney, "Canton Asylum," 4.

33. "Susan W——. File," undated letter, RG 75, CCF 1907–39, box 16, file 52844, NARA-DC.

34. Burch, *Committed*, 34.

35. Putney, "Canton Asylum," 16.

36. Samuel Silk to Commissioner of Indian Affairs, April 13, 1929, NARA, State Archives of the South Dakota State Historical Society.

37. Samuel Silk to Commissioner of Indian Affairs, April 13, 1929, 7–8.

38. Putney, "Canton Asylum, 1902–1934"; Yellow Bird, "Wild Indians," 5.

39. Jerome C., statement entitled "Trouble with a Girl," dated September 6, 1923, "Jerome C——. File."

40. For more on competency commissions and Cato Sells, see *Annual Report of the Commissioner of Indian Affairs*, 1917, 3; McDonnell, "Competency Commissions"; Ellinghaus, *Blood Will Tell*; and Gregory, "Competency, Allotment, and the Canton Asylum."

41. Gregory, "Competency, Allotment, and the Canton Asylum."

42. Gregory, "Competency, Allotment, and the Canton Asylum."

43. Gregory, "Competency, Allotment, and the Canton Asylum."

44. Gonaver, *Peculiar Institution*; Hogarth, *Medicalizing Blackness*; Summers, *Madness*. For a discussion of medical experimentation on Black women during the antebellum era, see especially Owens, *Medical Bondage*.

45. See Prucha, *Americanizing the American Indians*, especially Secretary of the Interior Henry Teller's report, "Courts of Indian Offenses."

46. Whitt, Voyles, and Burch, "Settler Ableism."

47. See, for example, Akers, *Living in the Land of Death*; Crandall, "Captive Cousins;" Million, "'We Are the Land and the Land Is Us'"; Pengra and Godfrey, "Different Boundaries"; and Senier, "'Traditionally, Disability Was Not Seen as Such.'"

48. See Andersson, *Lakota Ghost Dance*; Coleman, *Voices of Wounded Knee*; and Maddra, *Hostiles?*

49. "Pawnee Medicine and an Indian Lodge."

50. "Pawnee Medicine and an Indian Lodge."

51. For an example of this line of thought, see *Annual Report of the Commissioner of Indian Affairs*, 1905, 3–4.

52. Carlson, "Institutions," 111–12.

53. Brown, "Tiny Taps and Noisy Hacks," 97.

54. "Protest against the Abolition of the Indian Dance."

55. Brown, "Tiny Taps and Noisy Hacks," 98.

56. "For Insane Indians."

57. "Insane Asylum for Indians."

58. Diane Putney notes in "Canton Asylum" that by 1916, Canton was expanded to accommodate eighty-five people (12); Burch reports that in the first decade of Canton's founding, dormitories were crowded. In 1909, in one example, the asylum confined twenty over capacity (*Committed*, 70, 146).

59. "Industrial Notes."

60. Millingen, "Miscellany," 94.

61. Jones, "Development of Insanity," 580–81.

62. Jones, "Development of Insanity," 580–81.

63. Peter G. B. (Sioux), essay entitled "Capital Punishment," "Peter G—. B—. File." This letter is reproduced in full in the appendix.

64. Gifford, "Gain in Indian Insanity," 44.

65. Gifford, "Gain in Indian Insanity."

66. Gifford, "Gain in Indian Insanity."

67. Burch, *Committed*, 34.

68. For a selection of contemporaneous political debates about Indian people, see Prucha, *Americanizing the American Indians*.

69. Veracini, *Settler Colonialism*, 23.

70. See Goeman, "Disrupting a Settler-Colonial Grammar of Place"; and Calderon, "Uncovering Settler Grammars."

71. Goeman, "Disrupting a Settler-Colonial Grammar of Place," 236–37.

72. Susan Burch explains, "Asylum officials and other settler medical professionals pathologized correspondence by [Elizabeth Alexis] Faribault and other Native people written in nonstandard English, justifying sustained confinement based on grammar and language. The mostly first- and second-generation Norwegian immigrant staff at Canton similarly described the Indigenous spoken communication they encountered as signs of disordered minds." Burch, *Committed*, 9.

73. Hummer was typically the subject of Indian office investigations; for example, Diane Putney writes that in October 1909, "thirteen employees at Canton, including [physician] Hardin, sent an affidavit to the Indian office, demanding an investigation of Hummer based upon a series of specific charges they leveled against him . . . [including] that he failed to issue the proper clothing and rations to patients, that the patients and their bedding were unclean, and that nonviolent patients were locked up for long periods of time." Putney, "Canton Asylum," 10–11.

74. R. E. Newberne, "Special Report on the Canton Asylum," April 14–15, 1918, RG 75, CCF-1907–1939, box 2, folder 35833, Canton Asylum, NARA-DC.

75. Allen, "The Misuse of Biological Hierarchies."

76. Newberne, "Special Report."

77. Newberne, "Special Report."

78. "Trouble with a Girl," "Jerome C—. File."

79. As medical historian Gerald Grob writes of commitment in the nineteenth century, "The diagnosis of insanity often did not involve the community. Nor were most com-

mitments begun by law enforcement personnel. Proceedings were usually initiated by members of the immediate family. Confronted with behavior that threatened the integrity of the family or situations with which they could not cope, relatives began the process of institutionalization as a last resort and with a vague understanding that it was the lesser of two evils." Grob, *Mental Illness*, 9.

80. "Edward J—. Student File," RG 75, series 1327, box 91, folder 4115, NARA, CISDRC, 13. Similarly, historian Caroline Norris described the Central Lunatic Asylum in Petersburg, Virginia, constructed for freedmen and women, as a "dumping ground for society's outcasts." Norris, "History of Madness," 159.

81. Hernández, *City of Inmates*, 10.

82. I draw upon Liat Ben-Moshe's definition of transincarceration as the movement from one carceral space to another, usually involuntarily. See Ben-Moshe, "Genealogies of Resistance"; Ben-Moshe et al., *Disability Incarcerated*.

83. Harry Hummer to Commissioner of Indian Affairs, June 30, 1919, RG 75, CCF 1907–1939, box 14, folder 57067, Canton Asylum, NARA-DC.

84. Harry Hummer to Commissioner of Indian Affairs, June 30, 1919, NARA-DC.

85. Burch also remarks on this act of courage in *Committed*, 61.

86. "Emma A—. File," letter from Emma to Hummer, October 20, 1929, RG 75, CCF 1907–39, box 18, folder 57404, Canton Asylum, NARA-DC.

87. Agnes frequently used this phrase in her letters to the commissioner.

88. Letter from Agnes to Commissioner Cato Sells, January 1, 1920, RG 75, CCF 1907–39, folder 91415, Canton Asylum, box 14, NARA-DC.

89. Harry Hummer to Commissioner of Indian Affairs, October 21, 1919, RG 75, CCF 1907–39, folder 91415, Canton Asylum, box 14, NARA-DC.

90. See Lombardo, *Three Generations*.

91. Harry Hummer to Commissioner of Indian Affairs, October 21, 1919, RG 75, CCF 1907–39, folder 91415, Canton Asylum, box 14, NARA-DC.

92. Theobald, *Reproduction on the Reservation*, 92.

93. Landrum's observation that Canton was "run like an Indian boarding school" is further evidenced by the fact that the "asylum" was not outfitted according to the standards of the era. In fact, as Theobald observes, sterilization procedures such as salpingectomies, or removal of the fallopian tubes, were overwhelmingly performed in institutions—such that historical knowledge of these sites and procedures obscure medical practices on reservations. Theobald writes, "That eugenic sterilizations in these years tended to be institution-based—that is, performed in state asylums, mental hospitals, or schools for the 'feebleminded'—also diverts scholarly attention away from reservations." *Reproduction on the Reservation*, 92. Putney, Yellow Bird, Riney, Leahy, and Burch have also noted that Canton's medical equipment departed from that found in similar contemporaneous institutions.

94. Yellow Bird writes that many of Canton's inmates were thirty years of age and under, and that "incarceration there was terminal: institutional policy declared these Native

people to be 'defectives,' and as such, procreation must be prohibited and they must be sterilized before they could be discharged. Since the superintendent did not know how to conduct sexual sterilization procedures, inmates simply remained until they died." Yellow Bird, "Wild Indians," 5.

95. It appears that sterilization could also be the primary reason for committing an individual to an institution. According to an article authored by J. H. Craft entitled "The Effects of Sterilization: As Shown by a Follow Up Study in South Dakota" in the *Journal of Heredity*, "In its practical application only those who seem likely to have children are sterilized. Patients that are expected to remain in the institution for the feebleminded, those who are well supervised at home, persons who are nearing middle age without showing any tendency toward sex offences, and defectives who are physically incapable or so unattractive that mating is improbable are not sterilized. . . . *Some patients who are committed for sterilization* are found to be physically unable to undergo an operation without jeopardizing their lives or health. In such cases the physicians are given the legal right of discretion to postpone or not perform the operation" (379, emphasis mine).

96. E. B. Meritt to Agnes Caldwell, November 24, 1920, RG 75, CCF 1907–39, box 14, file 722.1, Canton Asylum, NARA-DC.

97. Lombardo, *Three Generations*, 15.

98. E. B. Meritt to B. Fitzgerald, November 24, 1924, RG 75, CCF 1907–39, box 17, file 722.1, Canton Asylum, NARA-DC.

99. E. B. Meritt to B. Fitzgerald, November 24, 1924.

100. Harding, "American Protestant Moralism."

101. Lombardo, *Three Generations*, 17.

102. E. B. Meritt to B. Fitzgerald, November 24, 1924. For more on federal paternalism and popular discourses of "protection," see especially Cahill, *Federal Fathers and Mothers*; Haskins, *Matrons and Maids*; and Jacobs, *White Mother to a Dark Race*, "Working on the Domestic Frontier," and "Diverted Mothering."

103. As quoted in Theobald, "1970 Law."

104. Samuel A. Silk to the Commissioner of Indian Affairs, October 3, 1933, RG 418, Records Relating to the Department of the Interior, 1902–43, Canton Asylum, NARA-DC.

105. Yellow Bird, "Wild Indians," 5.

106. Burch, *Committed*, 98.

107. Private conversation between the author and Anne Gregory, August 3, 2023. Cited with permission.

108. Private conversation between the author and Anne Gregory, August 3, 2023. Cited with permission.

109. Ora Padgett to Harry Hummer, June 24, 1921, RG 75, CCF 1907–1939, box 15, folder 46420, Canton Asylum, NARA-DC.

110. There were no formal commitment procedures at Canton; only the approval of the commissioner of Indian Affairs was needed. See Dilenschneider, "Invitation to Restorative Justice."

111. Samuel Silk noted in a 1933 investigation that "many patients, young males and females, who have been in Canton for many years, were sent to that institution because of some difficulty at a school or agency—a fight with a white man, or a fight with a husband or wife.... Some of them never had any schooling, can neither read nor write." Samuel A. Silk, Report on Canton Asylum, October 2, 1933, RG 75, CCF 1907–1939, box 4, folder 7448, Canton Asylum, NARA-DC.

112. Child, "Boarding School as Metaphor."

113. Landrum, *Dakota Sioux Experience*, 96.

114. Silk, Report on Canton Asylum.

115. Based on available Canton documents, I have identified these boarding institutions as facilities that sent Indian people to Canton. It is unclear whether those sent from these institutions were local tribal citizens or students; in some cases, reservation schools were also the locus of the reservation superintendent's official activities.

116. Penrose, "Mental Disease and Crime"; Schildbach and Schildbach, "Criminalization through Transinstitutionalization." There were no formal commitment procedures at Canton; only the approval of the Commissioner of Indian Affairs was required.

117. Deleuze, *Foucault*, 26.

118. Grob, *Mental Illness*, 9.

119. Telegram from Charles F. to Hummer, regarding Mary M. F., July 5, 1918, RG 75, CCF 1907–39, box 14, file 55913, NARA-DC.

120. Putney, "Canton Asylum," 7.

121. Grob, *Mental Illness*, 10.

122. Dilenschneider, "Invitation to Restorative Justice."

123. Dilenschneider, "Invitation to Restorative Justice."

124. Letter from Oliver K. Chandler to Commissioner of Indian Affairs, March 27, 1923, RG 75, CCF 1907–1934, box 15, folder 21996, Canton Asylum, NARA-DC.

125. McDonnell, "Competency Commissions," 21–34.

126. In the scathing 1924 report, "Oklahoma's Poor Rich Indians," coauthors Gertrude Bonnin, Charles Fabens, and Matthew Sniffen wrote that at the conclusion of their investigation into the administration of Indian estates in Eastern Oklahoma, it was found "that when oil is 'struck' on an Indian's property, it is usually considered prima facie evidence that he is incompetent, and in the appointment of a guardian for him his wishes in the matter are rarely considered." Bonnin, et al., "Oklahoma's Poor Rich Indians," 7.

127. Bonnin, Fabens, and Sniffen, "Oklahoma's Poor Rich Indians," 5.

128. Bonnin, Fabens, and Sniffen, "Oklahoma's Poor Rich Indians," 38.

129. Bonnin, Fabens, and Sniffen, "Oklahoma's Poor Rich Indians," 38.

130. Bonnin, Fabens, and Sniffen note "that an examination of 14,229 probate cases in six counties where the Indian population is largest shows the average cost of administration to be TWENTY per cent, and in some instances it has been as high as SEVENTY per cent. . . . Incidentally, the cost for probating Indian estates in other sections of the country cannot exceed a total of $74. In most cases the cost is not over $20 . . . excessive and unnecessary administrative costs, unconscionable fees and commissions, are allowed by many of the County Courts to professional guardians, attorneys, et al." Bonnin, Fabens, and Sniffen, "Oklahoma's Poor Rich Indians," 5.

131. Bonnin, Fabens, and Sniffen, "Oklahoma's Poor Rich Indians," 27–28.

132. Harry Hummer to Superintendent of the Crow Creek Agency, July 14, 1925, RG 75, CCF 1907–1939, box 8, folder 51361, NARA-DC.

133. H. E. Wright to Commissioner of Indian Affairs, July 27, 1925, RG 75, CCF 1907–1939, box 8, folder 51361, NARA-DC.

134. Shakespeare, *Disability Rights and Wrongs.*

135. Livingston, *Debility and the Moral Imagination*; Puar, *Right to Maim.*

136. "Peter G—. B—. File," letter from Peter to Commissioner, RG 75, CCF 1907–39, box 8, file 54300, Canton Asylum, NARA-DC.

137. This occurred less frequently than did the forcible commitment of Indian women and men at the request of unrelated persons.

138. Newberne to Commissioner of Indian Affairs, regarding James H., March 22, 1920, CCF 1907–39, box 5, Canton Asylum, NARA-DC.

139. Newberne to Commissioner of Indian Affairs, March 22, 1920, NARA-DC.

140. Former superintendent Oscar Gifford was quoted as expressing a similar rationale for the increase in Indigenous insanity in 1904, under the heading "Worry over Family Affairs." Gifford, "Gains in Indian Insanity."

141. Newberne to Commissioner of Indian Affairs, regarding James H., March 22, 1920, CCF 1907–39, box 5, Canton Asylum, NARA-DC.

142. In the essay "Representing Whiteness in the Black Imagination," hooks writes, "Ideologically, the rhetoric of white supremacy supplies a fantasy of whiteness. Described in Richard Dyer's (1988) essay 'White' this fantasy makes whiteness synonymous with goodness. . . . Socialized to believe the fantasy, that whiteness represents goodness and all that is benign and non-threatening, many white people assume this is the way black people conceptualize whiteness. They do not imagine that the way whiteness makes its presence felt in black life, most often as terrorizing imposition, a power that wounds, hurts, tortures, is a reality that disrupts the fantasy of whiteness as representing goodness." hooks, "Representing Whiteness," 341.

143. Indian Territory at the time.

144. Billy the Kid (1859–1881) was an outlaw who gained notoriety for his involvement in the "Lincoln County War," a violent dispute between two rival factions in the territory of New Mexico. For more on Billy the Kid's life and death, see Nolan, *West of Billy the Kid.*

145. Tower, *Outlaw Statesman*, 146.

146. "Emily Waite File," RG 75, Canton Asylum, box 1, Records of Indian Inspector for Indian Territory, Case Files of Insane Indians, 1905–8, NARA-FW.

147. "Emily Waite File."

148. "Emily Waite File."

149. "Emily Waite File."

150. John T. Hill's last will and testament was disputed by his surviving family members. See *Hill v. Buckholts*, Oklahoma Supreme Court, 1920.

151. Debo, *And Still the Waters Run*, 13.

152. *Pauls Valley Democrat*.

153. Tower, *Outlaw Statesman*, 216.

154. Tower, *Outlaw Statesman*, 216.

155. "Emily Waite File."

156. For more on "intimate colonialism," benevolent violence, and other seeming antinomies, see Cahill, *Federal Fathers and Mothers*; Lowe, *Intimacies*; and Stoler, *Haunted by Empire*.

157. Private conversation between the author and Anne Gregory, August 3, 2023. Cited with permission.

158. According to Jogues Prandoni and Maureen Jais-Mick, archivists at St. Elizabeths, fifty Indigenous people transferred from Canton to St. Elizabeths lived out their remaining days there.

159. Burch, *Committed*, 104.

160. Burch, *Committed*, 98.

161. Yellow Bird, "Wild Indians," 3.

162. "Lucy G—. File," "History of Lucy G—. as written by herself," March 12, 1911, RG 75, Department of the Interior, Office of Indian Affairs, Canton Asylum for Insane Indians, Individual Patient Files, 1910–1916, box 8, case 124, Canton Asylum, NARA-KC.

EPILOGUE

1. "Fact Sheet."

2. Arias, Tejada-Vera, Kochanek, and Ahmad, *Vital Statistics Rapid Release*.

3. *Native Lives Matter*, 1–14.

4. *Native Lives Matter*, 5.

5. *Native Lives Matter*.

6. Peña, "ICE Wants to Show Public Citizens How to Arrest Immigrants."

7. Peña, "ICE Wants to Show Public Citizens How to Arrest Immigrants."

8. Bruni, "There's a New Surveillance State."

9. In yet another example of willful ignorance about the historical past, Florida's Department of Education announced in January 2023 that it would not allow an AP course on African American history to be taught in Florida high schools because, as it claimed, "the course is not 'historically accurate' and violates state law." See Mazzei and Hartocollis, "Florida Rejects A.P. African American Studies Class."

10. Office of the Chief, Tk'emlúps te Secwépemc, press release.
11. *Federal Indian Boarding School Initiative Investigative Report.*
12. On June 7, 2023, Senator Elizabeth Warren (D-Mass.) reintroduced Bill S. 1723, the Truth and Healing Commission on Indian Boarding School Policies Act, through the Indian Affairs Committee.
13. "Truth and Healing Commission on Indian Boarding School Policies Act."
14. Private conversations between the author and Deidre Whiteman, May 31; and July 18, 2023. Cited with permission.
15. Private conversation between the author and Rose Miron, July 18, 2023. Cited with permission.
16. Private conversation between the author and Megan Baker, July 26, 2023. Cited with permission of the Choctaw Nation of Oklahoma.
17. Gross, "'Reservation Dogs.'"

bibliography

Archival Collections

Ancestry.com
   Collections
Carlisle Indian School Digital Resource Center (CISDRC), Dickinson College, Carlisle, PA
   Dickinson College Archives and Special Collections
Cornell University Library, Ithaca, NY
   Division of Rare Manuscript Collections
   Morris Edward Oppler Papers, 1818–1997
Cumberland County Historical Society (CCHS), Carlisle, PA
   Carlisle Indian School History, Oral Histories
   Photographs
Digital Repository of Ireland (DRI)
   Magdalene Oral History Collection
The Henry Ford Archive, Dearborn, MI
   Ford Motor Company Serial Publications Collection
   Photographic Vertical File Series
Irish Film Archive, Dublin, Ireland
   The Father Delany Collection
Justice for Magdalenes Research Archive
Magdalene Oral History Project, funded by the Irish Research Council
   Transcripts and Audio Files, University College Dublin
National Archives and Records Administration (NARA), Denver, CO
   Canton Asylum, Records of the Consolidated Ute Agency, correspondence
   RG 75, Records of the Bureau of Indian Affairs
National Archives and Records Administration (NARA), Fort Worth, TX
   Canton Asylum, Central Classified Files, 1907–39
   Records of Indian Inspector for Indian Territory, Case Files of Insane Indians
   RG 75, Records of the Bureau of Indian Affairs
National Archives and Records Administration (NARA), Kansas City, MO
   Canton Asylum for Insane Indians, Central Classified Files, 1907–39
   Individual Patient Files, 1910–1916
   RG 75, Records of the Bureau of Indian Affairs

National Archives and Records Administration (NARA), Washington, DC

    Central Classified Files, 1907–39

    Canton Asylum for Insane Indians Boxes 1–20

    Records Relating to the Department of the Interior, 1902–43

    RG 75, Records of the Bureau of Indian Affairs

University of Hawaiʻi, Manoa, HI

    Social Movements, Archives and Manuscripts Collection

Published and Primary Sources

1964 Press Photo Otto T——. *Minnesota Convention Rep*, June 13, 1964. Photograph. Historic Images, accessed June 7, 2023. https://historicimages.com/products/dfpy68875?_pos=1&_sid=e34de75b3&_ss=.

Adams, David Wallace. *Education for Extinction: American Indians and the Boarding School Experience, 1875–1928*. Lawrence: University Press of Kansas, 1995.

Adams, Mikaëla. "'A Very Serious and Perplexing Epidemic of Grippe': The Influenza of 1918 at the Haskell Institute." *American Indian Quarterly* 44 (2020): 1–35.

Adkins, Karen. *Gossip, Epistemology, and Power: Knowledge Underground*. Cham, Switzerland: Palgrave Macmillan, 2017.

Aerial View of Ford Motor Company Highland Park Plant. 1923. Photograph. 84.1.1660.P.833.34974. From the Collections of The Henry Ford.

Akers, Donna. *Living in the Land of Death: The Choctaw Nation, 1830–1860*. East Lansing: Michigan State University Press, 2004.

Allen, Garland E. "The Misuse of Biological Hierarchies: The American Eugenics Movement, 1900–1940." *History and Philosophy of the Life Sciences* 5, no. 2 (1983): 105–28.

Andersson, Rani-Henrik. *The Lakota Ghost Dance of 1890*. Lincoln: University of Nebraska Press, 2008.

Annual Report of the Commissioner of Indian Affairs. Washington, DC: US Government Printing Office, 1905.

Annual Report of the Commissioner of Indian Affairs. Washington, DC: US Government Printing Office, 1907.

Annual Report of the Commissioner of Indian Affairs. Washington, DC: US Government Printing Office, 1908.

Annual Report of the Commissioner of Indian Affairs. Washington, DC: US Government Printing Office, 1917.

Arias, Elizabeth, Betzaida Tejada-Vera, Kenneth D. Kochanek, and Farida B. Ahmad. *Vital Statistics Rapid Release: Provisional Life Expectancy Estimates for 2021*. Report no. 23. National Vital Statistics System, 2022.

Aries, Philippe. *Centuries of Childhood: A Social History of Family Life*. New York: Vintage, 1965.

Arvin, Maile. *Possessing Polynesians: The Science of Settler Colonial Whiteness in Hawaiʻi and Oceania*. Durham, NC: Duke University Press, 2019.

Bauer, Natalee Kēhaulani. *Tender Violence in US Schools: Benevolent Whiteness and the Dangers of Heroic White Womanhood*. New York: Routledge, 2022.

Bauer, William J. *We Were All like Migrant Workers Here: Work, Community, and Memory on California's Round Valley Reservation, 1850–1941*. Chapel Hill: University of North Carolina Press, 2009.

Bell, Genevieve. "Telling Stories out of School: Remembering the Carlisle Indian Industrial School, 1879–1918." PhD diss., Stanford University, 1998. ProQuest Dissertations and Theses.

Benevolent Institutions 1904. United States Bureau of the Census. Washington, DC: US Government Printing Office, 1905.

Benevolent Institutions 1910. United States Bureau of the Census. Washington, DC: US Government Printing Office, 1914.

Benjamin, Walter. *Illuminations: Essays and Reflections*. New York: Schocken Books, 1968.

Ben-Moshe, Liat. *Decarcerating Disability: Deinstitutionalization and Prison Abolition*. Minneapolis: University of Minnesota Press, 2020.

Ben-Moshe, Liat. "Genealogies of Resistance to Incarceration: Abolition Politics within Deinstitutionalization and Anti-Prison Activism in the U.S." PhD diss., Syracuse University, 2011.

Ben-Moshe, Liat, Chris Chapman, and Allison Carey, eds. *Disability Incarcerated: Imprisonment and Disability in the United States and Canada*. New York: Palgrave Macmillan, 2014.

Beyer, C. Kalani. "The Connection of Samuel Chapman Armstrong as Both Borrower and Architect of Education in Hawai'i." *History of Education Quarterly* 47, no. 1 (2007): 23–48.

Biolsi, Thomas. *Power and Progress on the Prairie: Governing People on Rosebud Reservation*. Minneapolis: University of Minnesota Press, 2018.

Bonnin, Gertrude. *American Indian Stories*. Lincoln: University of Nebraska Press, 2003.

Bonnin, Gertrude, Charles H. Fabens, and Matthew K. Sniffen. "Oklahoma's Poor Rich Indians: An Orgy of Graft and Exploitation of the Five Civilized Tribes, Legalized Robbery." *Indian Rights Association, Publications,* 2nd ser., 127. Philadelphia: Office of the Indian Rights Association, 1924.

Brandt, Allan. *No Magic Bullet: A Social History of Venereal Disease in the United States since 1880*. Oxford: Oxford University Press, 2020.

Briggs-Wall, Henrietta. "American Woman and Her Political Peers, 1893." Postcard. Hutchinson, Kansas. Commissioned by Henrietta Briggs-Wall, 1911. Manuscript Division, Library of Congress (047.00.00).

Brockliss, Laurence. "Introduction: The Western Concept of Childhood." In *Childhood in the Late Ottoman Empire and After*, edited by Benjamin C. Fortna, 1–18. Leiden, Netherlands: Brill, 2016.

Brown, Kristen Rose. "Tiny Taps and Noisy Hacks: Listening to Zitkala Ša's Sonic Politics." *Resonance* 2, no. 1 (Spring 2021): 89–107.

Brunhouse, Robert L. *Apprenticeship for Civilization: The Outing Program at the Carlisle Indian School*. Carlisle, PA: Dickinson College Archives and Special Collections, 1939.

Bruni, Frank. "There's a New Surveillance State: It's Your Neighbor." *New York Times*, February 3, 2022.

Burch, Susan. *Committed: Remembering Native Kinship in and beyond Institutions*. Chapel Hill: University of North Carolina Press, 2021.

Burrage, Rachel, Sandra L. Momper, and Joseph P. Gone. "Beyond Trauma: Decolonizing Understandings of Loss and Healing in the Indian Residential School System of Canada." *Journal of Social Issues* 78, no. 1 (2022): 27–52.

Cahill, Cathleen D. *Federal Fathers and Mothers: A Social History of the United States Indian Service, 1869–1933*. Chapel Hill: University of North Carolina Press, 2011.

Calderon, Dolores. "Uncovering Settler Grammars in Curriculum." *Educational Studies* 50, no. 4 (2014): 313–38.

Carlson, Licia. "Institutions." In *Keywords for Disability Studies*, edited by Rachel Adams, Benjamin Reiss, and David Serlin, 109–23. New York: NYU Press, 2015.

Case, Martin. *The Relentless Business of Treaties: How Indigenous Land Became U.S. Property*. St. Paul: Minnesota Historical Society, 2018.

Chilcote, Olivia M. *Unrecognized in California: Federal Acknowledgement and the San Luis Rey Band of Mission Indians*. Seattle: University of Washington Press, 2024.

Child, Brenda. "The Boarding School as Metaphor." *Journal of American Indian Education* 57, no. 1 (2018): 37–57.

Child, Brenda J. *Boarding School Seasons: American Indian Families, 1900–1940*. Lincoln: University of Nebraska Press, 1998.

Coen, Mark, Katherine O'Donnell, and Maeve O'Rourke, eds. *A Dublin Magdalene Laundry: Donnybrook and Church-State Power in Ireland*. London: Bloomsbury Academic, 2023.

Coleman, William. *Voices of Wounded Knee*. Lincoln: University of Nebraska Press, 2000.

Colmant, Stephen, Lahoma Schultz, Rockey Robbins, Peter Ciali, Julie Dorton, and Yvette Rivera-Colmant. "Constructing Meaning to the Indian Boarding School Experience." *Journal of American Indian Education* 43, no. 3 (2004): 22–40.

"Color or Race, Nativity, and Parentage of Occupied Persons." In *Fourteenth Census of the United States Taken in the Year 1920, Volume IV, Population 1920, Occupations*. Department of Commerce, Bureau of the Census. Washington, DC: US Government Printing Office.

Contagious and Infectious Diseases among the Indians. United States Public Health Service. Washington, DC: US Government Printing Office, 1913.

Conway, Katherine. *In the Footprints of the Good Shepherd: New York, 1857–1907*. New York: Convent of the Good Shepherd, 1907.

Cowing, Jessica Louise. "Settler States of Ability: Assimilation, Incarceration, and Native Women's Crip Interventions." PhD diss., William & Mary, 2020. ProQuest Dissertations Publishing.

Craft, J. H. "The Effects of Sterilization: As Shown by a Follow Up Study in South Dakota." *Journal of Heredity* 27, no. 10 (1936): 379–87.

Crandall, Maurice. "Captive Cousins: Hoomothya, Wassaja, and a Lifetime of Unwellness." *Western Historical Quarterly* 54, no. 2 (2023): 117–36.

Cumberland County Prison (Jail). Photograph. 467A, no. 03, CCHS, Carlisle, PA.

Cummins, Kathleen. *Herstories on Screen: Feminist Subversions of Frontier Myths.* New York: Columbia University Press, 2020.

Davis, Angela. *Are Prisons Obsolete?* New York: Seven Stories Press, 2003.

Davis, Lennard. *Enforcing Normalcy: Disability, Deafness, and the Body.* New York: Verso, 1995.

Debo, Angie. *And Still the Waters Run: The Betrayal of the Five Civilized Tribes.* Princeton, NJ: Princeton University Press, 2020.

Deer, Sarah. *The Beginning and End of Rape: Confronting Sexual Violence in Native America.* Minneapolis: University of Minnesota Press, 2015.

DeJong, David H. *"If You Knew the Conditions": A Chronicle of the Indian Medical Service and American Indian Health Care, 1908–1955.* Lanham, MD: Lexington Books, 2008.

Deleuze, Gilles. *Foucault.* Translated by Seán Hand. Minneapolis: University of Minnesota Press, 1988.

Deloria, Philip, Jr. *Indians in Unexpected Places.* Lawrence: University Press of Kansas, 2004.

Deverell, William, and Anne Hyde. "The 1920s: Prohibition and the West." In *Shaped by the West*, vol. 2, *A History of North America from 1850*. Berkeley: University of California Press, 2018.

Dilenschneider, Anne. "An Invitation to Restorative Justice: The Canton Asylum for Insane Indians." *Northern Plains Ethics Journal* 1, no. 1 (2013): 105–28.

Dining Hall with Female Student Workers [version 2]. circa 1883. Photograph. CCHS, CCHS_PA-CH1-077C, CISDRC.

"Doing Nicely, Thank You!" *Ford Times* 9 (1915–16). Dearborn, MI: Ford Motor Company, 1916.

Dominguez, Laura. "Courtyard Sisters: Settler Fantasy and Experiment at the International Institute of Los Angeles, 1914–1940." *Western Historical Quarterly* 52, no. 4 (2021): 415–40.

Dowd, Gregory Evans. *Groundless: Rumors, Legends, and Hoaxes on the Early American Frontier.* Baltimore: Johns Hopkins University Press, 2015.

Eadle Keatah Toh 1, no. 3 (May 1880). CCHS, CISDRC.

Ellinghaus, Katherine. "Assimilation by Marriage: White Women and Native American Men at Hampton Institute, 1878–1923." *Virginia Magazine of History and Biography* 108, no. 3 (2000): 279–303.

Ellinghaus, Katherine. *Blood Will Tell: Native Americans and Assimilation Policy.* Lincoln: University of Nebraska Press, 2017.

Emery, Jacqueline. *Recovering Native American Writings in the Boarding School Press*. Lincoln: University of Nebraska Press, 2017.

Erevelles, Nirmala. *Disability and Difference in Global Contexts: Enabling a Transformative Body Politic*. New York: Springer, 2011.

Esch, Elizabeth. *The Color Line and the Assembly Line: Managing Race in the Ford Empire*. Berkeley: University of California Press, 2018.

"Fact Sheet: Disparities." Indian Health Service, October 2019, https://www.ihs.gov /newsroom/factsheets/disparities/.

Fass, Paula S., ed. *The Routledge History of Childhood in the Western World*. New York: Routledge, 2013.

Fear-Segal, Jacqueline. "Nineteenth-Century Indian Education: Universalism versus Evolutionism." *Journal of American Studies* 33, no. 2 (1999): 323–41.

Fear-Segal, Jacqueline. *White Man's Club: Schools, Race, and the Struggle of Indian Acculturation*. Lincoln: University of Nebraska Press, 2007.

Fear-Segal, Jacqueline, and Susan D. Rose. *Carlisle Indian Industrial School: Indigenous Histories, Memories, and Reclamations*. Lincoln: University of Nebraska Press, 2016.

Federal Indian Boarding School Initiative Investigative Report. US Department of the Interior. Washington, DC: US Government Printing Office, 2022.

"Fees Paid to Carlisle Police." RG 121, CCF Entry, no. 38426-1914-Carlisle-821, NARA, CISDRC.

Filter, John. *Child Labor in America: The Epic Legal Struggle to Protect Children*. Lawrence: University Press of Kansas, 2018.

Fine, Gary Alan, and Patricia Turner. *Whispers on the Color Line: Rumor and Race in America*. Berkeley: University of California Press, 2001.

Finley, Chris, and Camilla Townsend. "'All He Had Told Them . . . Was True': Native American History and the Witnessing of Abuse in the Archive." *Native American and Indigenous Studies* 9, no. 2 (2022): 95–123.

Finnegan, Frances. *Do Penance or Perish: Magdalen Asylums in Ireland*. Oxford: Oxford University Press, 2004.

Fischer, Claude S. *Made in America: A Social History of American Culture and Character*. Chicago: University of Chicago Press, 2010.

Fitzgerald, Maureen. *Habits of Compassion: Irish Catholic Nuns and the Origins of New York's Welfare System, 1830–1920*. Urbana: University of Illinois Press, 2006.

Fixico, Donald. *The Urban Indian Experience in America*. Albuquerque: University of New Mexico Press, 2000.

"For Insane Indians." *Red Man* 15, no. 1 (September 1898). CCHS, CISDRC.

Ford Model T Assembly outside the Highland Park Plant, circa 1914. Photograph. 84.1.1660.832. From the Collections of The Henry Ford.

"Ford 'Original Americans.'" *Ford Times* 9, no. 7 (February 1916): 305.

Foucault, Michel. *Discipline and Punish: The Birth of the Prison*. Translated by Alan Sheridan. New York: Vintage Books, 1995.

Freedman, Estelle. *Their Sisters' Keepers: Women's Prison Reform in America, 1830–1930*. Ann Arbor: University of Michigan Press, 1984.

Friedman, Moses. "The Carlisle Plan Makes for Independent Citizenship." *Red Man* 4, no. 3 (November 1911). CCHS, CISDRC.

Gaft, Samuel. "The History of the Henry Ford Trade School, 1916–1952." PhD diss., University of Michigan, 1998.

Garland-Thomson, Rosemarie. *Extraordinary Bodies: Figuring Physical Disability in American Culture and Literature*. New York: Columbia University Press, 1997.

General Hospital in Lancaster, PA, c. 1915. Postcard. From the author's personal collection.

Gifford, Oscar. "Gain in Indian Insanity." *Chicago Daily Tribune*, January 3, 1904.

Gilbert, Matthew Sakiestewa. *Hopi Runners: Crossing the Terrain between Indian and American*. Lawrence: University Press of Kansas, 2018.

Gilmore, Ruth Wilson. *Golden Gulag: Prisons, Surplus, Crisis, and Opposition in Globalizing California*. Berkeley: University of California Press, 2007.

Glover, James W. *United States Life Tables 1890, 1901, 1910, and 1901–1910*. Department of Commerce, Bureau of the Census. Washington, DC: US Government Printing Office, 1921.

Goeman, Mishuana. "Disrupting a Settler-Colonial Grammar of Place: The Visual Memoir of Hulleah Tsinhnahjinnie." In *Theorizing Native Studies*, edited by Audra Simpson and Andrea Smith. Durham, NC: Duke University Press, 2014.

Goeman, Mishuana. *Mark My Words: Native Women Mapping Our Nations*. Minneapolis: University of Minnesota Press, 2013.

Goffman, Erving. *Asylums*. New York: Doubleday, 1990.

Gonaver, Wendy. *The Peculiar Institution and the Making of Modern Psychiatry, 1840–1880*. Chapel Hill: University of North Carolina Press, 2019.

Gorman, Deborah. "The 'Maiden Tribute of Modern Babylon' Re-Examined: Child Prostitution and the Idea of Childhood in Late-Victorian England." *Victorian Studies* 21, no. 3 (1978): 353–79.

Grant, Madison, and Henry Fairfield Osborn. *The Passing of the Great Race; or, The Racial Basis of European History*. New York: Scribner, 1922.

Gregory, Anne. "Competency, Allotment, and the Canton Asylum: The Case of a Muscogee Woman." *Disability Studies Quarterly* 41, no. 4 (2021).

Grob, Gerald N. *Mental Illness and American Society, 1875–1940*. Princeton, NJ: Princeton University Press, 1983.

Gross, Ariela Julie. *What Blood Won't Tell: A History of Race on Trial in America*. Cambridge, MA: Harvard University Press, 2009.

Gross, Terry. "*Reservation Dogs* Co-Creator Says the Show Gives Audiences Permission to Laugh." NPR, September 19, 2022.

Guise, Holly Miowak. "Who Is Doctor Bauer? Rematriating a Censored Story on Internment, Wardship, and Sexual Violence in Wartime Alaska, 1941–1944." *Western Historical Quarterly* 53, no. 2 (2022): 145–65.

Haddad, George. "Medicine and the Culture of Commemoration: Representing Robert Koch's Discovery of the Tubercle Bacillus." *Osiris* 14 (1999): 118–37.

Harding, Susan F. "American Protestant Moralism and the Secular Imagination: From Temperance to the Moral Majority." *Social Research* 76, no. 4 (2009): 1277–306.

Harrison, Emily A. "The Usefulness of Saving Babies: A Reflection on Materials from a 1916 Campaign to Prevent Indigenous Infant Death." *Harvard Library Bulletin* (2021): 1–10.

Hartman, Saidiya. *Scenes of Subjection: Terror, Slavery, and Self-Making in Nineteenth-Century America, Race and American Culture.* New York: Oxford University Press, 1997.

Hartman, Saidiya. "Venus in Two Acts." *Small Axe* 12, no. 2 (2008): 1–14.

Hartman, Saidiya. *Wayward Lives, Beautiful Experiments: Intimate Histories of Riotous Black Girls, Troublesome Women, and Queer Radicals.* New York: W. W. Norton, 2019.

Haskins, Victoria K. *Matrons and Maids: Regulating Indian Domestic Service in Tucson, 1914–1934.* Tucson: University of Arizona Press, 2012.

"Henry Ford Trade School Information Brochure, 1931–1941." Brochure. From the Collections of The Henry Ford, Object ID 64.167.450.1 https://www.thehenryford.org/collections-and-research/digital-collections/artifact/373433#slide=gs-252397.

Hernández, Kelly Lytle. *City of Inmates: Conquest, Rebellion, and the Rise of Human Caging in Los Angeles, 1771–1965.* Chapel Hill: University of North Carolina Press, 2017.

Heywood, Colin. *A History of Childhood: Children and Childhood in the West from Medieval to Modern Times.* Cambridge: Polity, 2001.

Hill v. Buckholts. Oklahoma Supreme Court. *Oklahoma Reports: Cases Determined in the Supreme Court of the Territory of Oklahoma,* 196–204. Norman: Oklahoma State Capital Printing Company, 1920.

Hinman, Alan R. "1889 to 1989: A Century of Health and Disease." *Public Health Reports* 105, no. 4 (1990): 374–80.

"Hoe Handle Medicine." *Indian Helper* 1, no. 44 (June 11, 1886). CCSH, CISDRC.

Hogarth, Rana. *Medicalizing Blackness: Making Racial Differences in the Atlantic World, 1780–1840.* Chapel Hill: University of North Carolina Press, 2017.

hooks, bell. "Representing Whiteness in the Black Imagination." In *Cultural Studies,* edited by Lawrence Grossberg, Cary Nelson, and Paula Treichler, 338–46. New York: Routledge, 1992.

Horn, Katrin. "Dangerous Domesticity: Gossip and Gothic Homes in Edith Wharton's Fiction." *Edith Wharton Review* 35, no. 1 (2019): 22–46.

House of the Good Shepherd in Reading, Pennsylvania. Postcard. Postmarked September 8, 1909. From the author's private collection.

Hoxie, Frederick. *A Final Promise: The Campaign to Assimilate the Indians, 1880–1920.* New York: Cambridge University Press, 1989.

"Industrial Notes." *Arrow* 2, no. 19 (January 5, 1906). CISDRC, Cumberland County Historical Society.

"Insane Asylum for Indians." *Red Man* 15, no. 7 (July–August 1899). CCHS, CISDRC.

"Iti Fabvssa." *Biskinik*. Choctaw Nation of Oklahoma, September 1, 2018.

"Iti Fabvssa." *Biskinik*. Choctaw Nation of Oklahoma, April 1, 2019.

Jacobs, Margaret. "Diverted Mothering among American Indian Domestic Servants, 1920–1940." In *Indigenous Women and Work: From Labor to Activism*, edited by Carol Williams, 179–92. Urbana: University of Illinois Press, 2012.

Jacobs, Margaret. "Indian Boarding Schools in Comparative Perspective: The Removal of Indigenous Children in the United States and Australia, 1880–1940." In *Boarding School Blues: Revisiting American Indian Educational Experiences*, edited by Clifford E. Trafzer, Jean A. Keller, and Lorene Sisquoc, 202–31. Lincoln: University of Nebraska Press, 2006.

Jacobs, Margaret. *White Mother to a Dark Race: Settler Colonialism, Maternalism, and the Removal of Indigenous Children in the American West and Australia, 1880–1940*. Lincoln: University of Nebraska Press, 2009.

Jacobs, Margaret. "Working on the Domestic Frontier: American Indian Domestic Servants in White Women's Households in the San Francisco Bay Area, 1920–1940." *Frontiers: A Journal of Women Studies* 28, nos. 1–2 (2007): 165–99.

James, Jennifer C., and Cynthia Wu. "Editors' Introduction: Race, Ethnicity, Disability, and Literature: Intersections and Interventions." *MELUS* 31, no. 3 (2006): 3–13.

Joinson, Carla. *Vanished in Hiawatha: The Story of the Canton Asylum for Insane Indians*. Lincoln: University of Nebraska Press, 2016.

Jones, David. "The Health Care Experiments at Many Farms: The Navajo, Tuberculosis, and the Limits of Modern Medicine, 1952–1962." *Bulletin of the History of Medicine* 76, no. 4 (2002): 749–90.

Jones, Michelle, and Lori Record. "Magdalene Laundries: The First Prisons for Women in the United States." *Journal of the Indiana Academy of the Social Sciences* 17 (2014): 166–79.

Jones, Robert. "The Development of Insanity in Regard to Civilization." *American Journal of Insanity* 60, no. 4 (1904): 577–96.

Justice for Magdalenes Research: A Resource for People Affected by and Interested in Ireland's Magdalene Institutions. https://jfmresearch.com.

Juvonen, Jaana, Vi-Nhuan Le, Tessa Kaganoff, Catherine H. Augustine, and Louay Constant. *Focus on the Wonder Years: Challenges Facing the American Middle School*. Santa Monica, CA: Rand, 2004.

Kafer, Alison. *Feminist, Queer, Crip*. Bloomington: Indiana University Press, 2013.

Kaiser, Laurie. "The Black Madonna: Notions of True Womanhood from Jacobs to Hurston." *South Atlantic Review* 60, no. 1 (1995): 97–109.

Kappler, Charles. *Indian Affairs, Laws and Treaties*, vol. 4, *Laws*. Washington, DC: US Government Printing Office, 1913.

Keliiaa, Caitlin. *Refusing Settler Domesticity: Native Women's Labor and Resistance in the Bay Area Outing Program*. Seattle: University of Washington Press, 2024.

Keller, Jean. *Empty Beds: Indian Student Health at Sherman Institute, 1902–1922*. East Lansing: Michigan State University Press, 2002.

Kidwell, Clara Sue. "Allotment." Oklahoma History Society Encyclopedia, accessed February 2022. https://www.okhistory.org/publications/enc/entry?entry=ALo11.

Klotz, Sarah. *Writing Their Bodies: Restoring Rhetorical Relations at the Carlisle Indian School*. Denver: University Press of Colorado, 2021.

Kraut, Alan. *Silent Travelers: Germs, Genes, and the Immigrant Menace*. Baltimore: Johns Hopkins University Press, 1995.

Kunzel, Regina. *Criminal Intimacy: Prison and the Uneven History of Modern American Sexuality*. Chicago: University of Chicago Press, 2008.

Kunzel, Regina. *Fallen Women, Problem Girls: Unmarried Mothers and the Professionalization of Social Work, 1890–1945*. New Haven, CT: Yale University Press, 1993.

Lajimodiere, Denise. "A Healing Journey." *Wicazo Sa Review* 27, no. 2 (2012): 5–19.

Lake, Marilyn. *Progressive New World: How Settler Colonialism and Transpacific Exchange Shaped American Reform*. Cambridge, MA: Harvard University Press, 2019.

"Landmark Comes Down." *Reading Eagle*, May 17, 1973.

Landrum, Cynthia. *The Dakota Sioux Experience at Flandreau and Pipestone Indian Schools*. Lincoln: University of Nebraska Press, 2019.

Lappas, Thomas. *In League against King Alcohol: Native American Women and the Woman's Christian Temperance Union, 1874–1933*. Norman: University of Oklahoma Press, 2020.

Larkin-Gilmore, Juliet. "Hygienic Dispossession: Allotment and the Cherokee and Choctaw Health Drives of 1917." Unpublished manuscript.

Larkin-Gilmore, Juliet. "On the Borders: Towns, Mobility, and Public Health in Mojave History." *Journal of Arizona History* 61, no. 3 (2020): 511–34.

Leahy, Todd. *They Called It Madness: The Canton Asylum for Insane Indians, 1899–1934*. Baltimore: Publish America, 2009.

Leon, Carol. "The Life of American Workers in 1915." *Monthly Labor Review*, US Bureau of Labor Statistics, February 2016, accessed January 10, 2022. https://www.bls.gov/opub/mlr/2016/article/the-life-of-american-workers-in-1915.htm.

Littlefield, Alice, and Martha C. Knack, eds. *Native Americans and Wage Labor: Ethnohistorical Perspectives*. Norman: University of Oklahoma Press, 1996.

Livingston, Julie. *Debility and the Moral Imagination in Botswana*. Bloomington: Indiana University Press, 2005.

Loizides, Georgios Paris. "'Making Men' at Ford: Ethnicity, Race, and Americanization during the Progressive Period." *Michigan Sociological Review* 21 (2007): 109–48.

Lomawaima, K. Tsianina. "Domesticity in the Federal Indian Schools: The Power of Authority over Mind and Body." *American Ethnologist* 20, no. 2 (1993): 227–40.

Lomawaima, K. Tsianina. "Estelle Reel, Superintendent of Indian Schools, 1898–1910: Politics, Curriculum, and Land." *Journal of American Indian Education* 35, no. 3 (1996): 5–31.

Lomawaima, K. Tsianina. *They Called It Prairie Light: The Story of Chilocco Indian School.* Lincoln: University of Nebraska Press, 1995.

Lomawaima, K. Tsianina, Brenda Child, and Margaret Archuleta, eds. *Away from Home: American Indian Boarding School Experiences, 1879–2000.* Phoenix, AZ: Heard Museum, 2004.

Lomawaima, K. Tsianina, and Teresa L. McCarty. *"To Remain an Indian": Lessons in Democracy from a Century of Native American Education.* New York: Teachers College Press, 2006.

Lomawaima, K. Tsianina, and Jeffrey Ostler. "Reconsidering Richard Henry Pratt: Cultural Genocide and Native Liberation in an Era of Racial Oppression." Special issue, "Native American Boarding School Stories," *Journal of American Indian Education* 57, no. 1 (2018): 79–100.

Lombardo, Paul. *Three Generations, No Imbeciles: Eugenics, the Supreme Court, and Buck v. Bell.* Baltimore: Johns Hopkins University Press, 2008.

Lonetree, Amy. "Indigenous Child Removal: Narratives of Violence, Trauma, and Survivance." In *Violence and Indigenous Communities: Confronting the Past and Engaging the Present,* edited by Susan Sleeper-Smith, Jeffrey Ostler, and Joshua Reid, 245–60. Evanston IL: Northwestern University Press, 2021.

Lowe, Lisa. *Intimacies of Four Continents.* Durham, NC: Duke University Press, 2015.

Lui, Mary Ting Yi. *The Chinatown Trunk Mystery: Murder, Miscegenation, and Other Dangerous Encounters in Turn-of-the-Century New York City.* Princeton, NJ: Princeton University Press, 2005.

Maddra, Sam. *Hostiles? The Lakota Ghost Dance and Buffalo Bill's Wild West.* Norman: University of Oklahoma Press, 2006.

Magdalene Commission Report [The Quirke Report]. May 2013, Ireland Department of Children, Equality, Disability, Integration, and Youth, gov.ie.

Magdalene Restorative Justice Ex-Gratia Scheme. Ireland Department of Children, Equality, Disability, Integration, and Youth, gov.ie.

Magneto Assembly at the Ford Highland Park Plant, 1913. Photograph. 84.1.1660.P.833.167. From the Collections of The Henry Ford.

Mays, Kyle T. *City of Dispossessions: Indigenous Peoples, African Americans, and the Creation of Modern Detroit.* Philadelphia: University of Pennsylvania Press, 2022.

Mazzei, Patricia, and Anemona Hartocollis, "Florida Rejects A.P. African American Studies Class." *New York Times,* January 19, 2023.

McBride, Preston. "A Lethal Education: Institutionalized Negligence, Epidemiology, and Death in Native American Boarding Schools, 1879–1934." PhD diss., UCLA, 2020. Proquest Dissertations and Theses.

McDonnell, Janet. "Competency Commissions and Indian Land Policy, 1913–1920." *South Dakota History* 11, no. 1 (1981): 21–34.

McGarry, Patsy. "Nuns Who Ran Magdalene Laundries Have Not Contributed to Redress for Women." *Irish Times,* March 2, 2022.

McGettrick, Claire, Katherine O'Donnell, Maeve O'Rourke, James Smith, and Mari Steed. *Ireland and the Magdalene Laundries: A Campaign for Justice*. London: Bloomsbury Publishing, 2021.

Meriam, Lewis. *The Problem of Indian Administration*. New York: Eastern Association on Indian Affairs, 1928.

Meyer, Stephen. "Adapting the Immigrant to the Line: Americanization in the Ford Factory, 1914–1921." *Journal of Social History* 14, no. 1 (1980): 67–82.

Miller, Douglas K. *Indians on the Move: Native American Mobility and Urbanization in the Twentieth Century*. Chapel Hill: University of North Carolina Press, 2019.

Miller, Douglas K. "The Spider's Web: Mass Incarceration and Settler Custodialism in Indian Country." In *Caging Borders and Carceral States: Incarcerations, Immigration Detentions, and Resistance*, edited by Robert Chase, 385–408. Chapel Hill: University of North Carolina Press, 2019.

Miller, Douglas K. "Willing Workers: Urban Relocation and American Indian Initiative, 1940s–1960s." *Ethnohistory* 60, no. 1 (January 2013): 51–76.

Millingen. "Miscellany." *American Journal of Insanity* 4 (1847): 93–94.

Million, Dian. "Felt Theory: An Indigenous Feminist Approach to Affect and History." *Wicazo Sa Review* 24, no. 2 (2009): 53–76.

Million, Dian. *Therapeutic Nations: Healing in an Age of Indigenous Human Rights*. Tucson: University of Arizona Press, 2013.

Million, Dian. "'We Are the Land and the Land Is Us': Indigenous Land, Lives, and Embodied Ecologies in the Twenty-First Century." In *Racial Ecologies*, edited by LeiLani Nishime and Kim D. Hester Williams, 19–33. Seattle: University of Washington Press, 2018.

Moreton-Robinson, Aileen. *The White Possessive: Property, Power, and Indigenous Sovereignty*. Minneapolis: University of Minnesota Press, 2015.

Morrison, Minnie. "Life Story of Mrs. Minnie Morrison: Awful Revelations of Life in Convent of Good Shepherd, Indianapolis, Ind.; A True Story." Pamphlet, Toledo, Ohio, 1925. University of Hawai'i, Manoa, Social Movements Collection.

Native Lives Matter. Lakota People's Law Project, 2015.

Nichols, Robert. "The Colonialism of Incarceration." *Radical Philosophy Review* 17, no. 2 (2014): 435–55.

Nielsen, Kim. *A Disability History of the United States*. Boston: Beacon Press, 2012.

Nolan, Frederick. *The West of Billy the Kid*. Norman: University of Oklahoma Press, 2015.

Norris, Caroline. "A History of Madness: Four Venerable Virginia Lunatic Asylums." *Virginia Magazine of History and Biography* 125, no. 2 (2017): 138–82.

Nyongó, Tavia. *The Amalgamation Waltz: Race, Performance, and the Ruses of Memory*. Minneapolis: University of Minnesota Press, 2009.

O'Brien, Jean, and Daniel Heath Justice, eds. *Allotment Stories: Indigenous Land Relations under Settler Siege*. Minneapolis: University of Minnesota Press, 2022.

O'Donnell, Ian, and Eoin O'Sullivan. *Coercive Confinement in Ireland: Patients, Prisoners and Penitents*. New York: Manchester University Press, 2012.

Office of the Chief, Tk'emlúps te Secwépemc. Press release, May 27, 2021. https://tkemlups.ca/wp-content/uploads/05-May-27-2021-TteS-MEDIA-RELEASE.pdf.

Otto T—. "wwI Draft Card." 1917. Ancestry.com.

Owens, Deirdre Cooper. *Medical Bondage: Race, Gender, and the Origins of American Gynecology*. Athens: University of Georgia Press, 2017.

Patterson, Andrea. "Germs and Jim Crow: The Impact of Microbiology on Public Health Policies in Progressive Era American South." *Journal of the History of Biology* 42, no. 3 (2009): 529–59.

Pauls Valley Democrat 3, no. 26, September 13, 1906. Pauls Valley, Indian Territory. Gateway to Oklahoma History, Oklahoma Historical Society. https://gateway.okhistory.org/ark:/67531/metadc116141/m1/6/.

Pavilion (Bandstand) at Carlisle Indian School. 1870–1879. Photograph. Potamkin, PO no. 01, Cumberland County Historical Society, Carlisle, PA.

"Pawnee Medicine and an Indian Lodge." *Indian Helper* 3, no. 13 (1887). Dickinson College Archives and Special Collections, CISDRC.

Peña, Mauricio. "ICE Wants to Show Public Citizens How to Arrest Immigrants with 'Citizens Academy'—But Locals Are Fighting to Stop 'Xenophobic PR Stunt.'" *Block Club Chicago*, July 13, 2020.

Pengra, Lilah Morton, and Joyzelle Gingway Godfrey. "Different Boundaries, Different Barriers: Disability Studies and Lakota Culture." *Disability Studies Quarterly* 21, no. 3 (Summer 2001): 36–53.

Penrose, Lionel. "Mental Disease and Crime: Outline of a Comparative Study of European Statistics." *British Journal of Medical Psychology* 18, no. 1 (1939): 1–15.

Pfister, Joel. *Individuality Incorporated: Indians and the Multicultural Modern*. Durham, NC: Duke University Press, 2004.

Phillips, Nancymarie. "Education for Girls in the House of the Good Shepherd, U.S. 1940–1980." PhD diss., Cleveland State University, 2008.

Piatote, Beth. *Domestic Subjects: Gender, Citizenship, and Law in Native American Literature*. New Haven, CT: Yale University Press, 2013.

Pratt, Richard Henry. *Battlefield and Classroom: Four Decades with the American Indian, 1867–1904*. Edited by Robert M. Utley. Lincoln: University of Nebraska Press, 1984.

"A Protest against the Abolition of the Indian Dance." *Red Man and Helper* 3, no. 2 (August 22, 1902): 1–4. CCHS, CISDRC.

Prucha, Francis Paul. *Americanizing the American Indians: Writings by the "Friends of the Indian," 1880–1900*. Lincoln: University of Nebraska Press, 1978.

Puar, Jasbir K. *The Right to Maim: Debility, Capacity, Disability*. Durham, NC: Duke University Press, 2017.

Putney, Diane. "The Canton Asylum for Insane Indians, 1902–1934." *South Dakota History* 14, no. 1 (1984): 1–30.

"Real Ownership." *Ford Times* 9 (1915–16). Dearborn, MI: Ford Motor Company, 1916.

Reiter, Keramet, and Thomas Blair. "Punishing Mental Illness: Trans-Institutionalization and Solitary Confinement in the United States." In *Extreme Punishment: Comparative Studies in Detention, Incarceration and Solitary Confinement*, edited by Keramet Reiter and Alexa Koenig, 177–96. London: Palgrave Macmillan, 2015.

Reverby, Susan M. *Ordered to Care: The Dilemma of American Nursing, 1850–1945*. Cambridge: Cambridge University Press, 1987.

Riney, Scott. "Power and Powerlessness: The People of the Canton Asylum for Insane Indians." *South Dakota State Historical Society* 27, no. 1 (1997): 41–64.

Riney, Scott. *The Rapid City Indian School, 1898–1933*. Norman: University of Oklahoma Press, 1999.

Risling Baldy, Cutcha. "Mini-Kiwhe:N (For That Purpose—I Consider Things): (Re) Writing and (Re)Righting Indigenous Menstrual Practices to Intervene on Contemporary Menstrual Discourse and the Politics of Taboo." *Cultural Studies and Critical Methodologies* 17, no. 1 (2016): 21–29.

Risling Baldy, Cutcha. *We Are Dancing for You: Native Feminisms and the Revitalization of Women's Coming-of-Age Ceremonies*. Seattle: University of Washington Press, 2018.

Roberts, Samuel Kelton, Jr. *Infectious Fear: Politics, Disease, and the Health Effects of Segregation*. Chapel Hill: University of North Carolina Press, 2009.

Robertson, Stephen. "Age of Consent Law and the Making of Modern Childhood in New York City, 1886–1921." *Journal of Social History* 35, no. 4 (2002): 781–98.

Ross, Luana. *Inventing the Savage: The Social Construction of Native American Criminality*. Austin: University of Texas Press, 1998.

Rothman, David. *The Discovery of the Asylum: Social Order and Disorder in the New Republic*. New York: Routledge, 2002.

Ruggles, Steven. "Fallen Women: The Inmates of the Magdalen Society Asylum of Philadelphia, 1836–1908." In *History of Women in the United States*, vol. 10, *Sexuality and Sexual Behavior*, edited by Nancy Cott, 201–18. Munich: K. G. Saur Publishing, 1993.

Rules for the Indian School Service. United States Bureau of Indian Affairs. Department of the Interior, United States Indian Service. Washington, DC: US Government Printing Office, 1913.

Schildbach, Sebastian, and Carola Schildbach. "Criminalization through Transinstitutionalization: A Critical Review of the Penrose Hypothesis in the Context of Compensation Imprisonment." *Frontiers in Psychiatry* 9 (2018).

Scott, James C. *Domination and the Arts of Resistance: Hidden Transcripts*. New Haven, CT: Yale University Press, 1990.

"Secretary Haaland Announces Federal Indian Boarding School Initiative." Press release, US Department of the Interior, June 22, 2021.

Segrest, Mab. "Rebirths of a U.S. Nation: Race and Gendering of the Nation State." *Mississippi Quarterly* 57, no. 1 (2003): 27–40.

Sells, Cato. "Save the Indian Babies." Washington, DC: United States Government Printing Office, 1916.

Senier, Siobhan. "'Traditionally, Disability Was Not Seen as Such': Writing and Healing in the Work of Mohegan Medicine People." *Journal of Literary and Cultural Disability Studies* 7, no. 2 (2013): 213–29.

Shah, Nayan. *Contagious Divides: Epidemics and Race in San Francisco's Chinatown*. Berkeley: University of California Press, 2001.

Shakespeare, Tom. *Disability Rights and Wrongs*. New York: Routledge, 2006.

Simonsen, Jane. *Making Home Work: Domesticity and Native American Assimilation in the American West, 1860–1919*. Chapel Hill: University of North Carolina Press, 2006.

Sixsmith, Martin. "The Catholic Church Sold My Child." *Guardian*, September 18, 2009.

Slivka, Kevin. "Art, Craft, and Assimilation: Curriculum for Native Students during the Boarding School Era." *Studies in Art Education* 52, no. 3 (2011): 225–42.

Smith, Andrea. "Boarding School Abuses, Human Rights, and Reparations." *Social Justice* 31, no. 4 (2004): 89–102.

Smith, Andrea. *Conquest: Sexual Violence and American Indian Genocide*. Durham, NC: Duke University Press, 2015.

Smith, James. *Ireland's Magdalen Laundries and the Nation's Architecture of Containment*. Notre Dame, IN: University of Notre Dame Press, 2007.

Smith, Linda Tuhiwai. *Decolonizing Methodologies: Research and Indigenous Peoples*. London: Zed Books, 2012.

Steere-Williams, Jacob. "The Germ Theory." In *A Companion to the History of American Science*, edited by Georgina M. Montgomery and Mark A. Largent, 397–407. West Sussex, UK: John Wiley, 2016.

Stern, Alexandra Minna. "Making Better Babies: Public Health and Race Betterment in Indiana, 1920–1935." *American Journal of Public Health* 92, no. 5 (2002): 742–52.

Stoler, Ann Laura. *Carnal Knowledge and Imperial Power: Race and the Intimate in Colonial Rule*. Berkeley: University of California Press, 2002.

Stoler, Ann Laura, ed. *Haunted by Empire: Geographies of Intimacy in North American History*. Durham, NC: Duke University Press, 2006.

"Stopping Carousals of Carlisle Students." *Harrisburg Telegraph*, May 4, 1915.

Summers, Martin. *Madness in the City of Magnificent Intentions*. Oxford: Oxford University Press, 2019.

Tatro, M. Kaye. "Burke Act." Oklahoma History Society Online Encyclopedia, accessed January 5, 2023. https://www.okhistory.org/publications/enc/entry?entry=BU010.

Taylor, Frederick Winslow. *Shop Management*. New York: Harper and Brothers, 1911.

Teeters, Negley K. "The Early Days of the Magdalen Society of Philadelphia." *Social Service Review* 30, no. 2 (1956): 158–67.

Theobald, Brianna. "1970 Law Led to the Mass Sterilization of Native American Women. That History Still Matters." *Time Magazine*, November 28, 2019.

Theobald, Brianna. *Reproduction on the Reservation: Pregnancy, Childbirth, and Colonialism in the Long Twentieth Century.* Chapel Hill: University of North Carolina Press, 2019.

Thompson, Ian. *Choctaw Food: Remembering the Land, Rekindling Ancient Knowledge.* Durant, OK: Choctaw Nation Education Special Projects, 2019.

Tomes, Nancy. *The Gospel of Germs: Men, Women, and the Microbe in American Life.* Cambridge, MA: Harvard University Press, 1999.

Tompkins, Kyla Wazana. *Racial Indigestion: Eating Bodies in the Nineteenth Century.* New York: NYU Press, 2012.

Touillot, Michel-Rolph. *Silencing the Past: Power and the Production of History.* Boston: Beacon Press, 1995.

Tower, Mike. *The Outlaw Statesman: The Life and Times of Fred Tecumseh Waite.* Bloomington, IN: AuthorHouse, 2007.

Trafzer, Clifford. *Fighting Invisible Enemies: Health and Medical Transitions among Southern California Indians.* Norman: University of Oklahoma Press, 2019.

Trafzer, Clifford. *Strong Hearts and Healing Hands: Southern California Indians and Field Nurses, 1920–1950.* Tucson: University of Arizona Press, 2021.

Trafzer, Clifford E., Jean A. Keller, and Lorene Sisquoc, eds. *Boarding School Blues: Revisiting American Indian Educational Experiences.* Lincoln: University of Nebraska Press, 2006.

Trennert, Robert. *The Phoenix Indian School: Forced Assimilation in Arizona, 1891–1935.* Norman: University of Oklahoma Press, 1988.

"Truth and Healing Commission on Indian Boarding School Policies Act." National Native American Boarding School Healing Coalition, accessed August 2, 2023. www .boardingschoolhealing.org/truthcommission.

Veracini, Lorenzo. *Settler Colonialism: A Theoretical Overview.* London: Palgrave Macmillan, 2000.

Vučković, Myriam. *Voices from Haskell: Indian Students between Two Worlds, 1884–1928.* Lawrence: University Press of Kansas, 2008.

Wald, Priscilla. *Contagious: Cultures, Carriers, and the Outbreak Narrative.* Durham, NC: Duke University Press, 2008.

Welter, Barbara. "The Cult of True Womanhood: 1820–1860." *American Quarterly* 18, no. 2 (1966): 151–74.

Wexler, Laura. *Tender Violence: Domestic Visions in an Age of U.S. Imperialism.* Chapel Hill: University of North Carolina Press, 2000.

Whalen, Kevin. *Native Students at Work: American Indian Labor and Sherman Institute's Outing Program, 1900–1945.* Seattle: University of Washington Press, 2016.

White, Louellyn. "Who Gets to Tell the Stories? Carlisle Indian School: Imagining a Place of Memory through Descendant Voices." *Journal of American Indian Education* 57, no. 1 (2018): 122–44.

Whitt, Sarah. "'Care and Maintenance': Indigeneity, Disability, and Settler Colonialism at the Canton Asylum for Insane Indians, 1902–1934." *Disability Studies Quarterly* 41, no. 4 (2021).

Whitt, Sarah. "'An Ordinary Case of Discipline': Deputizing White Americans and Punishing Indian Men at the Carlisle Indian Industrial School, 1900–1918." *Western Historical Quarterly* 54, no. 1 (2023): 51–70.

Whitt, Sarah. "'Wash Away Your Sins': Indigenous and Irish Women in Magdalene Laundries and the Poetics of Errant Histories." *American Indian Culture and Research Journal* 46, no. 3 (2023): 1–23.

Whitt, Sarah, Traci Brynne Voyles, and Susan Burch. "Settler Ableism: Indigeneity, Unsettling the Archive, and Accountability in History." In *Cripping the Archive: Disability, Power, and History*, edited by Jenifer Barclay and Stefanie Hunt-Kennedy. Urbana: University of Illinois Press. Forthcoming 2024.

Witgen, Michael. "Seeing Red: Race, Citizenship, and Indigeneity in the Old Northwest." *Journal of the Early Republic* 38, no. 4 (2018): 581–611.

Wolfe, Patrick. "Settler Colonialism and the Elimination of the Native." *Journal of Genocide Research* 8, no. 4 (2006): 387–409.

Yellow Bird, Pemina. "Wild Indians: Native Perspectives on the Hiawatha Asylum for Insane Indians." *Center for Mental Health Services* (n.d.): 1–10.

index

pathologization, 17, 21, 83, 100–104, 123, 177, 186; and Canton Asylum, 23, 140, 151–52, 155, 159, 238n72; and Ford partnership, 87, 89, 93; and Indigenous lifeways, 72, 74, 77–78, 186

patriarchy, 57, 66, 113, 236n28

Patterson, New Jersey, 46

Pawnee people, 151–52

Peekskill, New York, 121

Peel, C.V., 94

Pennsylvania, 57, 97, 184. *See also* Carlisle Indian Industrial School; Cynwyd, Pennsylvania; Edgewood, Pennsylvania; Lansdowne, Pennsylvania; Reading, Pennsylvania; Tullytown, Pennsylvania

personhood, 34, 209n34, 217n134, 219n6

Pettigrew, Richard, 144–45

philanthropy, 4, 114, 144, 166, 181, 186, 234n113

Phillips, Nancymarie, 118, 121

Phoenix, Arizona, 81

photographs, 100–105, 102 fig.2.6, 103 fig.2.7, 225n107

Piatote, Beth, 123, 216n109

Pima School, Arizona, 171

Pine Ridge Agency, 119, 234n2

Pipestone Indian School, Minnesota, 162, 168–69, 171

Pleasant Point Indian Reservation, Maine, 44

policing, 41–44, 46, 51, 60, 69, 189–90, 215n86

poverty, 72, 77–78, 188

power, 24, 49, 128; and Canton Asylum, 140, 166, 168, 171, 181; and Carlisle, 28, 30, 35, 37–38, 41, 51, 69, 73; and Carlisle Outing system, 57–59, 63–64, 68, 126; and private sector, 92, 97–98; and settler institutions, 2–3, 7, 14, 16, 20, 23, 187, 218n138

Pratt, Richard Henry, 7, 12, 71, 104, 124, 153, 210nn15–16, 211n17, 221n44; and Carlisle, 32–33, 45, 57

pregnancy, 61–65, 121, 126, 191, 233n100

Presbyterianism, 61

Prescott, Arizona, 92

prisons, 22, 27, 111–12, 115, 118, 127–28, 132–33, 136, 188, 232n87. *See also* incarceration

private labor sector, 3, 20–21, 69, 72, 82, 97, 185, 222n46. *See also* Ford Motor Company; Lancaster General Hospital

productivity, 74, 80, 85, 224n86

Progressive Era, 10–11, 16, 18, 30, 34, 89, 109, 139, 166, 172, 184, 230n55

progressivism, 84

proletarianization, 28, 72, 222n46

prostitution, 113–14, 118, 121

Protestant Episcopal Church, 135

Protestant institutions, 113, 118–19, 121, 135, 187, 211n18

psychiatry, 18, 22, 100, 134, 145–48, 154–57, 160–62, 168–72, 187, 235n3

public health, 74–77

Public Health and Marine-Hospital Service, 77

punishment, 32, 183–84, 211n18; and Carlisle, 9–10, 20, 27–31, 36–45, 48, 59–60, 63, 69, 185; and Carlisle Outing system, 60, 68–69, 186; and Ford partnership, 84, 88, 93; and Good Shepherd Homes, 21–22, 111–13, 117, 127, 187; and racialization, 3–4, 6–7, 16–21, 81; resistance to, 24–25

Putney, Diane, 144, 147–48, 238n58, 238n73

Quakers, 57

Quapaw Indian Agency, 173

Quigley, Mike, 190

Quinton, Amelia Stone, 55

Quirke, John, 228n30

racialization, 28–30, 37, 50–51, 72, 96, 107, 140–41, 182, 189–90; and punishment, 3–7, 18–21, 81

transinstitutionalization, 16, 111, 119, 132–33, 137, 171, 188, 239n82

trauma, 33, 121, 169, 183, 192

treaty obligations, 77, 82, 175

Trenton, New Jersey, 39–41

tribal nations, 3–4, 7, 80, 110, 113, 136, 189, 216n109; colonial control of, 14, 20–22, 28, 33, 35; and healing, 183, 191, 219n4, 225n96; and land dispossession, 34, 146, 208n18, 212n26. *See also* Indigenous sovereignty

Trouillot, Michel-Rolph, 24–25, 131

truth, 143, 182, 194

Truth and Healing commissions, 67, 143, 193

Truth and Reconciliation Commission, Canada, 192

tuberculosis, 73, 75–77, 148, 234n2

Tuck, Eve, 24

Tuhiwai Smith, Linda, 19, 24, 131

Tullytown, Pennsylvania, 38–39

Turner, John, 147

Turtle Island, 25, 63, 143, 194, 196

Umatilla School, Oregon, 171

United States Indian Service, 123

unmarked graves, 148, 192, 228n26

"uplift," Indian, 7, 9, 21, 73, 79, 123–24, 144, 166, 186, 226n124; and Carlisle, 30, 54, 69

upward mobility, 72, 87

US Bureau of Land Management, 196

US Congress, 77, 145, 154, 168, 211n17, 212n29

US Department of Homeland Security, 189

US Department of the Interior, 32, 43, 91, 144, 172, 212n29; boarding school investigation, 22, 27, 110, 135, 137, 138 fig.3.6, 192–94

US federal boarding school system, 12, 22, 27, 33–35, 71, 131, 135, 140, 169, 192–94, 208n19; and health crises, 76–77; survi-

vors of, 110, 113, 136–39; and wage labor, 81. *See also* Carlisle Indian Industrial School

US federal Indian policy, 4, 7, 27

US Immigration and Customs Enforcement (ICE), 189–90

US National Center for Health Statistics, 188

US Supreme Court, 189

US War Department, 7, 27, 83, 118, 211n17

Valentine, Robert, 87

venereal diseases, 53, 89, 93

Veracini, Lorenzo, 16, 159

vigilantism, 50, 190–91

violence, 41, 63, 67, 104, 143, 146, 157–58, 189–90, 216n109, 243n156; colonial, 137, 182, 187

Virginia, 123

vocational training, 30, 35–37, 83–85, 184–85, 211n18, 222n46

Voyles, Traci Brynne, 74, 219n6

Vuckovič, Myriam, 15

wage labor economy, 80–82, 92–93, 185, 221n36, 221n44

Waite, Emily, 142, 177–82

Waite, Fred Tecumseh, 178, 179 fig.4.4

wardship, 14, 82, 91, 97, 140, 149, 152–53, 174, 182, 214n59. *See also* infantilization

Warner, "Pop," 7

Warren, Elizabeth, 193

warriors, Indian, 32

Washington, DC, 1, 92, 144, 148, 211n17

Wauwatosa, Wisconsin, 110

Weaver D., 46

Welch, Gustavus, 42

wellbeing, 10, 53, 64, 151, 189, 191, 193

Welter, Barbara, 218n140

Wexler, Laura, 104, 230n54

Whalen, Kevin, 15, 81, 231n67

Wheelock Academy, 36

White, Louellyn, 7